The Organization in its Environment

Book 1 Structures, Resources, and Markets

McGraw-Hill Business Education Courses

Consulting Editor:
Graham Edwards
Principal, Kirby College of Further Education, Cleveland.

The Organization in its Environment

Book 1 Structures, Resources, and Markets

G. J. Edwards, MSc(Econ), FCIS, MBIM
Principal

A. C. Kellar, LLB, ACMA
Principal Lecturer

both of Kirby College of Further Education, Cleveland.

McGRAW-HILL Book Company (UK) Limited

London . New York . St Louis . San Francisco . Auckland . Beirut
Bogatá . Düsseldorf . Johannesburg . Lisbon . Lucerne . Madrid
Mexico . Montreal . New Delhi . Panama . Paris . San Juan . São Paulo
Singapore . Sydney . Tokyo . Toronto

Published by McGraw-Hill Book Company (UK) Limited

MAIDENHEAD . BERKSHIRE . ENGLAND

British Library Cataloguing in Publication Data

Edwards, Graham James
  The organization and its environment.
  Book 1: Structures, resources and markets. —
  (McGraw-Hill business education courses).
  1. Organization
  I. Title II. Kellar, A C
  301.18'32'024658   HM131   78-40809

  ISBN 0-07-084601-4

12345 8079

Printed and bound in Great Britain

Contents

Foreword to the Series

Course structures devised by the Business Education Council present an exciting new challenge to lecturers, students and authors alike. The Council has considered it no longer appropriate to educate for a career in business by means of academic disciplines which, however appropriate in themselves, were brought into at best a loose interrelationship, and which were capable of being taught in a fashion, academically sound, but perhaps insufficiently applied to the situations which students might find in the business world.

The new course structure identifies, at all levels (General, National, Higher National), four important Central Themes an understanding of which, it is argued, is central to all business education, and which underlie all academic disciplines. These Central Themes are Money (including the most efficient use of the resources which money can buy); People (and their human relationships as producers and consumers); Communication (embracing a much wider concept than mere 'Business English'; and Numeracy (not just 'Business Mathematics' but a logical and numerate approach to business problems). Additionally, the BEC philosophy is that academic disciplines must be interrelated if they are to be meaningful in the solution of business problems.

An important aim of the BEC course structure at both General and National level is therefore:

to encourage the development of the understanding and skills implicit in the Central Themes, with particular emphasis on the improvement of the student's standards of literacy and numeracy.

A further aim at General level is:

to develop basic work competence through practical assignments which relate the knowledge, skills and understanding derived from various parts of the course to business situations.

This, at National level, becomes:

to develop the student's ability to interrelate knowledge, skills and understanding from various parts of the course through practical assignments derived from business contexts.

The modular course structure itself encourages this interrelationship by breaking down traditional subject barriers. The exciting new challenge to authors and lecturers is to adopt the BEC philosophy without abandoning the integrity or the essential content of subject disciplines. Side by side with Common Core Modules, applicable to all students at a particular level, run Board Core Modules and Option Modules. There is a need to integrate subject matter both within and across the modules in order to produce a coherent pattern of study. This must be just as relevant for students ending their studies at this point as for those progressing to a higher BEC level or to examinations for and membership of professional bodies. The challenge to students is to grasp the intricacies of interwoven Central Themes, subjects and modules and to emerge with the knowledge, skills and understanding which will enable them to solve practical problems.

All the authors in this series have met the challenge in their own way. Each has, however, covered the general objectives and the learning objectives of the relevant BEC module in a way which makes for a logical teaching and learning progression, while bearing in mind the need for interconnections between the modules. Books at both General and National level stand, not only in their own right, but as part of a package. They contain their own assignments designed to integrate subject disciplines within the module and based on practical example. Books in the same series also contain common cross-modular assignments in order to carry integration still further.

The consulting editor and the authors are well aware that there is no unique solution to the challenge posed by the BEC course structure. Some people would advocate throwing caution to the winds and, abandoning much that was good and relevant in the existing schemes, would seek out change for the sake of change. Others would attempt to mould BEC courses to their own skills and teaching methods, thus frustrating change altogether. We have decided on what we believe to be a sensible middle way; our approach seeks to enable teachers to plan and present the new course structures effectively, thus enabling students to learn more easily and, above all, to consider BEC courses relevant to their jobs and careers.

Preface

Books 1 and 2 of *The Organization in its Environment* are primarily intended for students taking National Certificate and Diploma courses of the Business Education Council. They meet the requirements of the double modules 3/4 at that level in both content and philosophy.

The BEC is concerned to ensure that students acquire knowledge in a way which will be relevant to their present or future work situation. These books, therefore, follow the stated aim of modules 3/4:

1. To help the student to appreciate his/her own organizational role, through an understanding of the characteristics, function, and structure of different types of business and administrative organization.
2. To enable the student to appreciate the overall business and social context within which he/she works, and to provide a framework for developing understanding of the nature of business and its environment both within the course and subsequently.
3. To encourage the student to regard academic disciplines as contributors to the analysis and solution of business problems, by requiring him/her to relate them as part of an overall approach to such problems.
4. To assist the student to apply his/her understanding to the working environment, so as to become an effective contributor member of his/her employing organization.

The double module 3/4 represents work over two years of the course. In devising these books the authors have taken into account the need to assess the degree of weighting to be given to the general objectives of the module, to the learning objectives within each general objective, and to the five sections into which the double module is divided.

Book 1—*Structures, Resources and Markets*—as a first-year text, is concerned largely with the basic framework of the environment within which organizations operate. It deals with many of the learning objectives in the module specification which require a student to 'list', 'state', 'describe' or 'identify'. The essential elements of law, economics, and public administration are integrated and presented in such a way as to make them usable in 'the analysis and solution of business problems'.

Book 2—*The Complex Society*—builds upon the ground prepared in Book 1. It concerns itself with 'evaluation' and 'analysis'. The integration of the essential elements, begun in the first book, is taken further. Much of the material is presented by means of a study of the actions and reactions of organizations in industry, commerce, and local and central government. This is done by a study of original material drawn from a variety of sources. The whole book is written around the topics of 'objectives', 'policies', 'accountability', and 'constraints'. The countervailing effect of these factors on organizations in every sector of the economy is shown, together with their effect on individuals, illustrating fully the complex society about which Book 2 is written.

Assignments are an important feature of the courses of the BEC. For this reason, both books feature samples of such assignments. These are carefully graded to give confidence to students in the early stages of their course. The Cross-Modular

Assignments in these books also appear in the companion books in this series concerning Common Core Modules 1 and 2. They follow the aims and objectives for such assignments and concentrate upon the analysis and solution of interdisciplinary problems. The problems thus presented are realistic and varied in type and complexity.

Graham Edwards is the author of *Framework of Economics,* also published by McGraw-Hill. The book has successfully met the needs of students through three editions over a number of years. Much of its content is particularly relevant to the new BEC courses and the authors have taken the opportunity to incorporate some of its tried and tested material into *The Organization in its Environment,* Books 1 and 2.

Students and teachers alike will meet many difficult problems in the ordering, presentation, and assignment work inherent in this new approach to business education. It is hoped that the organization of the subject matter in these books will be of real assistance in solving these problems.

Although these books are intended primarily for BEC students, it is hoped that they will also be useful to students preparing for business studies examinations at Ordinary and Advanced level. The new approach to subject disciplines, the ordering of material, the summaries at the end of each unit, and the integrating sections at the beginning of each part may also be of use to the general reader.

GENERAL OBJECTIVES TESTED BY ASSIGNMENTS IN BOOK 1

	10 BAKERY INDUSTRY	10 ORGANIZATIONS–LOCATION ETC.	25 SOCIAL TRENDS–USE OF STATISTICS	25 POPULATION TRENDS–LEA IMPLICATIONS	39 SMALL FIRMS PROBLEMS	51 LOCAL AUTHORITY SERVICES	60 CONTRACT FOR RESOURCES	68 RISKS	84 T.V. GAMES	98 SEX DISCRIMINATION	99 CONTRACT OF EMPLOYMENT STATEMENT	99 DISMISSAL	113 LEGACY	121 REDEVELOPMENT OF TOWN CENTRE SITE	129 LOCATION REPORT	137 MEETING DEMAND	149 GARDEN TOOLS	149 CAR SPARES MARKET	162 FARMER–DEMAND FORECAST	162 UNPRODUCTIVE CIVIL SERVANTS	171 EXCLUSION CLAUSES
A	ALL OBJECTIVES TOUCHED UPON	✓			✓	✓															
B																					
C					✓	✓															
D			✓	✓										✓							
E							✓	✓	✓	✓	✓	✓	✓	✓	✓	✓					
F																	✓	✓			
G																		✓	✓	✓	
H																					
J																					✓
K						✓													✓	✓	
L																					
M																					
N							✓			✓	✓	✓									✓
P										✓	✓	✓									✓
Q																					

LEARNING OBJECTIVES COVERED

Learning Objectives / UNIT NO	1	2	3	4	5	6	7	8	9	10	11	12	13	14	15	16	BOOK 2
THE ORGANIZATION																	
A1	P		P	P													P
A2	P		P	P													P
A3			P	P													P
A4			P	P													P
A5			P	P													P
B1	P	P	P	P													P
B2	P	P	P	P													P
B3	P		P	P													P
C1																	F
C2																	F
C3																	F
ORGANIZATION AND DEMOGRAPHIC FACTORS																	
D1		F															
D2		P															P
D3		P												P			P
D4		P															P
D5		P		P										P			P
THE ORGANIZATION AND ITS RESOURCES																	
E1	P					P											
E2								P	P	P	P	P					P
E3						F											
E4							F										
E5							F										
E6							F										
E7							P				P						
E8								P									P
E9								P									P
E10			P	P													P
E11																	F
E12										F							
E13										P							P
E14										F							

P = partly covered   F = fully covered

LEARNING OBJECTIVES COVERED

Learning Objectives	UNIT NO 1	2	3	4	5	6	7	8	9	10	11	12	13	14	15	16	BOOK 2
E15																	F
E16																	F
E17								P									P
E18								P									P
E19								P									P
E20								P									P
E21																	F
THE ORGANIZATION, ITS MARKETS, CUSTOMERS AND CLIENTS																	
F1													P	P			
F2													P	P			
F3													F				
F4														P			P
F5														P			P
G1													P				P
G2														P			P
G3														P			P
G4														P		P	P
G5													F				
H1																	F
H2																	F
H3																	F
H4																	F
J1					P				P						P		P
J2					F												
J3									P						P		P
J4					P				P						P		P
J5																	F
J6																	F

P = partly covered   F = fully covered

LEARNING OBJECTIVES COVERED

Learning Objectives	UNIT NO 1	2	3	4	5	6	7	8	9	10	11	12	13	14	15	16	BOOK 2
THE ORGANIZATION, THE STATE AND THE COMMUNITY																	
K1				F													
K2				P													P
K3																	F
K4																	F
L1			P	P											P		P
L2																	F
L3																	F
L4																	F
M1																	F
M2																	F
N1					P			P	P						P		P
N2																	F
N3																	F
P1																	P
Q1								P									F

P = partly covered   F = fully covered

Part One   The organization and its structure

John Donne reminded us that no man is an island. Since his day, society has become even more complex. Individuals are hedged around by laws, by the customs of the times, by lack of the means to do exactly as they please. Yet, at the same time, the individual's decisions affect the lives of others, perhaps to a greater degree than ever before. If we are to be more informed citizens, there is a clear need to appreciate the overall business and social context within which we all live and work. Only in this way can we make a more effective contribution, as workers and as members of the community, to the general well-being.

But where to start? This book concentrates on an investigation of the characteristics, function, and structure of the different types of organizations within which most of us work. It investigates the economic, legal, social, and political framework within which such organizations operate. In doing so, it helps us to understand more clearly our own role within the organization, so that we may play a better part in helping it to overcome its problems and to reach its objectives.

So we start with a look at the nature of organizations—what they are and what they do. Later, we shall look more closely at the resources at their disposal and at the problems connected with their use. Finally, we shall investigate the needs and demands of their customers and clients. This part sets out to answer the following questions: What are organizations? What, why, where, when, how, and for whom do they produce? What are the economic, legal, social, and political constraints upon them? To this task we now turn.

1

Unit 1   The organization in its environment: a bird's-eye view

Are you at work or are you a full-time student? In either case, you belong to an organization. Are you part of a family? Do you belong to a club? Or a church? Again, you are part of an organization, which may be generally defined as 'a number of persons or groups having specific responsibilities and united for some purpose or work'. None of us can avoid belonging to at least one organization, the State itself. Most of us belong to some or many organizations.

The reasons why organizations are formed become clearer when we look more closely at the definition. First, they consist of 'a number of persons'. Of course, that number could be one, as in the case of the window-cleaner who has apparently little to organize except his bicycle, ladder, bucket, and cleaning materials. In fact, as we shall see, even his life is not quite so simple as that. More typically, however, organizations consist of several or many people, grouped together for 'some purpose or work'. The purpose may be mutual support. Like-minded people join clubs, form charitable groups, go to the same church, gang up at football matches. 'United we stand, divided we fall.' Mankind seems to be naturally gregarious. The purpose may equally well be greater efficiency. If people in the group have different aptitudes then by accepting 'specific responsibilities' they may work more purposefully together. This is the concept of specialization, or division of labour, which we shall meet again. Last, some groupings are involuntary; the army and prisons come to mind. But most organizations consist of people who associate freely. All seem to have some common characteristics.

Some characteristics of organizations

Every grouping must have a **structure.** The people making up the group are inter-dependent, and often, as we have seen, perform a particular task within the group framework. Second, organizations are capable of **decision-making.** The particular process of making decisions varies, of course. It may be through a committee or through a power hierarchy. The decisions may come from one man or woman, or from a ruling group. Sometimes the organization has built-in checks and balances. By this means, power and the decision-making function are diffused and no one individual or group is able to gain too much power. We can see an example of this in the interaction of the Cabinet, legislature and courts under the British Constitution. Indeed, every organization has a **constitution**, in the sense of having rules by which it operates. This constitution may be written or unwritten, vague or precise, within or outside the law, but it must exist if the organization is to fulfil its purpose.

Organizations: wealth and well-being

Organizations, as we have seen, may be formed for many different purposes. Our major interest is in those which are concerned with the **production of wealth**. At once

3

we need to be aware that apparently familiar words must, for our purposes, be more closely defined. Production, for example, means turning the world's resources into a form in which they can give satisfaction. In this special sense of giving satisfaction, production is the creation of **utility**. Put another way, production adds to the stock of wealth, which itself may be defined as anything which has *utility,* is *transferable* and is *scarce*.

If this seems rather complicated, perhaps an example will make it clearer. Let us suppose that an organization has as its purpose the conversion of crude oil into petrol and paraffin. Crude oil is useless in itself; it has no utility. The conversion process is production. If the process cost nothing in terms of use of resources and if crude oil were in limitless supply, the petrol and paraffin would be *free goods*, at everybody's disposal without cost. But, of course, this is not the case. Oil is 'scarce'; petrol and paraffin are produced only at a resource cost. This resource cost is called a **real cost** to distinguish it from a money cost, although both usually arise in the creation of utility. Does this mean that both petrol and paraffin are wealth? That depends. Certainly, both are scarce. Certainly, both may be transferred from the producing organization to somebody else. But suppose that nobody wants paraffin, while many people need, and are willing to pay for petrol. Then paraffin is not wealth; it has no utility. Petrol is wealth as long as people *need* it and are willing to *demand* it by paying for it. Note the distinction.

Not all organizations produce goods which have immediate utility to the final consumer. If we follow our example further, crude oil can only be tapped by the use of technology in the form of drilling rigs and all the other hundred and one pieces of equipment which are necessary, especially in the rigorous conditions of the North Sea. So we must distinguish between organizations producing such **capital goods** and those producing **consumer goods**.

A further distinction is between those producing tangible goods and those producing services. Solicitors offer a service; so do teachers and policemen. So, indeed, does the wholesaler who stores in bulk for supply in smaller quantities to the retailer. And here we must distinguish between the private sector of the economy, in which both the solicitor and the wholesaler operate, and the public sector, in which the State and local government operate. Organizations in the private sector may produce goods and services; so may those in the public sector. However, in the latter case, we come to the further area of well-being—the quality of life—as opposed to wealth. The possession of wealth by an individual may bring about material well-being—although, as Midas discovered, this does not necessarily bring happiness. Some of the organizations controlled by central or local government, like those in the area of national health, are directed at non-material well-being.

Let us sum up at this point. We are concerned with productive organizations which create either wealth or well-being in the form of goods or services. They may lie in the private or in the public sector; that is a question of ownership. If they produce goods, these may be either capital or consumer goods.

Organizations and resources

4   When engaged in the process of production, what do organizations organize? First,

they organize the people who work for them—managers, craftsmen, technicians, office workers, salesmen and so on. The list of specialized functions could be extended almost endlessly, down to the legendary saggar-maker's bottom knocker. Second, as we have seen, they use resources. These may be capital goods in the form of lorries, typewriters, computers, machine tools, buildings, land, and a host of other items. Resources used may also consist of capital in the form of raw materials, goods in the process of production, or stocks of unsold finished products. They may take the form of money assets. *Capital*, we are discovering, is another word with a variety of meanings, each of which must be carefully distinguished according to the sense in which the word is used. To the organization, any form of capital is part of its assets. Collectively, non-human assets may be considered as somebody's property. Whose, we will discuss later.

The process of production has been said to be that of people working with property to create wealth. Economic resources may thus be broadly classified into **work** and **property**. Work is the sum total of the tasks performed by everybody in the organization. Property is the collective name for all the assets used. Both must be used in the way which best fits the objectives of the organization.

The private sector

There is another equally important question to be asked: Who does the organizing? In part, this is a question of ownership, in part of management. In the private sector, which is not under State control, it is sometimes difficult to decide who is directing the organization. It is difficult because the 'someone' is not always the same kind of person or persons. If you bought this book from a small bookseller, it will be obvious to you that he runs his business personally. He may employ and direct the activities of half-a-dozen assistants, but it is his shop; he has provided the capital for the premises and fittings, for the stock and displays. Losses and profits are his alone. He decided what books should be held in stock, publicity is his responsibility and so on. However, if you ask who is the equivalent of this owner-manager in your town's largest bookshop, there may not be an easy answer. It is apparent that we need to analyse what the small bookseller is doing in running his own business and draw a parallel with the larger organization. You will remember that he takes decisions and also lives with the consequences of those decisions. If he is an enterprising individual and branches into new lines of books he will be uncertain whether he will make a profit or loss on the venture. He will have planned and calculated the expected financial consequences of his new venture, but he cannot be certain. It is in these areas of *uncertainty* and *organization* that we need to look to find the equivalent of our owner-manager in a large bookshop. This shop is probably part of a chain, which has similar shops in most large towns.

So far as the *organization* of the large shop is concerned, the most important long-term decisions are made centrally, perhaps at a head office. These decisions apply to all branches and are probably in the areas of wages and salaries, staffing, budgets, stock policies, advertising, and similar general matters. We need to ask ourselves who makes these important decisions? The answer is almost certainly the senior management of the organization; and it is equally certain that they are paid employees of the organization, in just the same way as the manager and assistants of the local branch.

5

Providing their decisions are sensible ones, and the organization prospers, they are not affected personally by the uncertainty attached to those decisions. Of course, if the organization does not prosper they may lose their jobs, but if a new line, which sells badly, is put into the shops, they do not lose by it. Equally, they do not usually profit directly from a good selling line. Their reward for decision-making and organization is a salary. This is their work in just the same way that the shop assistant's work is to sell to customers. Thus we can see that these senior managers—and, for that matter, branch managers—do some of the work done by the owner–manager of the small book-shop. They fill his role of manager; they do not bear the *uncertainty* which attaches to his other role, that of owner of the bookshop. In short, we have to seek the *owner* of the chain of bookshops.

A detailed study of the whole question of ownership in a variety of organizations needs to be left until later (see Unit 3). At this stage, let us say that it is likely to be the *shareholders* who own the chain of shops. They own just what the term implies, a share, or shares, in the business. Who these people are we will also consider later. The share which they own cannot be identified as so much stock or a few counters. It is a share in the total 'property' of the organization. We can now assert that shareholders bear the uncertainty attached to the business. If profits are made, they are usually rewarded; if losses, it is they who bear the losses. If the organization can no longer trade because of accumulated losses, they are entitled to share what is left when it is wound up.

There is one more aspect of the owner–manager's work which we need to consider. Since he combined the two functions he was able, as it were, to consult with himself. In the larger organization, this is not possible. Thousands of shareholders cannot be consulted about even the most important trading decisions of the organization. They are represented by a board of directors, which thus forms a link between the owners and managers of the organization. This is a rather simplified view of the role of a board of directors, but it will suffice at this stage.

The public sector

In identifying what the majority of organizations have in common, we have so far looked at examples in the so-called private sector of the economy—that is, at those organizations which are owned by one or more individuals or groups. However, the private sector represents only part of the vast number of organizations in the country.

We now need to consider the part played by local and central government in the setting up of trading and non-trading organizations. Keep in mind, however, that the three features of private sector organizations we have identified are present in the public sector also. These were ownership, management and consultation.

Governments have set up a large number of organizations for many reasons. For the present, it is only necessary to identify the major types, and to leave a detailed discussion on, for example, their financing and control until later (see Unit 4).

Among trading organizations, the nationalized industries play perhaps the most important role. It was the importance of the product of such industries as coal, electricity, and gas which led to their being taken into public ownership in the first place. This ownership now extends into the railways, part of road haulage and long distance coach operation, steel, air transport, and many other operations. For these industries, central government controls the capital and bears the uncertainty. It also provides a broad base of policy within which the industry works. Management is, however, separate from ownership, and is carried out by boards, which are themselves responsible to the appropriate government Minister.

The examples given above are the result of long considered policy decisions of government. However, we can now see examples of public ownership being extended for reasons of social policy. The acquisition of British Leyland by the National Enterprise Board is an example of this. For different reasons, the British National Oil Corporation was formed to regulate and control the oil exploration and extraction industry on behalf of the nation. Both these are examples of a quasi-autonomous national government organization (quango), dealt with further in Unit 4.

Other government organizations, both local and central, meet a need which the private sector is not likely to be able to satisfy. The payment of welfare benefits on the scale necessary in a modern society would not be feasible if it had to be carried out by an insurance company on a profitable basis. The provision of municipal housing and transport, with subsidized rents and fares where necessary, are other examples. It is to local and central government that we turn for the provision of these services, offered to ensure well-being.

The organization in its environment

Although we shall examine both private and public sector organizations in greater detail in later units, it should be clearly understood at this stage that they all have the common characteristics which we identified in the earlier sections of this unit. It should also be understood that they have other characteristics in common. They are located in these islands; the population of the country provides the workforce; they are all working within the law of the land; and the resources they use are shared out among them on the basis of supply and demand or by government decision. It is to these aspects that we now turn; to what might be called the 'environment' of the organization.

The organization and its location

Look around where you live or work and ask yourself this question: why is this factory here, or that office or shop there? The answer to this apparently simple question may be easy to find, but often it is very difficult. The owner of the small bookshop which we considered earlier may live in the same town and wish to live near his work. But why did the larger bookshop open in the town? And why is it in the particular place where you now find it? Consider a factory near you. Why is it where it is? How long has it been there? Is it expanding or contracting? Is it changing, through modernization? Is there a government office in your town? Why is it there, if the clients with which it deals live all over the country? As we said earlier, the answers to these questions are sometimes difficult to find, but it is important to try to work them out. In your career you will have to consider, and live with, the consequences of the location of your organization and that of others.

Having considered the location of an organization, we can look at its surroundings—its environment, in a much wider sense of the word.

Physical environment

Again, if you look around, you will see at once, that any organization must consider the limitations of its physical environment, and if necessary, live with them. The size of the existing site is an obvious limitation on plans to expand. There are, of course, others. Road and rail links must be considered. Can employees travel easily to work? Is there housing near? Is the area generally industrial or residential? Are there service industries near? The service industries themselves and local and central government departments must also consider communications. Can customers and clients travel to them easily if necessary?

Social environment

By social environment we mean the surrounding population. Here, the organization needs constantly to consider whether enough workers, with suitable skills, are available. And if customers or clients are local, are there enough of them? And are the activities of the organization acceptable? Pollution, by noise or smell, is of obvious concern to the surrounding community.

Legal environment

Every organization must work within the laws of the land; they form what might be called its legal environment. Thus, relations with employees, suppliers, customers, clients, and local and central government must all be conducted within a restricted legal framework. This framework may only affect the organization in particular ways. For example, it may have no patents to protect or trademarks to defend. But it may need to store certain chemicals or explosives, for which it must be licensed. Naturally our small bookseller has no need of such licenses. However, both organizations must be aware of the legal requirements of the **Health and Safety at Work Act 1974**, just to give one important example. An organization, whatever sector it is in and of whatever kind it is, must always consider its legal environment in all its actions.

Political environment

Under this heading we need to examine those factors which an organization must consider in its plans and actions, and which are under the control of local and central government. As we have already noted, there is a legal framework within which the organization must operate. However, there is also a large area of decisions which may be affected by government actions of one kind or another. The building of a motorway is an example of government action of this sort. Government plans may be changed, or scrapped, and the motorway never built at all. An organization which based its plans for expansion on the projected motorway would find them invalidated.

Another uncertain area is planning permission, which is generally under the control of local government. Plans for a supermarket may be turned down by a council. A government office may be opened and staff lost to it. Changes in the rates of indirect taxation may affect sales for good or bad.

The common factor among all the above examples is that they are the result of decisions by local and central government. For this reason, and others which we shall consider, organizations try to influence many government decisions. Once the decisions are made, they cannot escape their consequences.

International environment

Under this heading we can examine the effect on an organization of economic, social, legal, and political factors in other countries. At first sight it might seem, looking at our small bookseller, that he is little affected by decisions in these areas. This would be a totally false assumption, and we can use his example to show that individuals, communities, and nations are more interdependent than they seem on the surface. The bookseller may be near an educational institution which has a large number of overseas students. Suppose that for some reason the number of such students is limited to the level of previous years, or even reduced. Of course, other students may fill their places, but if they do not, book sales may fall. At the same time, other potential customers may find that they have less money available for books because of the rising price of commodities like coffee and oil. Again, book sales are affected.

The trading organization with large overseas markets, which imports some of its resources, must carefully consider the implications of decisions made by foreign governments. They may have severe repercussions on prices—think of the rise in price of oil for example. Licences may not be granted to overseas customers to buy from some countries. Import duties may be changed. Competitors may be breaking into some markets with a more acceptable product.

We can now see that the social, legal, and political environment of an organization can be almost world-wide. Its markets may be the populations of many countries; the laws of those governments must be considered; and the decisions of those governments can have far-reaching consequences.

The economic environment

So far, we have examined the organization with particular reference to the creation of goods and services. In the process of production, it uses other goods and services. Where is the starting point in this chain of goods which the organization uses? The starting point is, of course, the extraction of raw materials from the earth, for them to be worked on by man. However, the supply of such materials has physical limits. In the short-term, the quantity which the controllers of the supply are able or willing to extract and put onto the market is also limited. Another factor to consider is that raw materials (and, for that matter, many goods) have alternative uses. So the resources used in our organization are also in demand by many others. If the supply is fixed, or is reduced, prices inevitably rise as demand increases. We are immediately in competition with others for this fixed or declining supply. We can see immediately that choice has to be exercised, because human economic wants are more diverse and more numerous than the resources available to satisfy them. We have to try to use our limited raw materials in the manner best suited to reach a desired end. But, as we shall see later, the end desired by one community may be very different from that considered essential by others.

So we are back full circle to the basic economic problems of wealth, scarcity, and

9

choice, and the ways in which organizations attempt to solve these problems in a social, legal, and political environment in order to allow both higher standards of living and a better quality of life. Such problem-solving can only take place if we are aware of the basic framework of economic forces, legal requirements, and social and political constraints, and can integrate our knowledge in a meaningful way.

Summary

All organizations have certain features in common. They have a structure, a constitution, and can take decisions. The organizations in our study are those concerned with the production of wealth in the public and private sector of the economy. Organizations use resources in the form of work and property which must be managed. Property is owned. Ownership and management may be concentrated in one person or among many. If ownership and management are separate, consultation is necessary. Both the private and public sectors contain organizations producing goods and services. Some public sector organizations, for reasons of social policy, add to the well-being of the nation. All organizations work within an environment which places constraints upon its actions. A study of the organization in its environment will assist in solving some of the problems met by an organization in its activities.

Assignments

1. Your town will have one or more of the following:

   (a) a Job Centre
   (b) a department store
   (c) a launderette
   (d) a small factory
   (e) a local authority housing department.

   Consider each of the above with regard to:

   (i)   location
   (ii)   customers and clients
   (iii) workforce
   (iv)   expansion
   (v)   communications
   (vi)   ownership.

2. [*Note* This assignment is given at this point as a basis for discussion, both now and at later points in the course.] The bread industry has two parts. Giant groups hold about 70 per cent of the market and smaller independent and store bakeries hold the rest. There are now two major groups, but a while ago there were three. The story of the downfall of the third illustrates particularly well much of the content of the double module, *The Organization in its Environment*.

   Changes of taste and a general fall in *demand* over twenty years left the industry with *over-capacity* estimated at 20 per cent. This was despite gradual closure of bakeries. However, the three groups were each *vertically integrated* and the vast market for bread, shrinking though it was, formed an essential outlet for flour milled profitably by each group. The ability to sell bread is determined by the retail markets available. A group selling some of its output through its own shops is less vulnerable than one having to rely on sales to other *retail chains*. For this reasons, Group A, having many shops of its own, made some *profit* from baking. Group B just about *broke even*. Group C had accumulated losses of £26m from baking.

The *labour intensive* baking industry had to absorb part of wage rises under *counter-inflation legislation* of various governments. At the other extreme, prices were controlled. An application to the Price Commission by the *market leader* resulted in a price rise being allowed which was just about adequate for the applicant. This price would then determine the general level of bread prices. The other groups would have preferred higher prices but fierce *competition* and over-capacity ruled this out.

Two further sets of pressures began to bear upon the bakers. Considerable union activity resulting in a strike was almost the last straw for the management of Group C. They were already beset by problems, the major one being the bargaining power of large supermarkets, in the face of *over-supply*. Very large *discounts* had to be offered to obtain any orders at all. In this way, losses accumulated to a level beyond which they could not be borne. At this point, the decision to close the bakeries of Group C was made.

One invariable, and sad, result of the closures was the *redundancy* of many workers. The acquisition, by the other two groups, of some of the bakeries of Group C considerably reduced the number of jobs lost. The cash received was then available for *redundancy payments* and closure costs.

The two remaining groups are now in a dominant position in the industry, a situation which had to be accepted by the Minister concerned. Nevertheless, commentators have made the point that the industry is now much healthier.

Some points for discussion and clarification

(a) What is the technical meaning of the words in italics?

(b) What is the effect of the closures likely to be on bread prices in large supermarket chains?

(c) What is the effect of the closures likely to be on the profitability of the two remaining large groups?

(d) Where might the cash come from to buy up the bakeries taken over from Group C?

(e) Why would some of the bakeries be bought by the other groups if they were losing money for Group C?

(f) One bakery in the north-east produced both bread and cakes. The bread section was closed in the general shutdown. Three months later, the cake section was closed as it could not operate as a viable unit without bread production. Why should this have been so?

(g) What problems will the redundant bakery workers meet? How might they be overcome?

(h) In what respects could the industry now be said to be 'healthier'? Is the commentator's view an objective one or a value judgement?

Unit 2 People

Introduction:
Consumers and producers

Perhaps the most fundamental point to make about any organization is that it is composed of people. Each person within it has his or her own hopes, fears, ambitions. Each has to relate, well or badly, to others in order to pursue common objectives. Each is part of the resources of the firm or public service department, and by working provides an input to production. This input takes the form of some skill necessary to the particular process of production.

People, then, are producers. They are also consumers of the goods and services so produced. Their decisions about what to consume influence, and are influenced by, those taken by their fellow human beings. Thus, an understanding of population patterns, whether of a particular country or the world itself, is basic, because changes in the patterns of population can alter both standards of living and organizational structures.

Total population
The Malthus theory

The Reverend Thomas Malthus, writing at the end of the eighteenth century, believed that the rate of growth of the British population would be greater than that of resources, particularly foodstuffs. Indeed, he went so far as to suggest that, while population was likely to grow in a geometric progression (2, 4, 8, 16,....), food production would grow only in an arithmetic progression (1, 2, 3, 4,...). This was the beginning of the famous law of non-proportional returns which is considered in detail in Unit 7. The point which Malthus made was that in no circumstances could a fixed amount of agricultural land, however well cultivated, continue to support indefinitely a population growing as fast as he foresaw. A vicious circle would develop. If people were better off, they would have more children. Food production would be outstripped, standards of living would drop again, and population growth would be held in check by famine and disease. The only remedies which Malthus could suggest in his day were later marriages and moral restraint. He believed that, unless these remedies were forthcoming, part of the population would always be living on the edge of starvation.

Malthus could not, of course, foresee the immense increase in production which would take place in the UK in the nineteenth century. Previously, there had been a long period, back to about 1700, when production of goods and services was limited by scanty technical knowledge and capital resources. Standards of living were kept low. The period of the industrial revolution saw not only a rapid increase in population, but an equally rapid one in capital development. The rate of growth of production outstripped that of population; standards of living rose as the race between population and production was won by the latter. Thus, economic growth began to influence future trends in population, rather than the reverse. Industrialization, coupled with international trade, meant that the UK could import more and more of the foodstuffs needed for the growing population. The point at which the threatened fall in the standard of living would occur was being pushed further and further into the future.

Yet who is to say the Malthus was wrong, even in the case of the UK? **Figure 2.1** shows the past growth and future estimates of UK population. The most recent census figure of 1971 shows that at that time our population was approximately 55 700 000. By 1975, it had nearly reached 56 000 000, and by the year 2001 best guesses indicate that it will have risen to 58 300 000. However, the difficulties involved in making projections of this kind are so great that the estimated population of the UK at the turn of the century ranges from 53 500 000 to 62 200 000.

Reasons for concern

If further growth occurs, need this worry us? Why should not ever-increasing production of material wealth still continue to take care of the problem as it has in the recent past? First, there looms what has been called the 'energy crisis'. World supplies of coal and oil, the resources from which almost all energy is derived, are limited and are rapidly being used up. Despite the best efforts of pure and applied science, it is not at all certain that these energy sources can—or should be—replaced by, for example, nuclear fission. Second, the UK cannot, as in the past, rely upon her superior exporting ability to import cheap foodstuffs. In the 'seventies, world prices of food and raw materials rose sharply. In part, this was caused by increased demand in other countries, including those in which standards of living have been particularly low in the past. Setting aside these external worries, there are other reasons for being concerned about population growth in the UK. We do not need to be economists to appreciate the

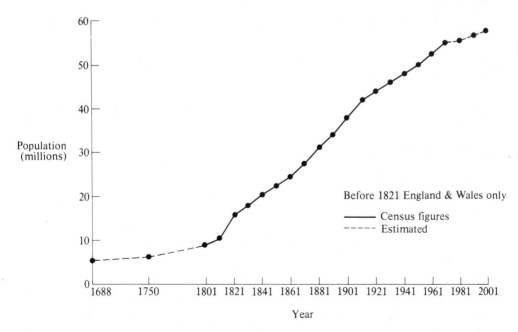

Fig. 2.1 UK population: past, present and future (Sources: Registrars-General and Government Actuary's Department)

problems of traffic congestion in our crowded cities and on our holiday routes.

Most of us have witnessed the air pollution caused by the internal combustion engine. We have seen the detergent froth on our rivers, many of which have been described as little better than open sewers. No wonder we now have a government department of 'the Environment' and an ever-growing concern at the damage which we are doing to our natural surroundings. Of course, not all this environmental damage can be ascribed to a growing population. Part of it is also caused by our striving for higher standards of living. Typically, our housing problem is partially due to growing numbers of people, but also partially to our desire to have more spacious surroundings. Should relatively affluent countries strive for higher standards of living at the expense of their own environment or of less affluent countries and communities elsewhere in the world or of both? If not, is it possible for standards of living to remain relatively stationary? The economist may be able to help in answering the second question but he is in no special position to answer the first.

Current estimates

Given the statistical evidence, it is still possible for different views to be held upon the probable effects of population growth in industrialized countries, such as the UK, the US and Western Europe. Not all social scientists predict that the quality of life in these countries will deteriorate. But no one country can live in isolation, and when we consider population trends in other parts of the world and for the world as a whole, the situation appears much more serious. It has been estimated that the population of Europe will increase from 462 million in 1970 to 568 million in the year 2000. Over the same period, it seems that Africa's population will increase from 344 million to 818 million and Asia's from 2050 million to 3778 million. In 1950, the total world population was 2486 million. In 1960, it had grown to 2982 million and in 1970 to 3632 million. By the year 2000, the projection is for a figure of 6494 million. If this figure is reached, the increase in world population between 1950 and the year 2000 will be 161 per cent. Since much of this population growth is centred on poor and underdeveloped countries, its indefinite continuance would lead only to the fulfilment of Malthus's prophecy.

Birth rates and death rates

If control of the population expansion, either within a particular country or in the world as a whole, is held to be desirable, we must first know how growth comes about. The population of any one country may increase partly as a result of immigration exceeding emigration, but the world population can grow only if there are more births than deaths. The most usual way of establishing the facts is through the use of birth rates and death rates.

Crude birth rate

Although statistical refinements are possible, an examination of the crude birth rate is sufficient for our purposes. By this is meant the number of births per year per thousand of the population. In one country at a particular time there might be 100 000 births in a population of 5 million. The birth rate would then be 20. At another time it might be 10 or 30.

This rate varies from time to time and area to area for many reasons, some of them sociological rather than economic. The age at which people marry is often decided by custom. Because the ability to have children declines with age, it is possible (but not necessary) that parents will have more children if they marry younger. In 1901, the average age at which men married in the UK was 27 and the comparable figure for women was 25. By 1974, these figures were 25 and 23 respectively. Again, in 1901 only 17 per cent of men and 29 per cent of women were married before their twenty-fifth birthday. In 1971, these figures had risen to 38 per cent and 68 per cent.

The trend towards earlier marriages in the UK apparently halted in the late 'seventies, and has not, as might have been expected, led to an increased birth rate. A minor complication is that the percentage of illegitimate births has risen steadily throughout the twentieth century and stood at over 9 per cent of all births in 1975. This aside, the birth rate at the turn of the present century was 28.6. Apart from short-lived changes caused by the unsettled conditions of the First and Second World Wars, there was then a steady fall to 15.5 in 1955, followed by a rise to a maximum of 18.8 in 1964. But in 1971 the figure had fallen to 16.2 and by 1975 it had reached the unprecedentedly low figure of 12.5. In terms of absolute numbers of live births, there were about 1 000 000 in 1964, but well under 700 000 in 1975. The total population in the year 2000 will be larger or smaller according to whether the declining trend in the birth rate is reversed or not.

Age structure

There is no single satisfactory explanation for the 'birth bulge' of the 'sixties and for the subsequent decline in the birth rate. Improved contraceptives and family planning services probably had an effect, together with a more tolerant attitude of society towards abortion. Numbers of abortions rose rapidly from about 13 000 in 1968 to about 30 000 in 1972, but then began to decline slightly. Whatever the reason the **age structure** of the UK population has been affected. Normally, with a growing population, one would expect to find more people in the lowest age group, say from 0-4 years old, followed by successively fewer in each older age group. The effect of a temporary increase in the birth rate, followed by a decline, is to produce a distortion in the pattern. In 1975, for example, there were approximately 4 000 000 in the 0-4 years old group and 4 500 000 in the 5-9 group. The mid 'sixties bulge is now (1978) in secondary schools, having already passed through primary schools. Soon it will go on to work or to further and higher education. Such a situation creates problems of educational and employment provision. The government has had to reduce, drastically, the number of teacher training places available. Also, special schemes to provide work for the young unemployed person have been devised; schemes which may be a feature of economic life for a while until the "bulge" has worked its way through.

Net reproduction rate

Another measure of population growth connected with birth is the **net reproduction rate.** If every girl during her child-bearing years produced precisely one daughter, this rate would be unity. A rate of, say, 1.9 would imply a growing population and one of 0.7 a decreasing population. However, perhaps more simple to use and understand is the measure of the size of family needed merely to keep the population steady. Allowing for early deaths and the fact that there are slightly more men than women in the British population, the average family size needs to be about 2.2 children for this purpose. It seems to have been slightly above this figure in the mid-'sixties, when the net reproduction rate was also slightly above unity at 1.2. The size of family seems to be related to the state of economic development in a particular country.

As the community gets richer and more goods and services become available, experience has shown that at first the size of family falls. Parents wish to bring up fewer children in a better fashion, while they themselves enjoy increased prosperity. Family planning becomes widespread, unless this runs counter to religious beliefs. As the status of women improves, more of them choose a career rather than marriage and a family. For a while, in the very richest countries, the average family size seemed to be increasing again. It is doubtful, however, whether this will turn out to be a permanent trend, given increasing awareness of social and environmental problems.

Crude death rate

The other factor which decides world population growth is the **crude death rate** which, like the birth rate, is calculated per thousand of the population. It indicates directly how many people survive and indirectly for how long. The great population increase in the UK between 1800 and 1900 was caused not by a large increase in the birth rate, but by a dramatic decline in the death rate. Previously, the high birth rate had been matched by a high death rate, particularly among children, and this prevented a rapid increase in population. By the mid nineteenth century, however, the death rate was already down to 24 per thousand of the population, and this itself was a great improvement on earlier years. Continuous decline down to the early twentieth century resulted in a death rate of 16. By 1976, it was further reduced to 12, and is unlikely to fall much further since people must die eventually, if only from old age.

Improved medical science, better diet, and a healthier environment are now doing for less developed countries what they have already done for the more prosperous ones. Improved transport allows a better distribution of foodstuffs and reduces the likelihood of local famines; this is particularly true if agricultural methods improve simultaneously. Better drainage and supplies of pure water make disease more rare. Apart from this general improvement in public health, the application of improved medical techniques lead to the elimination of illnesses such as malaria or tuberculosis. Unfortunately, such application is not yet within the reach of every country. It is expensive, requiring the provision of both hospitals and trained medical staff and a very poor country may be able to afford neither.

Relation between birth and death rates

In countries with a very high birth rate—such as India, China, and Puerto Rico—population is growing fast, particularly since the death rate is being reduced gradually. A vicious circle may then develop. There may be so many people that the living standard of each is low. It would be desirable to educate them into an understanding of the need to limit births, but this would demand the provision of more professional people than the country can afford. Without these, a temporary increase in the standard of living leads to more children being born at the same time as the death rate is falling. In such a situation, it is difficult to provide sufficient capital to make output more efficient, since nearly all goods produced must be consumed immediately.

In countries where a high standard of living has already been achieved—such as Sweden, the USA, or the UK—this problem has already been overcome. In these countries, the fall in death rate has been followed by a fall in birth rate for reasons already discussed. Indeed, in the UK by 1975, total births were only slightly greater than total deaths, giving very little natural increase. It begins to look as if a very rapid growth in population is a temporary stage in the development of a country, bound up with the standard of living which its people have achieved at the time.

Migration

Emigration and immigration also affect the size of population of particular countries, though not of the world as a whole. The rapid growth of the US in the nineteenth century and of Australia in recent years has been caused largely by the arrival from outside of people from many nations. Israel has been virtually created through an influx of Jewish people from the rest of Europe. The motive of migrants has always been the hope of bettering their position; in past centuries, the incentive was economic, political, religious, or that of plain adventure. In the nineteenth century in the US, for example, the young man 'went West' with the expanding frontier because there was a real possibility of making good. Migrants were welcomed because there were vast resources to develop. When the physical limits to expansion were approached, the community's attitude towards immigrants changed.

One country's gain may be another's loss. The UK has been concerned because of the drain of her best scientists to the US and other advanced countries. Before the building of the Berlin Wall, East Germany's steady loss of population was a valuable source of labour to West Germany. It is often the young, the adventurous, the skilled, who migrate. On the other hand, a country whose population is increasing rapidly by natural means, such as Jamaica, India, or Pakistan, may welcome emigration as a means of preventing standards of living from falling.

Of course, some people move into a country at the same time as others are moving out. During the present century, the population of the UK has normally experienced a net loss from migration. For example, in 1974 total immigrants numbered under 200 000, while the number emigrating was 260 000. Much of the movement was between the UK and Commonwealth countries.

Although migrants are a welcome source of manpower and, in the UK, often undertake employment which the indigenous population scorns, they nevertheless create social and economic problems. This is particularly so if they have language difficulties and congregate in a relatively few specific areas. Houses and schools are only two of their requirements and most of the burden falls on central and local government.

17

Age structure

It is useful for some purposes to divide the total population into three age groups; young persons up to 16, the 16-65 age group, and people aged over 65. The middle of these three age groups is, roughly speaking, capable of work; the others are either too young or too old. Not all the 16-65 age group are actually at work; quite apart from possible unemployment, many of this group are housewives, undoubtedly 'employed', but not classified as forming part of the working population. Other people may be living on incomes derived from the ownership of property; some may be permanently ill or otherwise unemployable; others are students or prematurely retired. In 1975, the total working population of the UK (including those registered as wholly unemployed) was 25 834 000 out of the total population of 55 900 000.

We have already noted that the age structure of the population, and thus the total number of people capable of work, is affected by changes in the birth and death rates. If birth rate is high and rising, while death rate is stable, each successive generation will be larger than the one immediately before it. The average age of the population will be falling.

Such a situation presents both opportunities and problems. As long as other resources are also increasing, a younger population is probably more adaptable to change, more able to move, and more enterprising. On the other hand, post-war experience in the UK, following two 'bulges' in the birth rate in the late 'forties and mid 'sixties has been of fluctuating pressure on the educational services. However, since it now appears that the birth rate of the 'seventies is likely to be considerably less than that of the 'sixties, the effect through to the end of the century will be that progressively more people will enter the working age group, as the 'bulges' move upwards through the age structure. For a time, at any rate, there will be a larger proportion of people of working age to support both the children and the retired.

However, this situation will not last indefinitely. If the decline in birth rate continues, then eventually the 'bulge' population will itself reach retiring age. Eventually, the falling birth rate will cause the total population to decline.

Declining population

Once capital and other resources have been established in an advanced economy, the problems of a **declining population** can also be serious. Such a decline usually means that the average age is rising. It could be caused, for example, by a very low death rate combined with a falling birth rate. Again, we are faced by the problem of combining resources with people in the right proportions. The UK electricity supply industry has, for example, installed new generating plant to cope with peak demands for power. This resource would still be available even if population declined, but would be 'wasted' since there would be little demand for its services. And it could not easily be transformed into some other form of capital which might be more urgently required. There need not be an absolute decline in numbers in order to bring this about. An ageing population would leave fewer members in the working group of 16-65. Just as a younger people might be more virile, mobile, and enterprising, so an ageing population might find it difficult to maintain momentum in a competitive world. The UK is lacking in many resources; her main asset is possibly the skill and enterprise of her people. Unless this were constantly reinforced by the younger members of her population, the country could find itself unable to trade sufficiently to buy essential raw materials and foodstuffs.

The types of goods and services demanded by an ageing population are not the same as those demanded by a younger community. Older people might demand more galoshes and less gum, more artificial teeth and less baby food. Yet only if enough people were willing and able to change their jobs and, possibly, homes, could this shift in demand be met; but an older population would be less likely to take kindly to the change. The effect on the pattern of demand caused by a change in the age structure is shown dramatically by post-war trends in the UK. Because of the sudden increase in the birth rate after 1945, there were about 750 000 more people in the 15-19 age group in 1964 than there were in 1959. The total spending of this age group in 1959 was already over £800 million, or some 5 per cent of all consumer spending. In the mid 'sixties, sales of records, record players, sports gear, and motor scooters expanded, reflecting, in large measure, the weight of teenagers' earnings. The 'baby boom' of the late 'forties was the best thing to happen to some industries for a long time. However, by 1968 numbers in the 15-19 age group had begun to decline and they have only started to increase significantly again from 1971. Demand for goods more appropriate to the 'young-marrieds' was then increasing, as the 'bulge' moved through into the next age group.

If a population declined and aged sharply, there would usually be less **capital accumulation.** Capital accumulation means the setting aside of part of current production in the form of machines, factories, and raw materials, in order to provide more efficient production in the future. Not only might total demand decrease, but older people would also probably be more cautious with their savings. If the accent were to be on security for savings, then more risky projects—possibly necessary to maintain a lead in world production—might be starved of money.

A declining population would also place an increasing burden on the 16-65 age group which, though supporting fewer children, would have to care for an ever increasing number of old people. Heavier calls would be made on the welfare services year by year. Larger amounts would need to be raised out of taxation in order to provide for more pensions and more hospitals. The process of redistributing incomes from workers to non-workers might, if carried too far, lead to loss of incentive to work and so to less, or less efficient, production.

Population size and the idea of optimum population

An **optimum population** is that which gives the greatest wealth per head for a given combination of resources, technical knowledge, and capital. If the population is too small in relation to resources, a state of *underpopulation* exists; if it is too large, a given country is suffering from *overpopulation*.

These notions seem fairly simple until we examine them more closely. An underpopulated country may exercise too small a demand for given goods to make production on a large scale profitable. The *market* is small. By way of example, we may point to the fact that New Zealand has no motor industry comparable with that of the UK. On the other hand, New Zealand's agricultural resources *are* used for the large-scale production of food, much of which is exported. New Zealand may, therefore, be

19

underpopulated as far as manufactures are concerned, but not in relation to agricultural products, because of the *nature* of its resources. Its standard of living is certainly not low. Again, Australia may appear underpopulated until we remember that a very large part of the continent consists of unproductive desert.

Recognition of optimum population

We have already seen that, in an overpopulated country, the increase in population, and thus in wants, is faster than the increase in the ability to satisfy these wants. The country has to 'run faster in order to stay in the same place', in the sense that increasing amounts of capital and new techniques are needed merely to *maintain* the present standard of living. Such a country will usually be an agricultural one in a 'Malthusian' situation, unable to obtain either more efficient agricultural production or make the changeover to industrialization. Such a situation is fairly easy to identify, but very difficult to improve.

Nevertheless, the idea of an optimum population is rather an unsatisfactory one. Conditions of technical knowledge, capital, and other resources are changing from decade to decade in every country; one can never tell when the optimum position has been reached. Two centuries ago, the UK would have been disastrously overpopulated with 50 million people; today, resources are so highly developed that we might feel alarmed if our population dropped much below that level. What may be the optimum level for an agricultural State is not that for an industrial one. Changes in birth rate, death rate, and migration are bound up with changes in living standards; such changes may well alter the ability of the population to produce maximum output per head. It is only situations of extreme overpopulation or underpopulation which can be easily appreciated; possible optimum levels are much more obscure.

Although we have noted possible problems arising out of the declining population in the UK, the world situation is such that some social scientists and environmentalists are now arguing that there should be no further population growth in this country. Such a growth has, in the past, given a dynamism to the economy. Pessimists would, therefore, argue that zero population growth means zero economic growth. The counter-argument is that economic techniques of handling the economy are now so sophisticated that the drive of a growing population is no longer necessary to keep production going. Of course, there are also those whose value judgement is that this relatively affluent society should no longer strive to obtain an increasing share of the world's wealth.

Occupational distribution

The **occupational distribution** indicates how the working population is earning its living. As the distribution changes over time, a good pointer is given as to which industries are becoming more or less important in a country. For example, if a country builds up its capital and technical knowledge, thus becoming more industrialized, it is likely that there will be fewer people employed in agriculture and more employed in manufacturing. This will not necessarily lead to reduced agricultural output, since more efficient techniques may be employed.

A striking feature of the most advanced economies is the number of people employed in producing services rather than goods. As standards of living rise, a lower proportion of total income is spent on food, housing, and clothes, while more is available for entertainment, holidays, and even law-suits! Again, the growth of State control over an economy will lead to a growth in the number of central and local government officers employed. The growth of the Welfare State is accompanied by a greater demand for both trained medical staff and for administrators. Another example might be the expansion of international trade which calls for more ships, insurance, and banking services.

There is also a relationship between occupational distribution, age structure, total population, and working population. If a large, youthful community provides many people capable of work, they are usually employed in those industries in which large amounts of labour can be used relative to other resources. Agriculture, for instance, may predominate. Where available numbers of people are small, the amount of other resources must be large in order to give a high level of output. We are back to the relationship between resources; this affects occupational distribution as much as standards of living.

Trends within the UK are a case in point. Over a century ago, the numbers employed in agriculture had begun to decline dramatically. In 1871, there were 1 700 000 agricultural workers in a population of 27 500 000 and the trend is still downwards. By 1971, the total population had virtually doubled, yet there were only 350 000 agricultural workers. For coal mining, there is a different picture; in both 1881 and 1971, about 430 000 miners were employed. Yet between 1900 and 1930, the figure was consistently over 1 000 000. In the century to 1971, the numbers employed in textiles fell by about a half to 650 000, and by 1975 this had declined by a further 100 000. Domestic servants, having numbered nearly 2 million, virtually disappeared from the records.

New occupations have emerged in the last 100 years. The chemical industry employed only 44 000 people in 1871. By 1971, the number had risen to 470 000, remaining fairly constant until 1975. However, perhaps the most dramatic changes were in the areas of service industries and public administration. These industries include not only such services as catering, but also financial, business, professional, and scientific activities. Public administration includes those employed in local as well as national government service. If we change our time scale, the percentage of total employees engaged in this sector increased from just over 25 per cent to about 32 per cent in the ten years after 1961. By 1975 this was around 35 per cent.

Geographical distribution

The place where a person lives within a country is often determined by the accident of birth. This is not so true, of course, of professional people, who tend to be rather more geographically mobile than manual workers. A second major influence on geographical distribution is industry and its location. Where agriculture predominates, population is likely to be spread relatively widely, taking advantage of the most fertile land. As soon as manufacturers grow up, on the other hand, the population tends to become more concentrated. (The question of industrial location is deferred to Unit 11.) The growth of services, like the growth of manufacturers, may also lead to a concentration in towns.

In 1975, 7100000 people lived in the Greater London area and 16900000 in the south-east of England. There were nearly 6.5 million inhabitants in the north-west of England, 5.2 million in the west Midlands and nearly 5 million in Yorkshire and Humberside. This compares with 5200000 in Scotland, 2700000 in Wales and 1500000 in Northern Ireland. Among the cities, Birmingham had a population of just over 1 million, Glasgow nearly 900000, and Belfast 370000. Only about one-fifth of the total population lived in rural areas. Some interesting facts emerge if geographical distribution and age structure are taken together. For example, the south coast of England has more than double the UK proportion of persons aged 60 or over, but is relatively underpopulated with persons of school age or in the age group 16–60. On the other hand, both the Home Counties and the West Midlands have a greater than average proportion of working population.

Population changes: the implications for organizations

We began this Unit by noting that organizations consist of people. Any change in the quantity or quality of people available therefore has an effect on the decisions made by organizations. A decision on where to set up production might be influenced by the location of manpower with a particular skill; one on how to produce (for example, whether to introduce labour-saving machinery or not) might be coloured by the existence of semi-skilled labour as opposed to craftsmen. This is only another way of saying that the geographical and occupational distribution of the workforce is an important consideration for organizations producing goods and services.

So, of course, is the total workforce available, the working population and, within that, the extent of employment. Workers and non-workers alike are consumers of the organization's products. Demands will always change as the age distribution alters or as the level of unemployment rises or falls. These demands fall on central and local government organizations as much as on private firms.

Government policy
Influence on population growth

Population growth is closely interrelated with government policy, and with government intervention through its organizations. Since the introduction of the National Health Service in 1948, medical care has for the most part been financed collectively. Medical research has led to a very low infant mortality rate and to the eradication of earlier scourges such as diphtheria, scarlet fever, and tuberculosis. The most important killer diseases—cancer and heart complaints—are now those of middle age. Such policies (and others such as the printing of health hazard warnings on cigarettes) have contributed to the position where a higher proportion of people than hitherto safely survives childbirth and has a greater expectation of life. On the other hand, policies such as legalized abortion and provision of improved contraceptives may possibly be having an effect on the birth rate. However, government policies directed towards securing a healthier population probably do not have a significant effect on population growth or decline.

Migration

A more pressing problem requiring government intervention is that of migration. In 1975, there were in the UK 1 800 000 immigrants from Pakistan and new Commonwealth countries other than Canada, Australia, and New Zealand, together with their offspring. Five per cent of the British population in 1966 had been born overseas as opposed to 2 per cent in 1931. It is natural that new immigrants to this country should seek their compatriots. In 1971, 6½ per cent of the population of Greater London consisted of people born in the new Commonwealth. This compared with 5 per cent for the west Midlands and 2 per cent for the UK as a whole. Since migrants bring both skills and labour but also a different way of life, social tensions are likely to arise, particularly in the specific areas, often decaying urban central areas, where they may be concentrated. Clearly, governments must have a migration policy, both for immigrants and emigrants, and, having decided their policy, must intervene to maintain it. Sometimes, of course, as in the case of the Ugandan Asians in late 1972, humanitarian considerations outweigh social and economic ones.

Occupational distribution

In an age of rapidly changing technology, government organizations must also concern themselves with, and attempt to influence, patterns of occupational distribution. Annual returns made by firms to the Department of Employment are used to ascertain the numbers in specified occupations. However, there was also one new feature of the 1961 census. By sampling—i.e., asking one household in ten—an attempt was made to find out how many people held technical and scientific qualifications. The answer turned out to be 287 610, of whom 255 940 were men. Not all these were working, so that the figure must be treated with some caution. Nevertheless, this was the first attempt to assess the country's trained manpower position. In the 1971 census, the question was extended to cover qualifications in all subjects other than those normally obtained at school, and a new question was asked about the possession of certain qualifications, such as the Ordinary National Certificate or Diploma, which are broadly equivalent to GCE Advanced level.

Retraining

The British government has done more than merely ascertain the facts. It has also intervened actively to help workers to change their jobs more easily. Employment exchanges have, of course, existed since before the First World War. In the past (and now, as Jobcentres) these government agencies have helped people to change their jobs more easily within their broad chosen sphere. However, government concern with retraining is a more recent development. In 1972, over fifty government Skill Centres were providing retraining for some 17 000 people. Additionally, the Training Opportunities Scheme, announced by the government in 1972, was specifically designed to retrain men and women from age nineteen upwards. This retraining takes place not only in the government Skill Centres, but also in colleges of further education; it can last for up to a year and is supported by a grant system. A rapid expansion of the Training Opportunities Scheme has taken place in the 'seventies and retraining will be provided for a great number of occupations.

Training is also undertaken, of course, by firms. In 1964 the Industrial Training Act set up Industrial Training Boards charged with the responsibility of exacting levies from and awarding training grants to firms in their industry. It was hoped that the cost of training would be shared more evenly between firms and that, as improvement in the quality and efficiency of industrial training took place, an adequate supply of properly trained men and women would become available in industry. Although improvements in both the quality and quantity of training appeared to have taken place between 1964 and 1972, in February of that year the Department of Employment proposed modifications to the scheme, including the establishment of the Manpower Services Commission with its associated Training Services Division, and the abandonment of the levy/grant system.

These examples are only a few of the multitude of population problems requiring government action. For example, we shall see in Unit 11 that the geographical distributions of industry and of population are interrelated and that the government has intervened to help regions with a maladjusted economic structure and above average unemployment rates. Whether one considers the National Health Service and public health, National Insurance, the provision of education through schools, colleges and universities, the encouragement of food supplies, retirement pensions, council houses, slum clearance, air pollution, or the provision of transport facilities, the same point emerges: government organizations are about people.

Any government policy, even if not a direct response to a population problem, influences one of the aspects of population which we have been discussing in this unit. The raising of the school-leaving age, some years ago, had an obvious effect on the size of the working population. However, changes in the rates of VAT and hire purchase deposits can have an equally important influence. Changes in demand for goods and services affect employment; this in turn can lead to retraining and movement within the UK and regional aid to promote employment; the problems associated with migration, which we have already examined, can follow fast.

Summary

The number of people in a country, in relation to available resources, is an important factor in the determination of standards of living. Equally important is the population structure, including the proportion at work, main occupations, and geographical distribution.

Total numbers are affected by changes in the birth rate and the death rate as well as by migration. Birth and death rates are themselves interconnected and are influenced by current living standards, by attitudes of mind, and by the state of medical knowledge.

Since the population structure must always be considered in relation to other resources, it is difficult to estimate an optimum population for any particular area. Conditions are always changing, for better or worse. In particular, the ideas of the Reverend Thomas Malthus must be subjected to critical analysis. Nevertheless, a rapidly increasing or decreasing population can lead to a serious decline in standards of living, since the economic structure of a country is often incapable of being adjusted rapidly enough to accommodate the change. While this is particularly true of such countries as India or China today, there is also the possibility that world population as a whole may be increasing too rapidly.

Population changes have implications for organizations because people are both producers and consumers of wealth. In particular, all policy decisions of central and local government organizations either influence or are influenced by such changes.

Assignments

1. From the statistical evidence provided in the latest available issue of Social Trends (Central Statistical Office: Annual), analyse any possible implications over the next ten years for:

    (a) the organization in which you work
              or
    (b) a firm producing hi-fi equipment
              or
    (c) a local government housing department
              or
    (d) a hypermarket
              or
    (e) British Rail.

2. Write a report, to be taken by a Director of Education to an education committee, dealing with the implications of population trends over the next twenty years for the local education service. (Consider school and college premises, staffing, and so on.)

Unit 3 Organizations in the private sector

As we have already seen, private and public sector organizations are devoted to the production of goods and services. The goods and services so produced are sold through markets or distributed by the State. Although organizations may be formed for one purpose, growth can take place, and the original purpose becomes diffused. A retail chain may set up its own wholesaling operation, and finally buy up manufacturing units until it controls a **vertically integrated** series of units of production. In a different way, a cigarette manufacturing organization may expand into the fast growing leisure industry. If an organization at the other end of the scale—for example a one-man business—wishes to grow, it may be limited by the personal skill and training of the owner. The differing forms of organization do not arise haphazardly; each has a purpose, and also advantages and disadvantages.

Why organizations are necessary

All organizations have at least one thing in common—they combine economic resources for the production of goods and services. This in turn means that somebody has to take decisions. In a society which believes in the institution of private property, the determination of what, where, when, and how to produce will be influenced by relative prices; in one which depends more on State action, the answers may come out of some central planning committee. In both cases, the policy decided upon must be carried out by organizations. Such organizations combine economic resources in the production of wealth.

Organizations usually endeavour to carry on production with a minimum of real cost, as resources must not be used wastefully. There is a continuing need for new and developing organizations because the economic situation is constantly changing, and invalidating yesterday's decisions. It may be right today to switch from the kind of production favoured previously. But that production may have involved the use of large amounts of capital equipment, which the new decision would make useless. For example, decisions made in the early 'seventies by the car industry to tool-up for the production of large cars now appear in a very different light given today's emphasis on energy conservation.

Where the situation is constantly changing there is bound to be uncertainty. The organization must live with this, try to anticipate change, and even take advantage of it. The risk of losing money sunk into the organization is always present. The reward for such risk, in the private sector, is profit. This reward goes to the entrepreneur, who bears the uncertainties of economic life and who is responsible for the policies of private sector organizations. As we shall see, the term 'entrepreneur' refers to different persons or groups in different organizations.

Types of organization: the private sector

Those organizations not controlled by central or local government are said to be in the private sector of the economy. The form which these organizations take depends very much upon what is being produced, and how much money capital is necessary. To produce steel, for example, demands a great deal of capital equipment, such as blast furnaces and rolling mills. It is unlikely, therefore, that a steel-producing organization would be very small or that any one person would have enough money to start it. On the other hand, a newly qualified accountant could set up in practice on his own, using a room in his house as an office. In brief, the form which an organization takes is usually related to its **scale of production**. This, in turn, is related to the amounts of money needed to form and operate the organization.

1. The one-man business

The distinguishing features of this form of organization are that one man raises the capital required to operate the business, and that the management and risks are borne by this one person. There may be employees in addition to the owner, but this does not alter the fact that the owner is the sole entrepreneur.

Although there are one-man organizations engaged in the production of goods, the vast majority are in the service industries. As living standards rise, societies demand a greater proportion of services, partly because more income is available for this purpose. The past decade has seen a mushrooming of travel agencies, shops selling take-away meals and convenience foods, hairdressing and beauty salons, and many other services. These frequently operate on a relatively small scale—often as one-man businesses. From the examples given it is clear that this type of organization predominates where the amount of money (capital) needed for the business is relatively small. Even within this category, amounts of capital required may vary enormously. For example, a newly formed estate agency needs far less capital than a new shop, which in turn needs much less capital normally than a business producing goods.

Funds

The main source of funds to start a one-man business is the savings of the owner. In addition, borrowing is possible, particularly to buy premises, and credit from suppliers can be used as a source of working capital. Financial support for small businesses is often available from government and other sources (which will be examined in later Units).

Once a business has been established on a sound footing an owner's thoughts will often turn to plans for expansion. For example, a shopkeeper may consider stocking a wider variety of goods, or perhaps opening another branch selling the same lines as those in the original shop. These plans need additional capital which would come mainly from profits in previous years ploughed back into the business. The owner could also use his own savings or borrow money to finance expansion.

Risk

Even in a successful business, a sole proprietor bears no small financial burden on his own. He can use the profits either for his personal needs and benefit or he can keep them in the business—he cannot do both. His employees must be paid promptly and

27

his suppliers will expect their bills to be paid on time. As his sales of goods and services are the source of funds, these must be maintained and, hopefully, expanded. He must try to get his own customers or clients to pay promptly. If he is not successful in his business, the risk of failure is his alone; his *liability is unlimited*, and he is responsible for his debts to the extent of all his business and personal possessions.

Management

In addition to the financial burden which the owner of a one-man business must bear, he is also responsible for the management of the organization. This may involve long hours of work for him, and often for members of his family. Finally, on the death of the owner, a one-man business may come to an end, particularly if taxes have to be paid on his estate. The return for this burden is the independence which many people seek— and, of course, the possibility of accumulating wealth.

In view of these problems and disadvantages, it is not surprising that many owners of one-man businesses seek ways of sharing the burden and removing some of the risks which they run. They may do this by entering into a partnership or by forming a limited company. It is to the first of these that we now turn.

HELP ON WAY FOR SMALL FIRMS

THE CHANCELLOR is to announce further measures to lift the weight of taxation from the "little man". He appreciates that difficulties are faced by small firms, a spokesman said. The Minister responsible for small firms is looking into ways in which more help might be given.

The most obvious way is in relation to VAT where the threshold is thought by many to be set too low at present. Other possibilities for action are . . .

2. The partnership

Partnerships may be formed for a variety of reasons. These include raising additional capital for expansion, bringing in a partner for the special skills he possesses, as well as the sharing of the management and risks attached to a business. Normally, the number of partners is limited to twenty; however, in the case of some professions there is no such limit. Solicitors, accountants, and estate agents, for example, fall in this category. Although the majority of partnerships exist for the provision of professional services, this form of organization is also common in small-scale manufacturing industries, in farming, and in the distributive trades.

While service partnerships do not generally require large amounts of capital, the limitation on numbers may seriously hinder the expansion of other partnerships. Also, each partner is personally liable for the debts of the partnerships to the extent of his private assets. All partners normally take a share in the management of the firm and the possibilities for disagreement multiply as the firm grows. This disagreement, or the death of a partner, may well bring the enterprise to an end.

It is possible to set up a **limited partnership**, in which some partners are only liable for the amount of capital which they have put into the business. There must, however, be at least one general partner in the firm and limited partners must take no part in the management of the business—they cannot, for example, enter into contracts on behalf of the firm. Although limited partnerships have not been popular in the past, there is now a growing interest in them. The affairs of the partnership still remain private but, at the same time, new capital can be attracted by offering limited liability to some partners.

Partnership agreement

Where care and forethought have gone into forming a partnership, the relationships between the partners are generally carefully set out in a **partnership agreement**. This contains, at the very least, profit-sharing arrangements, details of capital to be invested, partnership salaries, whether drawings in anticipation of profits are to be allowed, and, possibly, how disputes are to be settled—for example, by a majority vote. However, not all partnerships are carefully formed. Indeed, many exist without the people involved realizing that they are trading in partnership. In such cases, the relationships between the partners are governed by the Partnership Act 1890. This Act of Parliament applies to all partnerships, wherever there is a gap in the partnership agreement, if an agreement exists at all. For example, if the partners have not agreed about the sharing of profits and losses, the Act decrees that they should be shared equally. In the same way, it is assumed that all partners have the right to invest equal amounts of capital in the firm, and also the right to equal amounts of capital if the partnership comes to an end.

The terms of the agreement are legally binding on each of the partners and therefore, each can enforce the agreement against the others, by legal action if necessary. Equally, if the agreement is silent on the matter in dispute, the courts will enforce the rules of the Partnership Act on behalf of a partner.

3. The joint stock company

(a) General considerations

As we have seen, the owner of a business or the partners in a firm (except for limited partners), are subject to unlimited liability. The attraction of **limited liability**, available in this special form of a limited partnership, is very useful to encourage investment. The **joint stock company** is a form of organization which offers limited liability to investors, but which does not have the restrictions of a partnership.

At present there are two forms of joint stock company: the private limited company and the public limited company. Both types are regulated mainly by the Companies Acts of 1948 and 1967. Their fundamental structure is so similar that in considering basic principles they may be taken together.

Formation of a company

If it is wished to form a limited company, a **memorandum of association** must be completed by the promoters of the company. The memorandum must always state the proposed name of the company, the situation of the registered office, and the objects of the company. It must also indicate that the liability of the members is limited, both expressly and by including the word 'limited' in the company's name. Finally, it indicates the amount of share capital to be issued, the form that the shares will take, and the fact that the founding members (who must sign the memorandum) wish to form a company registered under the Companies Acts and are prepared to hold a stipulated number of shares in it.

By reference to a memorandum, intending future shareholders (i.e., members) can establish the objects for which the company was formed. A company is restricted in the ways in which it may change its original objects. Partly for this reason, objects clauses tend to be very widely drawn. In Unit 5, the objects of a company are considered in relation to contracts made by the company.

In addition to the memorandum, a set of **articles of association** must be compiled. The articles govern the internal constitution and operation of the company. A company may adopt a standard set of articles, known as Table A, contained in the Companies Act 1948, if it so wishes. Even if it prepares its own articles, the standard articles in the Act will apply whenever there are inconsistencies.

The memorandum and articles of association must be registered with the Registrar of Companies, who will issue a **certificate of incorporation**. This important document establishes the company as a legal entity in its own right, thus ensuring continuity. 'John Smith & Company Limited' may go on for centuries, despite the fact that, over the years, the 'company' will be composed of different individuals each with the right of limited liability.

Together with a *certificate of incorporation*, the Registrar of Companies also issues a **certificate of trading** after the founding members and the directors have taken up their shares. These shares can take several forms. The most commonly issued is an **ordinary share**. The purchaser of an ordinary share becomes a part-owner of the company, shouldering the uncertainties up to the limit of the purchase price of the shares, and participating in full in any distribution of profits. Somewhat more secure, though usually less lucrative (in good times), is the **preference share** which, if profits are made, limits the dividend entitlement to a stipulated percentage. Another variation is the **cumulative preference share**, which enables the dividend not paid in a year of loss to be carried on to a further year when a profit is made. The participating preference share is a hybrid, earning both a fixed percentage dividend and, under conditions of high profit, an extra dividend. A company may also raise capital by offering **debentures** for sale. These are quite different from shares, in the sense that the owner of a debenture is a creditor of the company, but not a part-owner. The debenture offers a fixed rate of interest irrespective of the profit or loss made in a given accounting period. It can thus be regarded as the least risky form of security to hold. Equally, if a company goes into liquidation, the debenture-holders must be repaid before the shareholders.

(b) Differences between private and public limited companies

A private company must have a minimum of two and a maximum of fifty shareholders.

On the other hand, a public company with a minimum of seven has no upper limit on the number of shareholders it may have. Thus a private company is still restricted in the amount of capital it may raise and is suitable mainly for small or middle-sized family enterprises. One of the great advantages of a public joint stock company is that the composition of its membership may be easily changed, as shares are freely transferable.

Small companies need more finance

EVIDENCE to the Wilson Committee shows that inadequate financial services may hinder the development of smaller companies. Problems in raising finance can lead to the acceptance of a take-over bid as an easy way out it was stated by a leading firm of stockbrokers. However, stock exchange rules allow trading in the shares of unquoted companies. In this way the availability of funds may be extended, it was said.

This form of trading was seen only as a second best to a full quotation.

To make their shares more marketable, many public companies (about one-quarter) seek a Stock Exchange 'quotation'. The Stock Exchange Council undertakes searching inquiries and has onerous requirements before it allows trading in a company's shares to take place. In particular, a company wishing to 'go public' and at the same time seeking a Stock Exchange quotation must issue a **prospectus,** which must state that a Stock Exchange quotation is being sought. It must also contain the most intimate details of the company's history and some forecast of its prospects. The prospectus will be accepted by, and registered with the Registrar of Companies. Nevertheless, when all the formalities have been successfully completed, the public joint stock company is in a better position than the private one whose shares may be transferred only if other shareholders agree. In addition, a public company, and particularly one with a Stock Exchange quotation, is able to raise further capital more easily because of the marketability of its shares.

4. Co-operatives

The co-operative movement may take one of two forms. **Producer co-operatives** are a means by which workers themselves undertake the uncertainties of production, acting as managers and entrepreneurs. Although producer co-operatives flourish outside the UK, particularly among farmers, they have failed to establish themselves in this country in exactly the same form. Skilled managers, capable of meeting changing economic conditions in open competition with joint stock companies, are difficult to find. Furthermore, the amounts of capital required for production on a large scale are often beyond the means of workers themselves. However, a hybrid form of co-

31

operative has recently come into existence. Following closure proposals, the workers in a firm have themselves set up the organization to run it, rather than accept closure. The capital has generally come from the National Enterprise Board, and also from the workers themselves. While some have been successful, others have suffered from the same problems as the former organization.

Consumer co-operation, on the other hand, took a firm hold in the last century. This business form, limited to the retail trade, is one in which the consumers themselves are the shareholders. Profits on the enterprise are returned to members in proportion to their purchases. The consumer co-operative movement started in the north of England, but is now widespread. In the mid 'sixties the enthusiasm which sustained it seemed to be evaporating to some extent. The advent of the supermarket and of other efficient organizations increased competition. Co-operatives, run largely by boards of management, sometimes suffered from their seeming inability to move with the times. Although they were backed by the Co-operative Wholesale Society, which distributes to the retail co-operatives, and although they were represented in Parliament, their share of important parts of the retail market was declining. This decline now seems to have been halted, and in some areas reversed. This has been done in several ways. Greater efficency has been achieved by merging societies into larger units. Television advertising has helped by creating a more up-to-date public image. Dividends have been distributed immediately by giving trading stamps on purchases. More important, the increase in the range of merchandise stocked, appealing to a wider range of consumer, has helped to boost sales. This has been done partly through separate cut-price discount stores operating outside the main framework of a society's shops.

The growth of organizations in the private sector

As we have seen, the form which an organization takes is often related to its size. Medium and large-sized organizations in the private sector are almost invariably joint stock companies. Where the unit of physical production, the **plant**, is large, then the organization of necessity is large. Large-scale production, say of ships, does not necessarily imply mass production. However, where this is technically possible and where sales are also likely to be great, large organizations are very likely to occur, irrespective of what they are producing. Business organizations, however, are rarely static. Often they grow from small beginnings, taking on some of the forms which we have examined. Sometimes they are established fully blown. It is now time to analyse the process of growth.

Reasons for growth

(a) Efficiency

Growth has a considerable effect on the costs of production, and we shall examine this more closely in Unit 7. It is sufficient, meanwhile, to refer to **economies of scale**.

Internal economies of scale arise from more efficient operations within the organization. Even when technical factors do not demand a large-sized firm, *technical economies of scale* can often be achieved during growth. Development in production methods, for example, invariably cuts costs by speeding up production. The carpet

32

industry has seen remarkable changes in technology in the last twenty years—years which have seen a decline in traditional weaving methods and the meteoric rise of tufted carpeting, following investment in new machinery. In this way, a more efficient combination of capital and manpower is achieved. The same argument has led to the development of the supertanker, which carries oil at less cost per unit weight than smaller ones. At its destination, the oil is refined in an integrated petrochemical plant which is more efficient in turning raw materials into a variety of products such as petrol and nylon. All these exemplify possible technical economies of scale.

Such technical economies of scale are usually expensive to finance. We noted earlier that as an organization grows it has easier access to large amounts of money capital, particularly as a joint stock company with a Stock Exchange quotation. Because of this it can usually also achieve *financial economies of scale*. Because large organizations are regarded as safer than smaller ones—sometimes wrongly so—they can usually obtain bank overdrafts on more favourable terms. Similarly, in relation to the raising of capital, it is often cheaper to raise large amounts than small ones through the machinery of the capital market.

Closely associated with specialized equipment and easier opportunities for finance is *specialized management*. The sole proprietor has to carry all the management on his shoulders. The large company, on the other hand, can afford to have separate works, sales, personnel, and purchasing staff. The professional associations of accountants, company secretaries, and the like stem from the growth of organizations which occurred at the end of the last century. Computers are now used by every large organization and their operation is usually under the control of skilled managers. Large companies are often broken down into divisions and the special skills of managers used in the production of different commodities. ICI Ltd, for example, has among its many divisions petrochemicals, agricultural products, paints, and pharmaceuticals.

The larger organization which we are considering can often obtain **marketing economies** because they can buy in bulk. They can take advantage of cheap prices for raw materials, stockpiling against the time when prices rise. Advertising campaigns can increase demand for products, and this can be backed by a large sales organization. Both stockpiling and advertising cost money, but such expenditure is worth while if income is increased by some greater amount. When an organization has products which are household names it will certainly have achieved marketing economies.

In the area of **risk-bearing economies**, the larger an organization is, the easier it is for it to overcome business uncertainties. Business economists may be employed to try to forecast future trends. Products may be diversified so not too many eggs are in one basket; expansion is possible into complementary industries. The smaller, specialized organization is very vulnerable to fluctuations in demand, for whatever reason, and cannot escape easily from the straitjacket of its size.

Another way in which a large organization may establish and maintain a cost advantage is by the use of its own *research and development* (R & D) department. Most inventions these days are likely to be produced by expert teams of scientists and engineers, heavily financed, and building on what has gone before. Research and development may result in improved equipment from which larger quantities of

33

cheaper products flow. Again, the R & D team may concentrate on the product itself—they may produce new and improved drugs, better paints, tougher carpets, new computers, soft margarine. It is also part of the R & D function to move ahead of, and thus create, demand. The development of the small calculator is a recent and important example of this. Research and development is an expensive business. Many millions of pounds may be spent developing a new drug or a new car. However, the growth arising from such expenditure exemplifies the cost-lowering processes of internal economies of scale. Scientific and engineering discoveries may lead to technical economies. The degree of specialization among research workers is an example of managerial economies. Market research may lead to marketing economies; new products help to spread the burden of uncertainty.

An organization may also be able to take advantage of *external* economies of scale. These are usually related to the area in which an organization is located. Many suppliers and customers of the organization will be fairly local. There will be opportunities for co-operation in the training of personnel. Service industries will develop which specialize in the needs of the area. Specialized transport facilities and marketing agencies will be there, and banks and insurance companies will be aware of local needs. Chambers of commerce will provide a forum for discussion. Local government will be aware of the need to keep a healthy variety of employment in the area. In a word, it is the infrastructure of the region in which the organization finds itself which provides external economies—or, in some cases, diseconomies—of scale.

It may be asked, in view of all the advantages of scale so far discussed, why small firms exist at all. One reason might be that small firms are in the early stages of their development and will grow eventually. Another, more general one, is that large organizations are just not necessary for many kinds of production. Their very existence would produce *diseconomies of scale*. We have already seen (page 27) that where the provision of services is concerned, a large organization is unnecessary. In the retail trade, small shops exist alongside large ones because of the specialized goods they offer, or because their customers come from the immediate locality, and are therefore limited .in number.

Where the production of goods takes place, the amount of possible sales must be considered. Thus, mass production of cars is quite feasible, large-scale (but not mass) production of ships is essential, but sporting guns still have care lavished upon them by craftsmen in small Birmingham workshops.

Other disadvantages concern **management**. Specialization carried too far may lead to higher, rather than lower, costs. Managers themselves must be managed. The extended chain of command may lead to more impersonal relationships and to failures of communication. As we have seen, large organizations are often subdivided, partly to avoid such problems. Marketing economies, too, are excellent as long as they succeed; but if conditions change, the large organization has more to lose than the smaller one.

Small firms will continue to exist where economies of scale are not important cost-reducing influences, or where constraints exist in terms of managerial skills, finance, or markets. If, as Adam Smith said, 'division of labour is limited by the extent of the market', this has its parallel in the size of firms.

34

(b) Market control

As organizations grow, they are usually able to take advantage of lower costs; indeed, this may be one of their objectives. Often, another objective is profit maximization. This can come from lower costs, but it can also come from higher prices. If an organization grows far enough, it gains a strong bargaining position, or even monopoly or semi-monopoly power. If a firm has no, or few, competitors—such as in the detergent industry—it is in a much stronger position to regulate prices in the absence of government intervention. If such an organization does not have competition, it does not have to allocate part of its resources to defend itself against such competition. Sometimes an organization will grow to achieve a quiet life, this being the objective of its managers. Having attained this, it will merely attempt to maintain its share of the market. At the other extreme, an organization may seek power, and to this end will grow aggressively. The scale of the vast multi-national company is such that governments must sometimes bow to their policies—for example, where the location and operation of new plants are concerned. This occurred in the case of the construction of oil drilling and production platforms in the north of Scotland.

The process of growth

During its growth, an organization may take on in turn each of the forms we have examined. Equally, it may start as a comparatively large joint stock company, and grow within that form. Both types of growth are the result of self-contained expansion; no other organization is involved. Such expansion leads, not only to a growth in the size of the particular organization, but also to a growth of the whole industry in which it operates.

More complicated is that method of growth which involves the coming together of two or more hitherto independent business units. In this case, the industry as a whole is not growing. The combination may range from a loose agreement to a complete amalgamation of two or more units. Furthermore, organizations may combine with others producing a similar product, with their suppliers, with their retailers, or in some other way. All these points must be considered separately.

We will first consider the ways in which combination is possible. The loosest form is an *understanding* between two independent firms which enables each to survive. This understanding may concern shares of the market, agreed selling areas, information sharing, or price-fixing agreements. Such associations, particularly if they have a common marketing system and operate a form of rationing of supply, are called **cartels**. Of more importance, in the British context today, is the amalgamation of two or more firms into a new unit. This might be carried out on the initiative of one of the firms using the method of the 'take-over' bid. An offer is made, to the shareholders of the other company, for their shares; the offer may take the form of cash or shares in the company making the offer, or both. If the offer is accepted, the two companies amalgamate. Often this form of amalgamation takes place amicably, with both companies seeing benefits from the **merger**. Another form of structure is possible, whereby a **holding company** is formed to control the operations of a number of companies. The companies themselves retain their separate identities, but may have some directors in common, thus forming what is known as an interlocking directorate.

35

The traditional analysis of the process of integration is to identify three forms: horizontal, vertical, and lateral. **Horizontal integration** takes place when firms combine with others making a similar product, such as bread. This may give each the opportunity to specialize—in areas of the market, for example. One result of such a merger may be economies of scale.

Vertical integration is said to take place when firms controlling different stages of a productive process combine. Unilever owns not only the factories which produce margarine; it owns estates for producing vegetable oil, and whalers for obtaining animal oils—raw materials used in margarine. It also has its own fleet of ships to transport these materials. Such backwards integration is paralleled by one of integration forwards when a manufacturer of women's clothing purchases the shops where the output is sold.

Lateral integration involves the amalgamation of organizations which are either making complementary products or providing complementary services or, more commonly nowadays, diversifying into new fields. The P & O shipping company, for instance, combined laterally with a travel firm. It then acquired a stake in North Sea and American oil. It is now part of a large and diversified group whose latest acquisition is a newspaper chain. The first of these moves is lateral integration; the second and third are diversifications into what is now known as a **conglomerate**. Force of circumstances may cause a brewery company to seek diversification into both food and leisure industries. It should be noted that combinations other than horizontal may not give the same opportunities for saving through economies of scale.

P & O income boosted by energy

THE P & O shipping group now gets about a quarter of its gross revenue from its energy division, compared with under two per cent only two years before. This dramatic increase has been brought about by expansion of its American oil and gas interests. The group is involved in both exploration and selling from around 3000 oil and gas wells through storage centres, a large road tanker fleet, and pipeline systems.

P & O is also moving rapidly into the oil supply business in Britain. At present, fuel is bought from the major oil companies and deliveries made mainly to commercial customers.

Multi-nationals

The growth of firms is not necessarily confined to national boundaries. Large firms may have associated companies or subsidiaries in other countries and thus become known as multi-nationals. Royal Dutch Shell, for example, by its very name indicates its British/Dutch link. Unilever also has strong Dutch connections, while ICI has major subsidiaries in Australia, North and South America, Canada, India, and Japan. The home country is that in which the head office is situated. As we shall see in Book 2, multi-national companies may pose major problems, in investment, taxation, and other areas, for national governments.

Problems of growth

It may be assumed that growing organizations consider that growth is good for them. We have seen that the advantages they seek to gain range from cost reduction to survival tactics, which may include diversification. It is by no means certain, however, that the anticipated gains always come about. The increase in total profit may not match the increased assets employed. There can be diseconomies of scale as well as economies, and costs may not fall as firms increase in size. Research and development expenditure, which we have examined, may not be justified by results. We should, therefore, be wary of assuming that it is a good thing for organizations to grow in size in an attempt to achieve lower costs.

This is particularly the case when we consider the positions of the consumer, of the organization, of the community, and the economy at large. Lower costs do not necessarily result in lower prices to the consumer, although government intervention through the Price Commission has had some effect. The results of growth may be somewhat antisocial. Not only may prices rise but consumers may find choice limited, because fewer firms are in existence. This may be all very well when it comes to washing powders, but is not such a good thing where, for example, drugs and medicines are concerned. Another result of growth is that large organizations may prevent newcomers from establishing a toehold in the market, despite the fact that the newcomers might be bringing in new ideas and new products. From the point of view of the community, it may be unhealthy for a large organization to dominate the area. There may be too much dependence, both in direct employment, and in other industries, upon the large firm. Its growth may result in fewer jobs, if capital-intensive expansion is planned to replace older, labour-intensive plant.

These are just some of the problems of growth, looked at from the point of view of the outsider. The emphasis has been on problems, rather than benefits, which equally can flow from growth. As so often in our studies, every case must be considered on its own merits.

The concept of optimum size

It might be thought, when looking at the question of growth, that there is, for every organization, a best size. That is to say, a size where production cost per unit is at its lowest, together with maximum benefit to everyone else concerned. Unfortunately, this concept of best, or **optimum** size is a nebulous one. First, economies of scale very rarely indicate the same size. What is best for technical production may be too small or too large for efficient marketing or management. Second, economic conditions are always changing. An optimum size achieved at one time may be wrong at another.

37

Third, organizations do not grow smoothly, but by a series of jumps. There may often be no middle way between being very small and very large. Another factor is that the size of an organization is not necessarily within its own control. The existence of a single, or dominant, customer will usually determine the scale of operation. Thus, although it is usually possible to see whether a firm should aim at being large or small and whether it should be organized by a sole proprietor, a partnership, or a joint stock company, one can rarely say that it has reached its optimum size. Still less can one say that it should sit tight—if it did, the tide of economic affairs would probably leave it high and dry.

Summary

Organizations are necessary in the process of production. Resources must not be used wastefully, and decisions must be made to meet changing conditions. Risk and uncertainty are involved and these are borne by the entrepreneur. In the private sector the entrepreneurial function can be seen in the sole trader, in partners, and in the members of a joint stock company. The public joint stock company is the most important type of private sector organization since it has a continuous life, can command larger amounts of money through the issue of shares and debentures, and its shareholders have the privilege of limited liability.

Each form of organization has a purpose and advantages. Partnerships, co-operatives, and joint stock companies enable people to combine in business. Their relationships are regulated largely by Acts of Parliament.

Organizations, once formed, are usually dynamic and grow. During this growth they may take one or more of the forms which we have examined. Growth is often linked with size and this depends on the nature of the productive process, the type of market served, and the opportunities available for specialization. There are two main reasons why growth is desired. The first, efficiency, is concerned with cost reduction through internal and external *economies of scale*. However, each organization is limited in such economies, after which diseconomies of scale set in. Thus, there is still a place for the small firm in the British economy. The second reason for growth is concerned with *market control*. This phrase covers a whole range of attitudes on the part of organizations, from the desire for higher profits to power-seeking.

Organizations may grow either by self-contained expansion or, more likely, by combining with others.

Such combinations may range in form from informal agreements, through mergers, to complete integration. Such integration may be horizontal, vertical, or lateral, leading to conglomerates.

Not all growth is necessarily beneficial to the organization. Equally, consumers, the community, and the economy may benefit from lower costs but may suffer from higher prices, restricted choice and problems related to employment. Although it is possible, theoretically, to conceive an optimum size of organization, this is rarely achieved or maintained.

Assignment

A government Minister is sometimes given responsibility for small firms.

(a) Explain why this is considered necessary.

(b) What problems do you think that small firms might have which could be helped by government action? (See press cuttings on pages 28 and 31).

Unit 4   Organizations in the public sector

We turn now to an examination of organizations in the **public sector** of the economy—that is, to those organizations which are controlled, directly or indirectly, by the State. Two major groups can immediately be identified: those organizations through which *central government* functions are carried out, and those through which *local government* operates. It should be noted at the outset that the organizations to be examined all function under powers granted to them by Parliament.

We shall see that there is as much variety and change in this sector as in the private sector. All governments carry out certain basic functions, such as tax collection and law enforcement to preserve the fabric of the State. However, there are many areas of policy in which the major political parties differ. Thus, a change of government inevitably brings about changes in the functions of existing public sector organizations; new ones will also be created.

The modern State, for political, social, and economic reasons, finds it necessary to extend its activities into areas other than pure government. The major one which we shall examine is that which includes the **nationalized** industries. Here, the State, through public corporations, controls the production of goods and services, more often than not without competition from the private sector. In addition, many government-appointed bodies carry out a wide variety of activities, and these will also be examined.

Central government organizations

General considerations

Following a general election, the leader of the majority party will be called upon to form a government. As *Prime Minister*, the leader will appoint Ministers from among his supporters. The majority of Ministers will be Members of the House of Commons, the balance being from the House of Lords. Not all Ministers are of equal rank. In modern governments, several *Ministries* are often grouped into a large **department**. Those in charge of such departments, (normally *Secretaries of State*), will be assisted by other Ministers bearing a variety of titles. In addition there are Ministers in charge of separate departments, and also appointments made without departmental responsibility. A number of senior Ministers will be invited to joint the *Cabinet* by the Prime Minister. In October, 1976, this number was twenty-three. Within the Cabinet, policies are put forward, discussed, and finally, decisions are made on how the policies will be implemented.

The Prime Minister, the Cabinet, and other Ministers constitute the government of the day. Ministers are responsible for ensuring that policies relating to their department are carried out. In addition, they are answerable to Parliament for the conduct of their departments. We can now examine the main features of these departments, and also the way in which government policies are given effect by them.

Central government departments: structure and functions

It is almost impossible to listen to a news bulletin or to read a newspaper without hearing or seeing a reference to a *government department*. During labour disputes, the Department of Employment is much involved. North Sea oil and gas are the concern of the Department of Energy. The Foreign and Commonwealth Office is responsible for much of Britain's overseas affairs. These are just three examples of the twenty or so major departments of State, whose influence extends to almost every aspect of our lives. As governments change, so does the way in which government activities are organized. New departments are created to meet new circumstances. The need for closer control of natural resources led to the formation of the Department of Energy. The drought of 1976 created a sudden awareness of the country's water supply problems; a Minister was immediately given special responsibility for water resources. Governments will create departments to put into effect a particular policy. Thus, we now have a Department of Prices and Consumer Protection—a department which did not exist separately before 1973.

Another cause of change arises when it is felt that separate Ministries would operate more efficiently if merged. This can happen when there is a close relationship between the functions of each Ministry. The present Department of Health and Social Security includes former Ministries of Health, National Insurance, Pensions, and National Assistance.

We can now examine the functions and structure of two of the departments mentioned, those of *Energy*, and *Prices and Consumer Protection*.

The **Department of Energy** is concerned with national energy policy and the development of new forms of energy production. It has particular responsibility for the

No bonanza in North Sea oil - BNOC chief

A DRAMATIC increase in oil prices is needed to produce a "bonanza" from the North Sea, the chairman of the British National Oil Corporation told the select committee on nationalized industries. Inflation and serious underestimation of the costs involved had resulted in "enormous overspend" on the development of North Sea oilfields, he said. As a result, now that the easier fields had been explored and developed, the future would be more costly. The BNOC might have to take a major role . . .

41

nationalized industries producing coal, gas, electricity, and atomic energy. Another major aspect of its work is the control of the exploitation of offshore oil and gas fields; this is done mainly through the British National Oil Corporation, a public corporation formed for this purpose. The department is split into divisions, each specializing in an aspect of the work. Thus there is a Coal Division and an Oil Policy (Home) Division among the eighteen or so major sections. In addition, there is one section, the Offshore Supplies Office, which has its headquarters in Glasgow. This section is concerned with ensuring that industry in Great Britain is capable of providing the specialized supplies and equipment needed in oil and gas exploration and production.

The formation of the **Department of Prices and Consumer Protection** arose out of an awareness that the government should take a positive role in these important areas. Some of the impetus came from the work of unofficial bodies such as the Consumers' Association; some came from the realization that government action seemed to be necessary to control prices and to redress the inequality between consumers and the organizations with which they deal. The department operates in the two major areas which its title suggests. Its control of prices is carried out mainly through the Price Commission, whose work the department supervises. Applications, by organizations, for price increases of their products are scrutinized by the Commission. The department also has powers regarding prices in the shops. Price control is, of course, one aspect of consumer protection. Other aspects include standards of products and the

Tea prices: Minister acts

VOLUNTARY cuts have been rejected by tea firms and the government is to force companies to cut prices. The Secretary of State for Prices and Consumer Protection is using his powers under the Prices Act 1974 and will fix maximum price levels. Price Commission recommendations will form the basis of consultation with the industry but only a week has been allowed for this. For their part, the major tea blenders reject the Commission's findings as inaccurate, pointing out that prices have already been cut considerably.

weights and measures by which such products are sold. The department has a division specializing in this work. It has also established the Office of Fair Trading under the control of the Director General of Fair Trading; the work of the Office is considered in detail in Unit 15.

The two departments whose work we have examined have a direct impact on the work of all organizations. However, they are far from being the only ones to have such an effect. A glance down a list of government departments will reveal **Departments of Trade, Industry, Environment, Transport,** and **Education**. There are **Offices** for **Scottish** and **Welsh** affairs which have a great deal of autonomy, being responsible for many functions carried out in England by separate departments. The Treasury, as the major financial department of State, has great influence on the work of all other departments and upon the policies of all organizations. Its advice to the government may result in measures which directly affect the level of economic activity in the country. These, then, are the major departments through which government policies are carried out.

Central government departments: Ministers and civil servants

As we have seen, each major department has at its head a Minister of the government in power. Under the doctrine of ministerial responsibility, the Minister, as political head of the department, assumes personal responsibility to Parliament for all actions taken by the department. In its everyday form this results in his answering Parliamentary questions and speaking in parliament and the Cabinet on major policy matters concerning his department. Under-secretaries and Ministers of State in the department are also concerned with Parliamentary questions on those matters for which they have responsibility. In addition, Ministers frequently have to defend their department and justify a course of action which has been taken. This responsibility is accepted and merely private action is taken against any civil servant whose mistake or misconduct has occasioned criticism.

The Ministers in a department (rarely more than five), have the responsibility of communicating government policy to their senior officials, the senior civil servants in the department. These men and women advise on the ways in which that policy can be made effective. This may be done by a new Act of Parliament or by making further regulations under existing powers. New staff may be required or existing staff retrained. Ideally, every action of the officials at all levels should be within a policy which is known and understood. Equally, Ministers need the advice of officials who often have very long experience of public affairs and of the department in which they are working. The advice which they give to Ministers can be based on such experience and on a knowledge of how well the department is serving the community. Officials at all levels are aware of social and economic problems affecting the work of the department, often through consultations with interested groups. By channelling this information to Ministers, any necessary action can be taken to enable the department to serve the community more effectively.

Local government organizations
General considerations

In our examination of central government organizations we have seen that some of   43 them are much in evidence at local level. The offices of the Department of Health and Social Security are one such example. This illustrates one problem which faces every government—which of the many essential functions need to be administered centrally and which are best run locally? Some—such as defence, social security, and energy—are obviously of national rather than local concern. Other functions will necessarily be restricted to a relatively small geographical area. Local bus services and the provision of libraries are examples of this. But not every function of government is so easily identifiable as being solely of national or of local concern. The setting and maintaining of national standards in education is important. However, local knowledge is essential to decide on the number and siting of schools. It can thus be appreciated that, even though local administration is desirable in some instances, central government supervision may still be necessary.

The re-organization of local government

A major re-organization of local government took place in recent years. This was largely on the basis of the recommendations of the Redcliffe-Maud Commission on Local Government. One reason for the reform was that many local authorities, because of their small size, found it difficult to maintain an adequate level of services. This often resulted in a disparity of standards of provision between neighbouring authorities. It was, therefore, a matter of urgency to establish a system of local government which reflected modern patterns of population and social needs. Since 1974, the whole of England and Wales (outside London) has been divided into counties, each county being further split into districts. Six of the counties (consisting of the major conurbations) are designated metropolitan counties, the subdivisions of which are metropolitan districts. While the non-metropolitan counties are generally based on the old counties (with some amalgamations), there has been a positive attempt to produce districts which broadly reflect patterns of settlement, transport, and work. Before the work and organization of the counties and districts are examined, it is worth noting that districts are not subordinate to counties. We shall see that the functions allocated to local government have been divided between the two.

Metropolitan counties and districts

The **metropolitan counties** are relatively small but densely populated areas. They are: Tyne and Wear, West Yorkshire, South Yorkshire, Merseyside, Greater Manchester, and West Midlands. In establishing these counties, the government referred to 'areas of continuous development' being drawn within the boundaries. Thus towns which previously might have been separate local government units, became, for some purposes, part of a larger unit, the metro-county. It was the need to consider physically adjacent areas as a whole which led to the allocation of certain functions to the metropolitan county. These functions are, principally, highways, traffic, transport and the police and fire services. In addition, the preparation of the main structure plan for the area is a county function. Refuse disposal is also a responsibility, but may be carried out by the districts.

The **metropolitan district** carries out functions which have been allocated to the smaller area, mainly because the need for these services can differ, even in adjoining

44

districts. The major functions are housing, control of local planning within the county plan, and refuse collection. In addition, metropolitan districts have responsibility for education, social services and libraries. A shared function, and one which is growing in importance, is that of arts and recreation.

Non-metropolitan counties and districts

Non-metropolitan counties, as might be expected, are generally larger in area than their metropolitan counter-parts. On the other hand, many of them are relatively sparsely populated, containing perhaps only one or two large centres of population. Others would almost merit metropolitan status. (In early re-organization proposals, South Hampshire, including Southampton and Portsmouth, was a proposed metropolitan area). Thus it can be appreciated that the allocation of functions between county and district in non-metropolitan areas does not always produce an ideal administrative result. This is particularly the case when a county is geographically very large.

The functions allocated to non-metropolitan counties are the same as those given to the metropolitan county. In addition, the former are responsible for education, libraries, and social services. These additional functions are given to the county because it is considered that district populations are too small to sustain the organization required to maintain an adequate standard of service.

Non-metropolitan districts form the major subdivision of the counties. Districts may range in size from compact urban centres of population to widespread rural areas. The functions allocated to them include housing, local planning and development, and refuse collection. In Wales, libraries and refuse disposal are district functions.

Parish councils

Those parish councils existing before re-organization have been retained; they have also been given wider powers. The most important of these is the right to be informed of planning applications within the council area and thus be able to make representations to the district council where necessary. One effect of reorganization has been to make the parish council attractive to larger communities within a district. Such villages and small towns are able to request the formation of a parish council and thus provide a forum for the discussion of community topics. Certain functions may be allocated to the parish council by the district also. In Wales, parish councils are known as **community councils**.

Greater London Council (GLC) and boroughs

The reorganization of local government in London preceded that in the rest of the country by some ten years. The structure is two-tier, with the GLC having responsibility for fire and ambulance services, major roads, and major aspects of planning. Some planning functions, and also housing responsibilities, are shared with the London boroughs which comprise the second tier. The boroughs carry responsibility for local roads, social services, local health services, and libraries. As will be appreciated, there is considerable similarity with the two-tier structure of metropolitan areas. The major difference is in the administration of education. The area covered by the former authority, the London County Council (LCC), has been used as the basis for a unified administrative structure in education. The result is that, in central boroughs, education is administered by the Inner London Education Authority (ILEA), which is a committee of the GLC. Each outer London borough has responsibility for education in its own area, as in metropolitan districts.

Local government in Scotland

Scotland has not been immune from local government re-organization. The previous structure of local government had begun to suffer the same defects as that in England and Wales. Following the investigation of the Wheatley Commission a new structure was proposed which was accepted by the government. It is a two-tier structure; the major divisions are the regions (seven) each of which is divided into districts. The functions discharged by each tier are very similar to those in non-metropolitan areas in England and Wales.

Councillors and officials in local government

So far we have examined the structure of local government from a legal point of view. Each authority exists, in law, as an incorporated association. It is given legal powers and duties; it can sue and be sued in its own name. However, it can only act through a human agency—that is to say, through those persons who are associated with the authority. We can draw a parallel with central government and identify two groups— those elected to serve the authority and those employed by it.

Councillors are elected by the voters of the area which they wish to serve. *County councillors* represent a **division** of a county. *Councillors* represent a **ward** in a district. As the titles suggest, councillors are elected to serve as members of a county or district council. It is the council which is granted powers and has duties imposed upon it. The way in which it carries out its obligations is a matter for each individual council; however, there is a general pattern in all local authorities which can be identified.

Following election, a council appoints a **chairman** from its members. In districts which have acquired borough status, a **Mayor** is appointed instead of a chairman. A council acts as a policy-making body. It sets up the machinery to ensure that its policy decisions are carried out, and it gives its approval to acts done in its name. It establishes a *committee structure* which covers the council's major functions. This structure includes social services and education committees (which must be formed), together with a considerable number of others, including housing, transport, and planning. Each council is free to set up whatever committees it considers necessary. In addition to functional committees, there are others which relate to matters of a general nature; finance and personnel are among these.

In addition to councillors, membership of some committees may include non-councillors, co-opted for their special knowledge. Another feature of the committee system is the formation of *subcommittees* for special aspects of the work of a large main committee. The education committee normally has a number of subcommittees, including primary, secondary, and further education. Each committee has a chairman who acts as spokesman for the committee, both in council debates and in public. The decisions of committees usually have to be confirmed by the full council. However, the council may *delegate* some of its powers to a committee; in this event, committee decisions would be final.

The **chairman** of each committee, in addition to the duties mentioned above, has what is perhaps an even more important function. It is his duty to maintain contacts between himself, his committee, and the permanent officers of the council. We now need to examine the work of these officers.

All **officers** of county and district councils are full-time paid officials, and work within one of the many departments through which the work of the authority is carried on. Each department or group of departments has at its head a *chief officer*. The work of the chief officers is co-ordinated and led by the senior officer of the authority. He is often designated *chief executive* in a county and *secretary* in districts.

In the discharge of its responsibilities, the council must use the committees of elected members and the departments of the authority efficiently. To do this, it needs to appreciate that each has a different role. In broad terms, each committee discusses and puts forward policy proposals to the council. When approved the department for which it is responsible carries them out. In practice, however, the division cannot be so sharply made, and the relationships between committee and department often depend on the personalities of the chairman and chief officer. The chief officer has considerable experience in the work of his department. He should be able to foresee developments in the need for services and thus be able to offer valuable advice to the relevant committee. His expertise and that of his department can also be used for the investigation of, and reporting on, particular problems. He may be asked to give his recommendations to the committee on such problems. Equally, he can seek the help and advice of the committee chairman in matters of difficulty. In this way, a high standard of service to the public can be maintained.

Other public sector organizations

So far, our examination of the public sector has concentrated on the direct provision of services by central and local government departments. The immediate control and responsibility of Ministers and councillors is an important feature of these organizations. There are, however, many other activities in the public sector in which this form of supervision would not work satisfactorily. When the State owns productive industries, for example, it is not necessarily a good thing to allow enterprise by civil servants. Equally, parliamentary intervention in the day-to-day running of a business is neither desirable nor practicable. For these reasons new forms of organization and control have been developed which leave only broad supervision in the hands of Ministers and Parliament. We can now examine the most important of the organizations in this area, the *nationalized industries* in which the government has taken over as entrepreneur.

Nationalized industries

The method generally chosen to remove these State-owned industries from immediate government control is by the formation of a **public corporation** to run an industry. Public corporations have been set up at various times and the main sectors of the economy so controlled are: the Bank of England, gas, electricity, coal, broadcasting, civil aviation, rail and (partially) road transport, cables and wireless, and atomic energy. Among the newest are shipbuilding (with the formation of the British Shipbuilding Corporation), British Aerospace, and the British National Oil Corporation. Although the organization differs in each case, the general outlines are similar. A **board** is established as a corporate body with a *legal identity*. Like a joint stock company, the board has a life of its own. It can own assets and is charged to operate those assets in the public interest, to provide an acceptable supply of goods and services, and make neither excess profits nor losses from inefficient operation. (Some losses may be dictated by a government which, for example, is operating a prices and incomes policy.) A Minister is empowered, by Act of Parliament, to appoint the board and to supervise its functioning in a broad sense. The Minister, through Parliament, usually authorizes the raising of money capital from various sources. General Treasury funds are made available for capital expenditure; borrowing from sources in this country and in EEC countries is now used as an additional source of finance. The board is responsible for the day-to-day running of a nationalized industry. In addition, it plays a major role in planning and the formulation of policy for the industry.

Reasons for nationalization

The main single reason for nationalization is the desire of the State to control the 'commanding heights' of the economy. A government that wishes to influence and plan future economic growth must have control over investment in those areas. Too little investment may lead to an excessive amount of unemployment and under-usage of resources; too much investment may lead to rapidly rising prices. The need for the economic control of particular industries has been a major argument for the nationalization of the so-called **public utilities**, such as electricity and gas production.

The avoidance of private **monopolies** has been another argument for nationalization. Private profit might be put before public interest and the community held to ransom by the witholding of essential supplies to force up prices. Such industries might be working efficiently, but there is a stronger case for taking over inefficient industries engaged in essential production. Some industries can only operate efficiently on a large scale. The nationalization and central control of coal mining has led to investment for development and reorganization. In this way, production can be concentrated in low cost coalfields. Prior to nationalization, this was not possible, and many mines were too small to make a profit. Another argument has been that labour relations may be better if people feel that they are employed by the nation as a whole rather than by a private employer.

None of the above arguments for nationalization has gone unchallenged. Investment can also be influenced through taxation and monetary policies. It is considered possible to control private monopolies by other means. Where there is no profit motive, efficiency may suffer. Rationalization and modernization has led to a decline in manpower in several nationalized industries. These industries are not immune from economic trends in this country and elsewhere. Nor, since the Second World War, have labour relations in the nationalized industries necessarily been better than those in the private sector.

48   The nationalization of industry has presented Parliament with many problems.

Included among these are questions of control and accountability. Too close a control would be unnecessary and stifling. On the other hand, nationalized industries must be accountable to the public through Parliament. The balance between these two ideals has not necessarily been achieved and these problems and the way in which some attempt has been·made to solve them will be examined in Book 2.

Quasi-autonomous National Government Organizations (quangos)

> ## QUANGOS A GROWTH INDUSTRY
>
> IT has been revealed to a persistently questioning MP that there are 20 000 members serving on around 900 quangos. Fees and expenses for those members amount to over £20 million a year. The MP agreed with an eminent quango chairman that many were necessary and did a useful job. Also that all governments in this country made such appointments.

As we have already noted, State intervention in a modern society invariably grows. New policies are devised, new problems arise, and the government of the day must develop the organization to meet these new situations. One way in which this is done is to remove the operation of some services from direct government control and place them in the hands of semi-independent bodies. This form of organization has been dubbed **quango** by many writers. The expansion of this name (see heading) explains the important features of these organizations. They are formed by central (i.e., national) government, and give the impression that they are independent of ministerial control, but yet some control exists. In general, their services are those which are best operated without the restrictions which might be present in a government department. Local and regional conditions can be taken into account and a certain degree of commercial risk accepted where this is necessary.

The **National Enterprise Board (NEB)**, the first of these organizations to be examined, is of relatively recent origin (1975). Its activities are concerned with direct investment in individual companies, which retain their own identity. The form which such investment takes is almost exclusively the purchase of shares in a company. In this

49

way, a permanent investment is made which, in the judgement of the NEB, will be profitable. As we have seen, it is often difficult for joint stock companies to raise capital unless they are 'quoted' companies. The NEB is able to fill this gap after satisfying itself that the operations of the company will benefit the region in which it is situated. The benefit may be to bring new products to the area, or to expand existing industries and to generally improve employment prospects. The Board has regional offices which deal with cases in the northern and north-western areas of the country. The London office deals with applications from the rest of the country. Perhaps the most eye-catching investment at the time of writing is that in British Leyland. However, investments of up to £1.5 million in individual companies have been equally important in helping to solve both economic and social problems in areas badly in need of such direct assistance.

The **Manpower Services Commission** is another newcomer to the ranks of quangos. Set up in 1974, under the provisions of the Employment and Training Act 1973, it took over responsibility for public employment and training services. These had previously been the direct responsibility of the Department of Employment. One purpose behind this move was to involve users in the planning and operation of these services. The Commission includes representatives of trade unions and employers associations together with members representing education and local government. The commission operates through two arms, Training Services Division and Employment Services Division. This form of organization attempts to replace consultation by responsibility, combined with an advisory role.

These are just two of the many quangos which exist in this country. The National Health Service is run by Regional Health Authorities; water resources are the responsibility of Regional Water Authorities; Development Corporations plan and administer the new towns. There are many more, but they all have much in common. They are the result of a deliberate attempt to remove direct responsibility for a great number of services from Whitehall. Whatever the reasons, and they include commercial expertise, social needs and local and regional democracy and knowledge, quangos now play a major role in public sector administration.

Summary

The two major areas of the public sector of the economy are central and local government. Central government functions are discharged through departments of State. Government Ministers bear ministerial responsibility to Parliament for the operation of their departments. Government policies are carried out through these departments which are staffed by civil servants. Some government functions are allocated to local authorities which, in England and Wales, are mainly metropolitan or non-metropolitan counties and districts. (In Scotland, regions and districts are the local government organizations.) Counties and districts have responsibility for different functions. At the heart of local government is the committee system. Full-time officials carry out council and committee policies and act as advisers to committees.

The nationalized industries are under broad State control and form an important part of productive industry. Reasons for nationalization include the control of private monopoly, more efficient production (often on a larger scale), and the need for the State to ensure full employment with better labour relations. However, nationalized industries are a public monopoly, they are not necessarily efficient, and they are as much affected by economic trends as the private sector.

The control of many forms of government activity is in the hands of quangos. Major examples include Regional Health Authorities, Regional Water Authorities, the Manpower Services Commission, and the National Enterprise Board. This form of organization removes the day-to-day operation of a service from government departments which are then left responsible for broad policy and financial control.

Assignment

1 (a) Your county and district or borough councils will each have a lengthy entry in a telephone directory. From these entries list the major public services provided:

    (i)   only by the county
    (ii) only by the district or borough
    (iii) by both councils jointly.

  (b) From list (i) or (ii) select one service. Consider the arguments for and against transferring that service to the other council or operating it jointly. Write a brief report setting out your arguments and conclusions. Headings under which the matter might be considered could include: finance, convenience for clients, local knowledge and control, geography, and staffing.

Unit 5   Organizations and contracts

The universality of contracts

Part Two of this book is concerned with the organization and its resources. In the acquisition, use, and disposal of resources every organization enters into contracts with other organizations as suppliers or customers. Contracts are made with individuals, usually as employees or customers. As individuals, we frequently make contracts with other individuals and with organizations. Yet few people would actually recognize a contract even if they were in the middle of making one. As a consequence of this, not many people would accept that they were legally bound by contract in many everyday situations. We shall see that the most common daily transactions form the basis of contracts. If the agreement forming the basis of these contracts is not honoured, legal action can be taken against the person or organization breaking the agreement. In short, there may be a breach of contract.

It may sound rather dramatic to apply the words 'breach of contract' to the failure of a customer to pay a bill for newspapers delivered during the month. However, the law does not take any account of the size of the transaction in deciding whether a breach of contract has taken place. It is concerned with the principles of law which can be applied to any transaction. It looks at the intentions of the parties concerned, through their negotiations, in deciding whether a contract exists between them. This Unit examines the basic legal rules which apply to all contracts.

As commerce has developed, particularly in the last 150 years, the courts have heard many disputes, often involving entirely novel contractual situations. From the decisions in these actions, and from Parliament, the law applicable to contracts of all kinds has been, and still is, in a state of continuous development. In later Units we will examine some of these developments with particular reference to contracts made by organizations in the public and private sectors of the economy.

The nature of a contract

As was mentioned in the previous section, a very large number of contracts are made and performed daily. People are rarely aware of the fact that these agreements give rise to obligations which are legally enforceable if necessary. However, it is just these features which make a contract unique and help us to examine its nature. It is an **agreement** with **obligations** which can be **legally enforced**. The intention of the parties is what matters. If they intended that the agreement should not be legally enforceable, the courts generally do not help in the event of a breach of the agreement. There will be no contract to enforce. For this reason, family arrangements and social agreements between friends are not enforced by the courts. The people concerned do not say, in so many words, that they do not wish the agreement to be legally binding but the circumstances may imply this. However, the courts have had to draw a line between normal family arrangements and agreements which, although between members of a family, should be considered to be binding contracts. The line seems to be drawn between ordinary arrangements—for example, about the family budget—and those which are made in less normal circumstances—for example, when a husband and wife have separated and problems such as maintenance and joint property have to be settled. The courts examine the circumstances rather than the words used.

Everyday contracts

The word 'contract' often conjures up a vision of an imposing document, bound by red tape, probably with a seal affixed, and drawn up by a lawyer. There are, indeed, some contracts which must be in this form. There are some contracts, such as credit sale agreements, which must be in writing. However, the vast majority of contracts made in everyday circumstances are made orally; there may be no written or printed details at all.

Most of us enter daily into several contracts. Buying a paper in the morning; travelling by bus or train; buying lunch at mid-day; finally, perhaps, going to see a film. All these transactions are contracts. There may be more—shopping at lunchtime for clothes; taking a taxi; ordering some goods; arranging to have clothes dry-cleaned—the list is endless. The fact that we are making contracts has a further significance as we have seen—we are legally bound in all these situations. So are the people or organizations with whom we contract.

It may sound improbable that the purchase of a newspaper may form the basis of a contract. If you were given yesterday's paper in error you would, of course, demand the correct paper or your money back. You are merely enforcing your rights, you may say. The source of those rights is the contract with the newsagent. Using our earlier definition, there is an agreement which the law will enforce if necessary. The newsagent has not kept his part of the bargain, and there has been a **breach of contract**. In this case the breach is easily remedied.

Offer and acceptance: the formation of agreement

It is usual, when determining whether the parties to a contract are in agreement, to analyse their negotiations in the following way:
(a) An **offer** is made by one party;
(b) An **acceptance** of the offer is made by the party to whom the offer was made (the offeree);
(c) If the offer and acceptance are about the same thing and in the same terms, there is an **agreement**.

Applying this analysis to the previous example, the purchase of a newspaper: the *offer* is made by the customer; *acceptance* is by the newsagent; they are usually in *agreement* over the subject-matter, and the customer takes away the newspaper. The contract has been performed.

The offer

An offer can be made in any form. It may be a telephone call, a letter, an order from a customer, in some cases even an advertisement. The offer may be made, as it is

53

sometimes put, 'to the world in general'. This means that the offer is open to anyone to accept. An offer may be made to a particular group of people and can only be accepted by members of that group. Finally, an offer may be made to one person only, and therefore can only be accepted by that person.

An offer to the world in general is frequently made by means of an advertisement in the form of a reward notice. These are sometimes seen in banks and post offices. The offer is made to anyone who happens to read the notice; it would be accepted by carrying out the terms of the offer, usually by giving information which leads to an arrest and conviction. Similarly, offers may be made in coupon form in a magazine; the offer is accepted by cutting out the coupon and using it as part-payment for certain goods. Advertisements for goods are generally not offers, as we shall see in Unit 9. However, in some circumstances, the courts will deem an advertisement to be an offer to the world in general. Such an offer can thus be accepted by anyone complying with the terms of the offer. The most famous offer of this kind was made in the 1890s by a company manufacturing a device called a 'Carbolic Smoke Ball', whose purpose was to ward off influenza. They offered £100 to anyone who caught influenza despite using their Smoke Ball. A Mrs Carlill purchased a Smoke Ball and, despite using it according to instructions, caught influenza. Several ingenious defences were put forward by the company: that it was only an advertising stunt; that they did not intend any agreement to be legally binding; that contracts could not be made with all the world. Despite all these efforts the High Court decided against the company; the Court of Appeal did likewise in 1893. Mrs Carlill was held to be entitled to the £100 offered by the company. A contract existed between her and the Carbolic Smoke Ball Co. which had been broken. The company had failed to perform its obligations under the contract.

An offer to a group may be made for the particular reason that the offerer wishes to restrict the terms of the offer to certain persons or organizations. For example, a company may wish to raise further capital by an issue of shares. It can give its existing shareholders the right to buy the shares earlier than outsiders, or at a lower price. Such an offer can be accepted only by individuals in the group to whom it is made, and not by other members of the public.

An offer to a particular person can only be accepted by the person to whom it was made, that is, the offeree. An offer of goods at a special price to shopkeeper A cannot be accepted by B who bought the shop from A after the offer was made.

Acceptance of an offer

As we have seen, an offer can only be accepted by the person to whom it is made. We now need to examine the legal rules relating to such an acceptance.

The most important of these rules is that *acceptance must be in exactly the same terms as the offer*. Nothing must be added or taken away; no new conditions attached. If the purported acceptance is in different terms from the offer, it is considered to be a **counter-offer**—that is, an offer in return which is itself capable of being accepted. In making a counter-offer, the offeree is rejecting the original offer. It cannot later be accepted if his counter-offer is itself rejected. Once an offer is rejected, it is said to be lapsed. To be capable of acceptance, it must be made again by the offeror. As an example, in the negotiations for a second-hand car, an original offer of £950 may be made by an intending purchaser. The seller may insist that he wants £1000. This may be met by another counter-offer of £975, which may again be rejected by the seller. The buyer may finally offer the £1000 originally requested, but this again is only a counter-offer; it is not acceptance of the seller's earlier counter-offer of £1000. The seller is still free to continue bargaining or to accept the £1000.

Quite often an *offer is made with a time-limit given for acceptance*. A dealer might give a customer a day to think about buying a car. The offer lapses after that time and cannot be accepted later, unless the dealer makes it again. If a phrase such as, 'think it over and let me know' had been used, the offer would lapse after a reasonable time. A day or two would probably be reasonable in such a case.

Normally, the offeror must hear about acceptance of the offer; *acceptance must be communicated to the offeror*. Of course, if the offeror is not concerned about communication of acceptance he is free to say so, as in Carlill's case. Here, purchase and use of the article constituted acceptance. He cannot go further and make up the offeree's mind by saying, for example, 'If I hear no more from you I'll assume you want the car.' If nothing more was said, he would be trying to make a one-sided contract by making up the offeree's mind for him.

When *acceptance is made by post* special problems arise which the courts have had to consider. Use of other methods of communication has also meant that legal principles appropriate to one method of communication have had to be applied to other methods. Many of the contracts for goods and services made by an organization are arranged by postal or similar means, and such contracts are dealt with in Unit 9.

Consideration: an outline

All contracts made without the formality of a deed must be supported by **consideration**. That is to say, each party to the contract must do or provide something of value. A deed, to which the familiar words 'signed, sealed and delivered' refer, does not need consideration to support it. Thus a gift made by deed can be legally enforced even though one of the parties to the arrangement did not provide consideration; it is a purely one-sided contract. The law requires the formality of a deed in these circumstances to ensure that rash impulsive promises can be the subject of second and more serious thoughts.

Consideration can be further illustrated by means of an everyday transaction, the purchase of a book. The price paid and the book itself each form the consideration on which the contract is based. If the buyer and seller each provides consideration in this way, the contract is immediately performed, and is said to be executed. A different situation arises if the book is ordered and paid for in full immediately. The buyer's consideration is executed; the seller, in return, promises to try to obtain the article. His promise forms his consideration, and he can be sued upon such a promise. If only a deposit is paid on an order, both parties are bound by their promises; the buyer to pay the balance and the seller to try to obtain and hand over the book. The promises form the consideration provided by each side and each can sue the other if a promise is not kept.

In these examples it is clear that consideration exists, and it is also clear that the courts would not be asked to consider any question relating to consideration in such

55

cases. Sometimes, however, the problem is not so easily solved. For example, the courts have had to determine whether consideration must have a fair value. The payment of £1 per annum rent plus a promise to keep a house in good order and repair has been held to be good. It was held that consideration must have some value, but within this rule the parties are free to make any bargain they wish. It is this same rule which the courts have followed in deciding that agreements to repay a debt in instalments, which is already due in total, are void for lack of consideration. The promisor suffers no loss at all by agreeing to do even less than he is bound to do anyway. Again, the courts have held that payment by cheque is no different from payment in cash, and cannot thus be consideration for an allowance to be made from a due debt.

The application of the rules relating to consideration to contracts made by organizations is considered in Unit 9.

Capacity of organizations to make contracts

When considering whether an organization is bound by contracts into which it has entered, it is necessary to look at the form of the organization. We can examine this with regard to each of the organizations reviewed in Units 3 and 4.

A sole-trader or one-man business is bound by all contracts made, whether or not they are for the purposes of the business. So long as they are legally valid, the firm must meet the obligations which it has undertaken. As we have seen, all assets used in the business can be used to meet the firm's obligations, and in addition most of the owner's private possessions can be seized to meet his or her business debts.

A partnership is bound by its trading contracts when these are within the scope of the ordinary business of the firm. Thus, a firm of estate agents would be bound by property advertising contracts with a newspaper. It might be different if they were to hire a luxury coach. In this case, the partner placing the order would be personally liable unless he could show that he was authorized by his fellow partners to place the contract.

A limited company (public or private) can make contracts in just the same way as an individual. However, as we have seen, the 'objects' clause of the Memorandum of Association defines the limits within which a company may operate. Contracts made within these limits—that is, for purposes within the objects clause—are valid. Contracts outside the clause are said to be **ultra vires,** or beyond the powers taken by the company in its Memorandum. Before Parliament passed the European Communities Act 1972, the distinction was of importance to a person dealing with a limited company. Now, protection is given by Section 9(1) of the Act: 'any transaction decided on by the directors' is considered to be one which the company has power to enter. So, in most circumstances, contracts may be enforced against the company, since it is not allowed to shelter behind the *ultra vires* rule. However, it seems that a company cannot enforce such a contract. If this were possible, the company would be suing on a contract not permitted by its own objects clause, a situation which the law does not allow.

In practice, most large companies have a very wide objects clause, which allows almost any conceivable activity to be carried on. The rule, of course, applies to any limited company, however small. The objects clause of such a company may be quite narrow. The 1972 Act has thus given a wide protection to those dealing with limited companies.

Local authorities, such as counties and districts are, like limited companies, *legal persons* in the eyes of the law. A local authority can only act through individuals as members of councils and committees, and through employees. The *ultra vires* rule outlined above applies to contracts made on behalf of the authority; such contracts must be within the powers given by Parliament to that authority. However, in practice the powers are very wide and are further extended by the use of subsidiary powers. These have the effect of extending the powers of a local authority to include acts which are necessary to achieve the principal objects. An authority may employ additional staff and rent extra accommodation. These actions might be necessary to enable the authority to carry out a new service for which it has been given a broad general power by Parliament.

Nationalized industries must work within the powers given to them by the particular Act of Parliament under which they were formed and operate. The powers, once again, are of such a wide nature that it would be a very strange contract to be *ultra vires* a statutory body such as the National Coal Board or British Railways.

Central government departments make contracts through the civil servants working in those departments. Such employees are considered to be servants of the Crown; the Crown can have no limit to its powers, and thus ordinary trading contracts with the Crown can never be void as *ultra vires*.

Terms: conditions and warranties

When the negotiations leading to a contract are concluded there are, either in the minds of the parties, or written down, a fair number of points about the contract which are considered to be important. These might include the name of a book ordered, its price, the date by which it is required, whether it is a paperback or hardback edition, the number of the edition, and so on. In addition, such a contract is subject to the Sale of Goods Act, 1893 (see Unit 15), which implies certain terms in contracts for the supply of goods.

In law, terms in a contract are classified either as conditions or warranties. The parties to a contract rarely state that a particular term is a condition or a warranty—it is left to the courts to decide in the event of a dispute. On the other hand, the 1893 Act specifies that certain **implied terms** are to be treated as conditions. The distinction is important when a term of a contract is broken. Suppose that the book ordered is delivered a week late and is the wrong edition. That there has been a breach of contract there is little doubt but is it a breach of a condition, of a warranty, or of both? *A condition is a term basic to the whole contract; a warranty is a less important term.* The fact that the book is the wrong edition is almost certainly a breach of condition. The late delivery is probably a breach of warranty.

The consequences of each type of breach are different. The breach of condition allows the injured party to treat the contract as at an end and to seek compensation in the form of damages. A breach of warranty, on its own, allows for damages only. It is worth noting that the time of delivery could just as easily have been a condition if the words, 'I must have the book by Friday week' had been used. If no time is mentioned, a reasonable time would be allowed for delivery.

Effect of misrepresentation

Representations are often made in contractual negotiations, to induce the other party to enter into a contract. The important point to remember about such representations is that they may or may not become terms of the contract—that is to say, conditions or warranties. If they do not, they are classed only as representations, and no higher. The parties to the negotiations do not intend to be bound by their statements of this nature.

Examples of representations might be:

1. A sale of a painting by X 'who has exhibited his work widely.'
2. 'Planning permission has been given for ten detached dwelling houses' said during negotiations for the sale of land.
3. 'The business is making about £5000 per annum.'
4. 'Orders are normally delivered in three to four weeks.'

It should be noted that the representations we are considering are representations of fact.

Representations made during contractual negotiations *must be true*. If they are not true they can only be false, and thus become misrepresentations. A misrepresentation, to have any effect in law, must have actually misled the person to whom it was made. For instance, the intending purchaser of a business may obtain an accountant's report on its financial soundness. He cannot afterwards complain of misrepresentations by the vendor regarding matters covered by the report if he goes ahead with the purchase. He did not rely on the vendor's statements but upon the report.

Misrepresentations may be quite *innocently* made; they may also be made *negligently*; they may even be deliberately *fraudulent*. Whatever the cause, the person who has been misled can refuse to perform the contract. However, if the contract has been performed before the misrepresentation is discovered, he has to persuade the other party that the deal should be called off and the subject-matter restored. He may be driven to seek the help of the courts, asking that the contract should be *rescinded*, or set aside. The remedy of rescission is only given at the discretion of the court. It must be sought quickly, before third parties have acquired rights in the subject-matter, and while the parties can be restored to their former position. If a car is sold 'having a recently reconditioned engine', the purchaser may discover quickly that this is not true, and incur repair costs. The seller may have made the representation quite innocently, but nevertheless he can be made to take back the car. In other words, the contract can be rescinded. This may seem a rather drastic remedy for a minor matter and the law recognizes this. *Damages* can be awarded instead. A reduction of the price would be a fair settlement of the dispute.

As was stated earlier, representations which turn out to be false may be made quite innocently, or they may be the result of negligence. During the negotiations leading to a contract, statements may be made more in the hope that they are true than with the certainty of truth. For example, a promise may be made that an order can be delivered within three days, without a check being made that this is so. In the case of both innocent and negligent representations, the person making them must be able to prove that there were reasonable grounds for believing them to be true. If this cannot be proved, damages can be awarded, when loss has occurred, whether or not rescission of the contract is possible.

The third class of misrepresentation consisting of those which are fraudulent, always results in damages if fraud is proved and loss is incurred. Obviously someone who makes a statement with a deliberate attempt to defraud does not himself believe the statement to be true. However, the restrictions discussed earlier on the right to an order for rescission apply equally to contracts induced by a fraudulent misrepresentation.

Mistakes which do not affect the validity of the contract

As we have seen, offer and acceptance must be in the same terms for agreement to take place. However, mistakes can arise in contractual negotiations. The courts have heard many actions in which one of the parties has alleged that a mistake has been made and that no contract came into existence. There are several kinds of mistake which have this effect of making a contract void, and these are examined in Unit 9. Here we look at mistakes which do not affect the agreement reached by the parties.

A mistake made by one of the parties when making a contract can first be considered. A builder, in putting in a tender for a job may make an error in his estimates and quote too low a price. If his tender is accepted, he is bound by it, and must be the loser. This is only fair, since he has made the error. The same reasoning applies in a situation where an article is sold at a bargain price. If the seller is unaware of current values, then he must stand by his price. As we shall see, a line must be drawn somewhere in such circumstances. If the tender or price is so low that the buyer must realize that an error had been made, a different situation arises.

A failure to read a document and thus to be mistaken about its contents does not mean that a person can escape the obligations of a contract. In the absence of fraud or a trick, we are all bound by the contents of documents which we sign, whether we read them or not. The moral is, to read the print, small or otherwise, before signing. If it is not understood, advice should be sought. In the same way, everyone is presumed to know the law; 'ignorance of the law is no excuse' means just what it says. We cannot escape our legal obligations just because we do not know what they are.

When a **mistake is made in the identity of the person with whom we are dealing**, the law will take no account of this unless *identity is important to the contract*. The most usual situation in which this problem arises is when a smooth-tongued rogue persuades a seller to part, with, say, a car in return for a worthless cheque. The car is then invariably sold quickly to an innocent buyer for cash. The rogue escapes with the proceeds. The problem which the courts have had to solve is a very difficult one: who must suffer in this situation, the seller or the buyer? If no contract exists, the innocent buyer cannot become the true owner of the car. That is to say, in law he cannot acquire a good title. On the other hand, if the original sale to the rogue is good, the buyer acquires a good title, and the seller is the loser. The law steers a middle course between these extremes. To show that no valid contract exists, the seller must prove that identity was very important to the transaction. He must show that he intended to deal only with the person the rogue pretended to be, and with no-one else. If he cannot do this, it does not mean that a fully valid contract exists, which cannot be upset. The contract is said to be voidable. If the seller acts quickly, before a third party buys the car and acquires a good title, the contract with the rogue can be avoided. The seller can only be required to take reasonable steps to avoid the contract. Informing the police and the motoring organizations would be one way of dealing with the problem. If this action is taken, the courts would probably consider the contract to be avoided; a buyer could not then acquire a good title.

In retail sales to customers—sales by, for example, a shop or a garage—the above problems are side-stepped, to a certain extent, by the use of cheque guarantee cards. Even if a cheque book and card have been stolen, the owner of the cheque book or the company issuing the card usually bears the loss on any transaction made by the thief. The innocent shopkeeper does not lose in this situation, whatever was said during the transaction.

Summary

We all enter daily into contracts for goods and services. The basis of such contracts is agreement between the parties. Agreement takes place when offer and acceptance are in the same terms. In addition to agreement existing, the parties to a contract must provide consideration, which must have some real value, however small. Any contract can be made by a one-man organization, providing it is within the general law of the land. Other organizations are limited in the contracts which they can make. These must be broadly within the objects or purpose for which the organization was formed. There is no limit upon the capacity of the Crown to contract.

Not all terms of a contract are of equal importance. They may be conditions or warranties. A breach of a condition can bring a contract to an end; a breach of either can bring an award of damages. Some statements of fact may not become terms of the contract, but may induce the other party to enter into a contract. These representations must be true; if not the contract may be set aside and/or damages awarded (in some circumstances). Mistakes regarding value, the nature and contents of a document, and identity, do not generally affect the validity of a contract.

Assignment

Your organization has been considering the purchase of replacement office furniture. It is planning to trade in some of the existing furniture in part-payment for the new. It is essential that delivery is made after completion of alterations to the layout of the offices, and before the office is occupied, two weeks later. Following letters of enquiry to several firms, replies were received from three. The letter from one firm, Offurnsup & Co., contains the following statements:

'We are suppliers to HM Government and to many local authorities, nationalized industries and leading companies.'
'All furniture is made to the highest standards, using best quality materials and skilled workmanship.'
'Our prices, for furniture required, are as follows:
   10 office desks (ODP 12) at £85 ea.
    8 standard chairs (SCO 2) at £17 ea.
    2 de luxe swivel chairs (SDO 1) at £32 ea.
Part-exchange prices as agreed by telephone with your Mr Johnson.
Delivery: two weeks from receipt of order.'

(a) Draft an order, in the form of a letter to Offurnsup & Co., setting out what you consider to be essential details. You may assume your letter is acknowledged in due course.
(b) From the negotiations identify:
    (i)   offer
    (ii) acceptance
    (iii) consideration
    (iv) representations
    (v) conditions
    (vi) warranties.

Part Two   The organization and its resources

More signposts: a look ahead

Part one was concerned with the reasons for and the forms of organizations producing goods and services in the public and private sectors. In Unit 5 we discovered that, whatever the nature of the organization, it is involved in making contracts. This point should be borne in mind now that we turn to the decisions which organizations must make when acquiring resources, because contractual obligations are clearly involved in the hiring of manpower, the purchase of raw materials, the commissioning of a mail-order warehouse, or the host of other activities which organizations may undertake.

These activities may be regarded as economic ones, but, as Unit 1 pointed out, they take place in a political, social, and legal environment. The economist concentrates on efficiency—that is, on making the best use of scarce resources to satisfy the expressed demand of customers and clients. Units 6 and 7 adopt this viewpoint in explaining the nature of resources and the problems of cost. However, it should always be remembered that decisions desirable in economic terms alone may be modified when political and social considerations are taken into account. For the sake of efficiency, it might be as well to disband British Steel, British Shipbuilders, and British Leyland, but what would then become of British industry? Decisions on what, how, when, where, and for whom to produce goods and services cannot always be made on economic grounds alone, as we shall see in Units 8 to 12. This is particularly true for those organizations in the public sector which deal with people's needs through, for example, the Welfare State. Yet without efficient production the amount of wealth created might be insufficient to sustain a Welfare State at all. This typical political and social dilemma should not be forgotten even though we turn now to economic considerations.

Unit 6   Economic Resources

Production

Production, as we discovered in Unit 1, can be defined as 'the creation of utility'. It can also be regarded as 'the creation of wealth', since wealth was defined as anything which, possesses utility, is scarce and is transferable. The physical scientists tell us that matter can neither be created nor destroyed. Thus, production can only be concerned with changing the form of something, or the place or time at which it becomes available. Raw materials, such as iron ore, have no power to satisfy the wants of a motorist; they have no utility for him. Once converted into a car, available in his locality at a time when he wants to buy it, these materials have gained utility. Production has taken place.

It is important to note that *place utility* or *time utility* are just as desirable as *form utility*. During the energy crisis of 1973, petrol was available in northern garages, but this did nothing to ease the problems of motorists in London. Equally unhelpful was the promise of North Sea oil by 1976. It follows, therefore, that the merchants storing bulk supplies were performing a productive **service**. Services as well as goods have the power of being desired. Teachers, policemen, and solicitors all do productive work. (It has even been remarked that when coin was acutely short during the eighteenth century, the English forger was a public benefactor!) *Any* activity is productive as long as people are prepared to pay for it—as long as it satisfies a want. The difficulty here is that some activities satisfy a want but are not paid for. The services of housewives are an obvious example. We have to say, regretfully, that because these activities are not exchanged between buyers and sellers through some form of market, and because they cannot be measured in money, we must leave them out of account.

Characteristics of resources

From an economic standpoint, resources have two major characteristics. The first of these is that they are generally **scarce**. Sometimes, indeed, as in the case of fossil fuels, they are finite and irreplaceable. Some informed estimates indicate that no organization will be able to use oil in a century's time if the present rate of world consumption continues. Other resources, mainly raw materials, may be recycled, and land, for example, may be used over and over again. However, the total land area cannot be increased and some of it is so inhospitable as to be of no practical use. In any case, as we noted in Unit 1, there is a **real cost** involved in using resources, whatever the extent and nature of the scarcity. This is best described as the *sacrificed alternative*. If resources are used for one purpose, they cannot simultaneously be used for another. This real cost is translated into **money cost** as far as organizations are concerned. Because resources are scarce, their owners have to be paid for their use. This would only be untrue in the case of resources which were so abundant that they were free for the taking.

The second major characteristic of many resources is that they are specialized and thus an imperfect substitute for one another. This is, of course, less true of raw

63

materials. It is easier to substitute fibreglass for wood than it is to substitute a machine tool for a computer, or a solicitor for an airline pilot. The implications for organizations of specialized resources are explored in Unit 7. Meanwhile, let us turn to a classification of resources.

The traditional classification of resources

The traditional classification of resources (or factors of production) was fourfold, into **land**, **labour**, **capital**, and **enterprise.** This grouping has a long and distinguished history, and it has the superficial advantage of relationship with the respective rewards of rent, salaries and wages, interest, profit. On the other hand, such a classification no longer fits the economic facts of life very well, and it is our ultimate purpose to suggest an alternative classification.

First, however, we must note that *any* broad classification is a vast oversimplification. Inside any grouping are countless numbers of individual resources distinguished more or less sharply from each other. For example, inside the group called labour are doctors and dieticians, carpenters and clowns, zither makers and zoologists. All these, although highly specialized, are grouped together because they gain an income predominantly from work. If we wish to consider the forces which make a lawyer's income what it is, these may be in general terms the same as those influencing an electrician's pay-packet. But nobody can argue that a lawyer is the same economic resource as an electrician merely because they both gain an income from work. Indeed, not even lawyers are the same as each other. Similarly, each piece of land is unique, at least in location, and there are also endless variations in capital equipment. In a very real sense, therefore, each economic resource is unique.

Work and property

It may be, however, that for some purposes broad classifications are useful. We may wish to know just how much of the nation's wealth flows to owners of work and how much to owners of property—the latter being sometimes called the **rentier** classes. Of course, many people are in possession of mixed incomes. Part of the incomes may be derived from physical and mental work, and part from the ownership of property. The annual Blue Book on National Income and Expenditure (HMSO) recognizes this by giving mixed incomes a category all their own. Nevertheless, if all production is carried out by *people* working with *other resources* owned by somebody or some institution, and if all incomes arise from the ownership of the capacity to work or from the ownership of property (or a mixture of both), then it would appear more sensible to recognize this and to reduce our broad categories of resources to two, which we can call **work** and **property**.

Land, property, and rent

Why has land hitherto been distinguished from other forms of capital and given a special category of its own? The answer is that land was considered to have an income differing from all other forms of income in its origin, and called **rent**.

We may illustrate this older view by considering a single survivor from nuclear

64

warfare. At first, the whole of his area would be his property. It might contain land capable of being cultivated, as well as forest, rivers, and other natural resources. These gifts of nature might be lumped together as land. The survivor would pay nothing for them. Since they were already in existence, there would be no **cost of production**, in either real or money terms. At first, they might be too great in quantity for him to work single-handed, but in any case, they would be **fixed in supply**. As more survivors found their way to this oasis, they might commandeer some of the abundant resources. It is unlikely that conflict would arise, or that payment would be made, since there would be sufficient land for all. Eventually, however, newcomers would find that all available land was occupied and had become somebody's property. They would then have to pay a *rent* to the owner if they wished to use the land. Since there was no original cost of production, such a payment, it might be argued, would be entirely a **surplus over cost** arising from the fact that land which was fixed in total supply had become scarce in relation to the demand for its product. As money came into use, and as more people needed to be fed, the price of foodstuffs might rise. More people, in competing for the use of land (the product of which was becoming more profitable to produce), would drive up the rent of land, the supply of which could not be increased. The rent would be *determined by* the price obtainable for the product of land, but would play no part in *determining* that price. It would be fixed by demand alone, not by supply.

In summary, the argument was as follows:

1. Land and other gifts of nature have no real costs of production.
2. Land is fixed in supply.
3. Therefore, the rent of land is a surplus over costs, arising from demand for the use of land.
4. This demand is *derived* from the demand for the product of land.

On the face of it, this argument is convincing. It is associated with the name of the economist David Ricardo, who lived at the time of the Napoleonic Wars. Ricardo saw marginal land being brought into use at a time of growing population and during hostilities. Such land was farmed at a high cost, which was only just covered by the high price of grain. Better land, farmed at lower cost, could be leased for ever increasing rents, especially if it was easily accessible. No wonder that Ricardo distinguished rents of **fertility** and **location.**

Modern economists usually modify Ricardo's arguments. While agreeing that the *land in total* is virtually fixed in supply, they point out that it is also capable of alternative uses. Land *for a particular use* is in most cases *not* fixed in supply. Not only is it capable of growing any one of a number of crops, but it is also available for building and other purposes. But, if this is true, once it is put to a particular use, a *real cost* to the community is involved in terms of the sacrificed alternative. In Unit 1, we defined wealth as being transferable and possessing utility. Real cost is involved in transferring a resource from one use to another and is often referred to as the resource's **transfer earnings.** Part of the land-user's payment, representing transfer earnings, is now called **commercial rent.** Furthermore, it is unusual today to find land in its virgin state. In most cases, capital (in the form of fertilizers, hedges, buildings) has been employed in its development. Therefore, another part of the payment for the use of land is interest on capital. This is particularly true in the case of rent being paid for the use of a house to live in. Of course, it is quite true that some land is in an advantageous position with regard to either location or fertility. An acre near Piccadilly Circus will let for more than an acre in Cornwall because it can be put to a more profitable use. *This surplus over costs payable for the use of a factor of production in fixed supply* is called **economic rent.**

So far we have argued that not all payment for land is, as Ricardo thought, economic rent. Now we should note that other resources may equally earn economic rent. A doctor, visualizing as transfer earnings an income of £10,000 a year, may train as a specialist. The cost of persuading him to work in a particular field is this figure. If, because of a shortage in his particular specialization, he eventually earns £15,000 a year, then £5,000 of this is a surplus over cost, or an economic rent. Again, if demand for cargo space suddenly increases, existing ships will earn higher freight rates, since they are in fixed supply in the short run. Eventually, however, if the demand continues more ships will be built. The economic rent will then disappear. Such a situation gives rise to what is called **quasi-rent** or economic rent in the short run. Oil-producing countries, we well know, may gain an enormous rent in the price of oil during a world shortage.

It has been shown that not all the rent of land is necessarily economic rent and, further, that any other resource may earn an economic rent, at least in the short run. In these circumstances, there seems very little point in continuing to classify land as a separate resource because of its peculiar form of income. It might just as well be lumped with all other capital under the heading **property.**

Enterprise, work, and property

Now let us turn to a consideration of the reasons why enterprise has been considered a separate factor of production. It could be argued that other resources are of little use unless they are organized. Somebody has to bring them together and manage them in the furtherance of production. Somebody has to hire them and take a chance that what is produced may be sold at a profit. In short, enterprise can be considered to consist of two separate functions, those of **organization** and **risk** (or uncertainty) **bearing.**

All this might have been valid a century ago and it is possibly true in certain instances today. There are still many small firms run by their owners, as we saw in Unit 3. These single-handed managers both organize their businesses and take the risks of failure. Even in such cases, however, the businessmen pay themselves *salaries* for their organizing ability, even though they may not bother to distinguish these as such within their total earnings. Furthermore, it is their *property* which is being put at risk and it is for this uncertainty that they hope to earn a profit. The situation in the case of a joint stock company is different. Here, organization is largely in the hands of salaried managers, while shareholders bear the risk. In other words, the two parts of enterprise are carried out by different groups of people.

Risk and uncertainty

At this point, it would be as well to distinguish between risk and uncertainty. Risks, such as those arising from the possibility of fire or theft, can be insured against. Even if one particular factory never burns down, it is certain that some factory, somewhere, will do so. Thus, by the payment of a premium, a factory owner can pool the risk with other similar owners. Business uncertainty, on the other hand, is uninsurable. It arises from changes in demand, from the actions of business competitors and from many other manifestations of the play of economic and market forces. It is such uncertainty that must be borne by somebody—in the case of joint stock companies, as we saw in Unit 3, mainly by the owner of ordinary shares. Profit, the reward for uncertainty-bearing, is one of the several types of income which may be earned by property owners. It differs from the others in that it may be negative and cannot be the subject of a contract in advance of dividends being declared. Salaries, the reward for management, are paid for work of a high order. In neither case does there seem much need to distinguish enterprise as a separate resource, since the functions of enterprise can now be included elsewhere; organization is carried out by managers who receive a salary and thus are included under the title of *work;* while uncertainty-bearing is one aspect of capital or *property* ownership.

An alternative classification

Our reclassification is now complete and is as follows:

Work: This group of resources is enlarged to include all human physical and mental activity which contributes to production. In particular, it includes management and organization, previously grouped under the heading of enterprise.

Property: Since, in the final analysis, only people and things contribute to production, this group comprises what is generally known as capital in the form of machines, raw materials, semi-finished and finished goods, and any other wealth owned by firms. It also includes land and any other gifts of nature.

The resources listed immediately above are acquired by a firm by means of money which it has obtained in one of two main ways (apart from its own savings). Either the money is borrowed, in which case **interest** is payable, or it is forthcoming from people who have bought shares in the firm and expect a dividend by way of **profit.** Profit, interest, and (in our classification) rent are *alternative* rewards for the use of property, while wages and salaries are the rewards for the use of workers of all types. We are now in a position to consider, in Unit 7, the economic implications, for organizations, of scarce and specialized resources.

Summary

Production is the creation of form, place, or time utility, and hence of wealth. The resources used in the productive process are scarce and specialized to a greater or less degree. Although they may be classified, the traditional fourfold classification of resources no longer fits the economic facts of life. Land can now be considered as part of the classification **property,** since it is no longer held that all its earnings are economic rent. Part may be commercial rent. Furthermore, other resources may yield an economic rent, at least in the short run. This short-run economic rent is called quasi-rent.

Enterprise consists of both management and uncertainty–bearing. (Risks may be insured against.) Management is salaried and is a higher form of work. Uncertainty arises from changes in economic conditions with the consequent chance that property may be hazarded. This hazarding of property must be paid for in some way. Such payment may take the form of rent, profit, or interest.

All production consists of people working with other resources (or factors of production). A new classification could divide resources into (a) work, and (b) property.

Rewards for these groups take the form of (a) wages or salaries, and (b) rent, profit, or interest.

Assignment

Explain the following in report form:

(a) the difference between insurable and uninsurable risks
(b) the difference between earned and unearned income
(c) the link between uninsurable risks and unearned income
(d) the reason why an ordinary shareholder cannot sue a public joint stock company if dividends are not declared.

Unit 7 Products, time, and costs

All organizations, large or small, producing goods or services, in the private or public sectors, have fundamental decisions to take. These are, what, for whom, how, when, and where to produce. The what and for whom depend mainly on the demands of the community and consideration of these questions is deferred to Part 3. Likewise, we consider questions of where to produce in Unit 11. In the present Unit we concentrate on the equally important considerations of how and when to produce. In other words, we are looking at the nature of supply, and the problems which businesses encounter in their attempts to produce as efficiently as possible.

These problems centre around the effort to use scarce resources so as to produce as much as possible using as little as possible. Once more, we return to the question of real costs. If resources are used wastefully, the final product costs more, not only, as we shall see, in terms of money, but also in terms of what has to be sacrificed in order to obtain the product. An example may make this clear. If a coal-miner, working for a wage of £90 a week, adds nothing at all to output, it is clearly uneconomic to employ him. This is particularly so if, for the same wage, he could add appreciably to the production of fuel oil. The community, in using a resource wastefully, is sacrificing energy needlessly.

Specialization and exchange

We noted in Unit 6 that resources, human or otherwise, are usually specialized. We, as individuals, do not produce all we need but must exchange our products for those of other people. Production takes place through the efforts of people working with other resources. These include not only what nature has provided, in the form of land, coal, wood, and the like, but also man-made resources, such as machinery, factory and office buildings, computers, and tools. All these aids to production are owned by somebody—an individual, a firm, a local authority, or the central government. So we called these aids *property*.

Specialization of work

Population trends at any time determine the size of the potential working population. Whether this is used to the best advantage depends on how far unemployment is avoided, how much property is available to work with, and how skilled the labour force is. Skill itself is bound up with specialization, or **division of labour.**

At first, you remember, our survivor from the nuclear disaster found himself alone. It was only when he was joined by other people that production could be shared out more efficiently. Even in this primitive society, some people would concentrate on the provision of food, others on building, clothing, and so on. Similarly today, doctors, teachers, and shopkeepers are specialized by occupation.

As a community becomes more advanced, further specialization is possible. Property, in more and more complicated forms, is produced. Mechanical diggers take the place of spades; the computer replaces the abacus. Not only are occupations more and more subdivided—specialized mathematicians becoming computer programmers—but there is also a distinction between one *process* and another. Workers produce parts of a complete product, rather than the whole of it. Cars are produced from the assembly of parts made by specialized workers, often organized in specialized firms. Production which is 'broken up' like this is said to be **disintegrated.** Workers or firms concentrating on particular processes, passing goods along, stage by stage, to the finished state, are said to be *vertically disintegrated.* Workers or firms producing different goods at the same level of production—such as woollen cloth, as opposed to worsted cloth—are horizontally disintegrated.

An advanced economy is thus highly complex. Primary producers, such as coal-miners or those drilling oil wells, are exploiting the gifts of nature. In 1973, we had a sharp reminder that however complicated an economy becomes, we still all rely in the final resort on those producing energy and food. Without the gifts of nature, no secondary production, whether it is the manufacture of a suit of clothes, an advanced aircraft, or the Channel Tunnel, can take place. Still less would there be a place for those involved in tertiary production—i.e., the service industries such as banking, insurance, transport, medicine, social services, education, and entertainment.

Advantages of work specialization

1. Increased production of wealth

Specialized workers are able to produce more than non-specialized ones; concentration on what they can do best would therefore seem to be sensible.

Up to a point, this is true. The business executive may be left to carry on the task of management, leaving his trained stenographer to produce his letters for him. We are assuming that each is better than the other at the special job performed; each has an **absolute advantage** over the other. Even if the executive happened to be a better typist than his stenographer, it would still be better if each specialized as long as some **relative advantage** existed. Supposing, for example, that the executive was ten times as good a businessman as the stenographer, but only twice as efficient at shorthand and typing. He has a relative advantage greater in management than in stenography. The community is better served by his specialization in management.

This is all very well, as long as the community is willing to demand management and pay for it. If this were not the case, the executive would be well advised to look for a job as a stenographer, particularly if these were greatly in demand. Division of labour does not always mean that people should concentrate on doing what they can do best, since there are cases in which nobody wants their product. In more technical terms, they should concentrate on production in which they have the greatest relative advantage, *given the state of demand.* We have already noted that 'division of labour is limited by the extent of the market'. This means that a high degree of specialization is only possible where a large demand for a product exists. Modern mass-production methods are based on this observation. But the statement can equally be taken to mean that a particular skill may not be wanted.

2. Increase in skill

It remains true, of course, that specialization can *develop* natural ability. The economics teacher, after ten years' experience in the classroom, may well wonder how

70

he dared to face a class when he had just gained a degree. Similarly, the apprentice motor mechanic develops into the skilled engineer, and the student doctor into the specialist.

3. *Other advantages*

Some occupations are wholly absorbing and satisfying. The professional man is often thoroughly wrapped up in his work, being motivated more by his interest in it than by the reward. Where the worker is a specialist at only one process or operation, the same interest may not be present, as we shall see later. Nevertheless, he can concentrate on only one job and does not waste time in moving from one task to another. Other resources are used more economically if, for example, the lathe operator concentrates on his one job, since fewer lathes are required than would be the case if labour remained unspecialized and more people used lathes for part of their working day. These fewer machines can also be used more continuously.

It has been argued that fatigue is reduced by specialization. This is often but not always the case. Some factory workers operating semi-automatic machinery may indeed gain such dexterity that they can be thinking of anything but the job in hand. On the other hand, the specialized teacher may find himself exhausted by furious mental activity throughout a day, even though he has done no physical work whatsoever. Similarly, the surgeon dare not let his thoughts wander and is unlikely to be very fresh at the end of a major operation. Circumstances alter cases. The main advantage of specialization must be increased and more efficient production; other advantages vary according to the nature of the skill and specialization involved.

Disadvantages of work specialization
1. *Frustration and boredom*

One of the causes of social unrest in nineteenth-century England stemmed from the fact that it was becoming increasingly difficult for a worker to move up the economic ladder and become a master. As firms expanded and used increasing amounts of other resources, so workers found it impossible to gather sufficient money or knowledge of the market to branch out on their own. The same situation exists today. While a painter and decorator may still found his own firm with comparative ease, the printing operative is unlikely to start a newspaper. If it is true that specialization may lead to initiative and invention (as through the suggestion box instituted by many firms), it is equally true that it may cause boredom, discontent, and frustration. Workers and management may become so divorced that the attitude of 'them' and 'us' develops, the two sides warring rather than co-operating.

2. *Industrial unrest*

Production in an advanced economy is the result of co-operative effort. In the car industry, for example, components are **mass produced** on a continuous-flow basis, using largely automatic processes which are often controlled and monitored by computer. These components are then brought together and assembled elsewhere, often in another part of the country. Any small group of workers controlling the output of components is therefore in a position to exert disproportionate pressure in pursuit of

71

wage demands and, if necessary, to bring the whole industry to a standstill. This growing tendency to exert industrial power is not confined to workers in the mass-production industry. Nor is all-out strike action necessary. The combined effect of a 'go-slow' by both miners and engine drivers at the end of 1973 was enough to force an energy crisis which put the whole of British industry on to a three-day working week.

3. Unemployment

Unemployment among specialized workers can thus come about by the action of their fellow workers. It can also come about by change in demand for the product which they make. Local and central government, for example, can greatly influence employment of construction workers through the expansion or contraction of public building programmes. Whatever its other merits, a very large cut in **public expenditure,** such as that which occured in the mid 'seventies, can be expected to contribute towards unemployment among building workers. Work is the most perishable of all commodities. Once a day's work has been lost, it is gone for ever. And while it is possible to scrap machines or to keep them idle and maintained with no more than a touch of oil, the unemployed man suffers a great blow to his self-esteem. We return to these points in later Units. Meanwhile, of course, it is important to note that unemployment caused by changes in demand occurs only as long as workers are unable to transfer from one occupation to another.

Mobility of labour

If such a transfer is easy, then there is high **occupational mobility,** and specialization need not necessarily be a handicap. There is often a range of occupations open to a worker trained in one particular field. The chauffeur can become a lorry driver fairly easily, and might even make a pilot. He is less likely to become an efficient accountant, but the latter might transfer from his job to that of company secretary.

Other factors affect occupational mobility. The accident of birth plays a large part in determining a person's future career. Differences of intelligence and of education are also important, while applicants for some jobs may find that the way is barred by the insistence, by trade unions or professional bodies, on a long and costly training.

Industrial mobility is also important. Our lorry driver would have no difficulty in changing from the brewing to the haulage business as long as he could still drive his lorry, and as long as he could live in the same area. If he had to change houses, however, he might be less mobile. This concept of **geographical mobility** plays a large part in determining the ease with which people can change their jobs. In September 1977, for the UK as a whole, 6.8 per cent on average of the total working population was registered as unemployed. However, the figure for the north of England was 8.8 per cent, while in London and the south-east only 5 per cent of the working population was unemployed. This situation persists because it is impossible or distasteful for many workers to uproot their families, pay higher rents in the south, and leave the part of the country in which they were reared.

Territorial specialization

72   Areas may specialize as well as men. Cotton in Lancashire, oil refineries around the

coast, gun-making in Birmingham, cocoa growing in Ghana and Nigeria—all these are examples well known to most people. In Unit 11 we deal with location of industry, and in Book 2 with international trade. Here, in passing we may remark that specialist skills often tend to be grouped in particular areas. Geographical mobility may then be retarded. As the industry which once formed the mainstay of a region declines, governments are faced with the dilemma of whether to take new work to the area or to encourage the working force to move out. The former course may raise costs of production, and the latter will result in waste of social capital in the form of half-empty cities.

Specialization of other resources

It is not only men that may become specialized and less mobile. The same is true of machines and of any other resource. Indeed, the whole process of production in the creation of **form utility** consists of making resources more specialized. A tree's wood may be made into many different products. Once the wood is shaped into a table or a lamp standard, there is little possibility that it can be used for anything else. The die which shapes the whole side of a car is also highly specialized. Once a car model is changed, the die becomes useless. Paradoxically, the specialized machine may cause less specialized labour. The skilled woodworker engaged on shaping the bodies of early cars has been replaced by the less specialized (though still skilful) machine operative today.

This effect does not, of course, always take place. A computer is a highly specialized piece of equipment. Since the computer only does exactly as it is told, it needs a highly specialized programmer to give it instructions. Again, it should be noted that its calculations are done so quickly that there is no point in installing it unless sufficient work exists for it. Once more, we see that division of labour (this time, machine labour) is limited by the extent of the market.

Land is another resource which may be capable of only one use. The reason may be natural, as in the case of very sandy soils able to grow only pine-trees, or it may be due to man's activities. Once land is built on, for example, its use can only be changed with difficulty and expense, although the building itself may be used in one of a variety of ways. Geographically, of course, land is completely **immobile.** Other resources are to some degree less so. China clay, used in the production of pottery, is transported around the coast and inland to Stoke-on-Trent. On the other hand, a piece of heavy machinery was recently stranded in Carlisle because a bridge on its route was unable to bear its weight. Finally, a factory building is virtually fixed in one place.

Even **consumer goods** are specialized. Manufacturers deliberately use brand names to persuade their customers that their products differ from those of competitors. These products are then said to be **differentiated.** Quite apart from this, nobody would buy a television set expecting it to do the work of a washing machine.

The combination of resources

The television set is a most *imperfect substitute* for a washing machine. Similarly, skilled men and unskilled ones cannot do the same work; neither can taxi-cabs do the work of forklift trucks. Resources, human and non-human, must be combined

73

together in order to create utility. Some of these may be more specialized than others; some may be scarcer than others. The problems which arise when *proportions* of resources used together are altered will now be examined. Units 8 to 10 look at the payments made for resources. What has just been said is also relevant to that discussion.

Characteristics of resources: implications for production

The first point then, is the combination of scarce and specialized resources in the creation of utility. Plants may grow wild with no assistance from a farmer, but systematic agriculture needs manpower, buildings, fertilizers, and so on if it is to be successful. Similarly, a television set can only be produced by men working with machinery. As a general statement, we can say that production can only be achieved by people working with property of one sort or another.

Second, different resources are not perfect substitutes for one another. If we wish to produce more television sets, there are only two ways in which this can be done. Either we can use an existing factory more fully, with men working on a shift system so that the machinery is hardly at rest, or we can build another factory. Similarly, a farmer can produce a greater output of crops either by farming *intensively,* thus getting a higher yield from his existing acreage, or by farming *extensively,* bringing more land into cultivation. In this section we first consider intensive production, before turning to the problems of extensive production. (It is as well to note straight away that no responsible farmer would expect to go on producing a higher yield indefinitely, merely by combining more and more manpower or fertilizer with a fixed acreage of land. This would inevitably lead to soil exhaustion and ultimately to lower yields.) The more specialized or specific a resource is, the less it can act as a substitute for another resource. Oak might be a substitute for steel under some circumstances, but not if the oak has already been shaped into a garden seat and the steel into a car chassis.

These examples indicate the third important point which needs to be stressed. It is that some resources are **fixed,** at least in the short run, while others are **variable.** Another way of saying this is that some factors of production are available only in fairly large 'lumps' or units of productive capacity. For example, if our television firm wants to make only a few sets, it nevertheless has to install machinery capable of making a much larger number. The machinery is *indivisible,* in the sense that it cannot be broken down into smaller units without destroying its effectiveness. On the other hand, essential raw materials and manpower are much more divisible, so that the obvious way to step up production would be to combine more men with the existing machinery rather than the other way round. In this way, the machinery would be used to much greater *capacity.*

The law of non-proportional returns

Efficient use of resources can only be achieved if they are combined in the right proportions. The first four columns of Table 7.1 illustrate the point. We are assuming that increasing amounts of a variable resource are being combined with one fixed resource. Since this is a general argument, we do not need to specify exactly what these resources are. They may be men and fertilizer combined with land, or more men

Table 7.1 Non-proportional returns

1	2	3	4	5	6	7	8	9	10	11
Variable resources combined with one fixed resource	Total product	Marginal product	Average product	Total fixed cost £	Total variable cost £	Total cost £	Average fixed cost £	Average variable cost £	Average total cost £	Marginal cost £
1	1	—	1	100 +	20 =	120	100	20	120	—
2	8	7	4	100 +	40 =	140	$12\frac{1}{2}$	5	$17\frac{1}{2}$	$2\frac{6}{7}$
3	18	10	6	100 +	60 =	160	$5\frac{10}{18}$	$3\frac{6}{18}$	$8\frac{16}{18}$	2
4	32	14	8	100 +	80 =	180	$3\frac{4}{32}$	$2\frac{16}{32}$	$5\frac{20}{32}$	$1\frac{6}{14}$
5	45	13	9	100 +	100 =	200	$2\frac{10}{45}$	$2\frac{10}{45}$	$4\frac{20}{45}$	$1\frac{7}{13}$
6	54	9	9	100 +	120 =	220	$1\frac{46}{54}$	$2\frac{12}{54}$	$4\frac{4}{54}$	$2\frac{2}{9}$
7	56	2	8	100 +	140 =	240	$1\frac{44}{56}$	$2\frac{28}{56}$	$4\frac{16}{56}$	10
8	56	0	7	100 +	160 =	260	$1\frac{44}{56}$	$2\frac{48}{56}$	$4\frac{36}{56}$	infinity

1. Fractions unreduced so that calculations can easily be reworked.
2. Columns 1 to 4 refer to physical product. Columns 5 to 11 refer to cost in money terms.

3. Column 3 can be calculated from column 2. Column $4 = \dfrac{\text{column 2}}{\text{column 1}}$ Columns 2, 5, 6, and 7 are assumed figures. Column $8 = \dfrac{\text{column 5}}{\text{column 2}}$

Column $9 = \dfrac{\text{column 6}}{\text{column 2}}$ Column $10 =$ either columns $8 + 9$ or $\dfrac{\text{column 7}}{\text{column 2}}$ To calculate column 11, ask yourself: (a) How

many extra products are produced by one more variable resource? (b) How much extra do these products cost to produce?
(c) Finally, then, how much extra does *each one* of these products cost to produce?

working in a factory; the effect is the same. One variable resource (or factor of production) combined with a fixed factor gives a total product of one unit of output. If you think that this is not very realistic, remember that, since we are making a general point, it is as well to keep the figures as simple as possible.

In Table 7.1, column 4 shows that the average product of the variable resource, used in this particular combination, is 1. Suppose we now combine two variable resources with the fixed factor of production. Eight units are now produced. The average product of each variable resource becomes $^8/_2 = 4$. Furthermore, the effect of using a second variable resource is to obtain 7 extra units of product. This extra is called the **marginal product.** It is found in column 3. The marginal product can be defined as *the difference made to the total product by combining one more unit of a variable resource with a fixed resource.* In order to make sure that you follow the argument, work right through the figures in the first four columns of Table 7.1. When you arrive at the last line you will see that the addition of an eighth unit of variable resources produces no extra product. The total product remains at 56 and the marginal product is 0. The 8 units of variable resource produce 56 products; on average they produce 7 each.

Some interesting conclusions can be drawn from a study of columns 3 and 4. The marginal product begins by rising, but later falls. We have already seen why this should be so. At first, the indivisible fixed factor of production is being underused. Too few variable factors are being combined with it. Later, however, it is being overworked, eventually to such an extent that no addition to production is possible by the addition of more variable resources. Nor must it be assumed that successive units of the variable resource are in any way inferior because the marginal product falls. They may each be equally efficient; it is the *number* of them combined with the fixed factor which causes the marginal product to fall eventually.

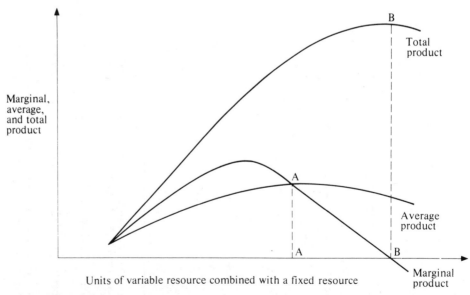

Fig. 7.1 (a) Where sufficient units of variable resource are employed to make marginal and average product equal (AA), the average product reaches its highest point.
    (b) Where total product is at its highest point, marginal product is nil (B), thereafter as total product falls, marginal product becomes negative.

The *average product* is related to the *marginal* one. This can best be illustrated by considering cricket scores. If the first batsman scores ten runs and the second twenty, then the average score will be fifteen. If the third man also scores fifteen marginal (or further) runs, the average remains fifteen. If a fourth batsman scores only three runs, the average falls to twelve. A little thought will show that the marginal and average numbers of runs are equal when the average is at its highest. Similarly, columns 3 and 4 show that average and marginal products are equal when the average product is at its highest.

What we have been discussing is known as the **law of non-proportional returns.** The word 'returns' is a quick way of saying 'marginal and average products'. Returns are non-proportional to variable resources employed. In other words, the marginal and average products do not remain constant, but rise and fall. One part of this law is called the **law of diminishing returns.** It is usually stated thus: *if more and more variable resources are combined with a fixed resource, then, after a while, the marginal and average product will fall.*

The relationships shown in the first four columns of Table 7.1 can also be expressed in the form of a graph. Figure 7.1 illustrates how this would look. As we would expect from the previous analysis, the marginal and average product curves intersect at the highest point of the latter. And when the total product curve ceases to rise, the marginal product is nil. Remember that the graph shows what happens to total, marginal, and average product when more variable resources are combined with a fixed resource. The units of variable resources used are plotted on the horizontal axis.

Products and costs

The fact that the marginal product eventually diminishes means that each successive addition of a variable resource leads to higher **real cost.** Not only are we sacrificing more and more of the resource's alternative product; we are also obtaining less and less addition to output. Obviously then, an organization seeking maximum efficiency has to produce using the best combination of fixed and variable resources. However, this combination is not necessarily that at which the average product is highest. A full discussion of why this is so must be postponed until we consider the organization's income. Meanwhile, however, it may be fairly clear from Table 7.1 that if the seventh variable resource cost £20 and the two extra products sold for, say, £30, a producer would certainly employ the extra resource, even though the average product was falling. The moral of all this is that we must now begin to translate changes in output into changes in costs of production.

Columns 5 to 11 in Table 7.1 are all expressed in terms of money. The fixed resource costs £100, which must be paid whether it is used or not. This is a **fixed cost.** Every successive unit of variable resource employed costs £20. The **total variable cost** appears in column 6. *Fixed cost plus variable cost equals the total cost of any given output.* Thus, the total cost of producing 45 units of product is the £200 shown in column 7. How much, then does each unit of product cost to produce? If 45 cost £200, then each costs $\frac{£200}{45}$. The answer, shown as $£4\frac{20}{45}$, appears in column 10. Thus:

$$\frac{\text{Total cost}}{\text{Total product}} = \text{Average total cost}$$

77

Let us work through this again, using another example. Assume that a factory costs £10000 to build. It employs 1000 men each paid £10 a week in wages, together with materials costing £5000. In a week, it produces 25000 shirts; the factory is then destroyed by fire. The cost of each shirt now works out at £1:

Fixed cost   = £10,000   £

Variable cost   = 1,000 x £10 for manpower   10,000

                  + for materials   5,000

                                        £15,000

Total cost   = £10,000 + £15,000 = £25,000

Total product   =   25000 shirts

Average total cost = $\dfrac{\text{Total cost}}{\text{Total Product}} = \dfrac{£25,000}{25000} = £1$

(cost per shirt)

How much of this £1 per shirt would be needed to cover the cost of the factory alone? £10,000 has to be divided among 25000 shirts:

$$\frac{\text{Total fixed cost}}{\text{Total product}} = \frac{£10,000}{25000} = 40\text{p} = \text{Average fixed cost}$$

And how much would be needed to cover payment of wages plus cost of material?

$$\frac{\text{Total variable cost}}{\text{Total product}} = \frac{£15,000}{25000} = 60\text{p} = \text{Average variable cost}$$

If we now return to Table 7.1, we see the same principles illustrated in columns 8 and 9. When two units of variable resource are used, for example, then:

$$\frac{\text{Fixed cost}}{\text{Total product}} = \frac{£100}{8} = £12.50 = \text{Average fixed cost}$$

$$\frac{\text{Variable cost}}{\text{Total product}} = \frac{£40}{8} = £5 \quad = \text{Average variable cost}$$

$$\frac{\text{Total cost}}{\text{Total product}} = \frac{£100 + £40}{8} = £17.50 = \text{Average total cost}$$

Our final problem is to calculate *marginal cost*. This appears in column 11 of Table 7.1. It may be defined as the *cost of producing the final unit of output*. But, of course, things are rarely produced one at a time. In other words, the marginal product hardly ever increases in steps of one. The third variable resource in our illustration produces ten extra (marginal) products when combined with the fixed resource, and two other variable factors of production. It costs £20 to employ. In order to find the marginal cost of the extra product, we do the following calculation:

$$\frac{\text{Increase in total cost in production of marginal product}}{\text{Marginal product}}$$

$$\frac{£20}{10} = £2 = \text{Marginal cost}$$

The seventh variable factor costs £20, but increases total product by only two units. The marginal cost of each of these is therefore £10. Can you now see why the marginal cost in line eight (column 11) is infinity?

As before, these relationships may be expressed in the form of the graph shown in Fig. 7.2. Movements in the various types of cost are plotted on the vertical axis against changes in output (or total product) on the horizontal axis. A glance back at Table 7.1 will confirm that, although average fixed cost is falling until the eighth variable factor is employed, average variable cost, average total cost, and marginal cost all start to rise at some earlier point. These cost curves become U-shaped on a graph. Furthermore, the marginal cost curve intersects those for both average variable cost and average total cost at their lowest points.

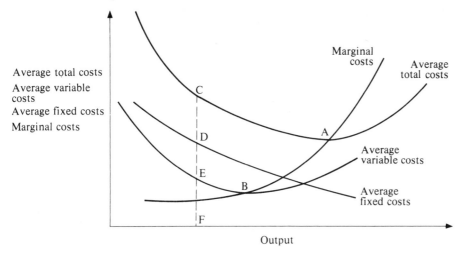

Fig. 7.2 (a) Marginal costs and average total costs are equal (A) where average total costs are lowest.
  (b) Marginal costs and average variable costs are equal (B) where average variable costs are lowest.
  (c) Average total costs minus average fixed costs equal average variable costs. Thus, for example, CF minus DF equals CD, but, since EF is also average variable costs, CD = EF.

The relationship between product and cost

This result is not accidental. As long as the marginal product increases, marginal cost falls, because the increase in total cost is being divided among a greater number of extra products. Similarly, when we come to the point of diminishing returns and the marginal product falls, then marginal cost increases. The same is true of the relationship between the average product and the average cost of each product. We have already noted that production under conditions of diminishing returns leads to higher real cost. Now it becomes obvious that money costs also rise in this situation.

We are now in a position to sum up the whole argument so far, regarding the relationship between product and cost. The assumptions on which we have worked are as follows:

1. A **short-run** situation exists. The short run can be defined in this context as a period

of time during which a firm cannot increase, decrease, or modify in any way the fixed resources which it employs.

2. There are no changes in techniques. Methods of production remain unchanged; greater efficiencies are not introduced. Thus, the combination of a fixed resource with a given amount of a variable resource always results in the same total product.

3. Production is achieved by the use of resources combined with one another. Such resources are not perfect substitutes for one another and may be relatively or absolutely indivisible.

If these assumptions are strictly adhered to, we find the following results:

(a) Firms have to increase production as best they can. This means the combination of more and more of the variable resource with the fixed one. At first, while the fixed factor is under-employed, both the marginal and average product will rise. So marginal and average costs will fall. The position is one of **increasing returns,** but the fixed resource is being used inefficiently.

(b) Eventually, a point of **constant returns** may be reached. Marginal *or* average product may remain unchanged, following the addition of another unit of variable resource. Marginal *or* average costs neither rise nor fall.

(c) Any increase in production past this point leads to **diminishing returns.** Both marginal and average product fall; marginal and average costs rise.

(d) In the extreme case, no further increase in total output is possible. The marginal product becomes zero or even negative. This situation results because the fixed resource has become so overemployed that a further addition of another variable resource is a hindrance rather than a help.

(e) This situation would hardly be allowed to arise, since all resources are scarce and have to be paid for. They have both a real and a money cost. It is, therefore, unusual for production to be carried on to the point where total production is at a maximum (or where the marginal product is zero).

(f) *Any* resource may be regarded as 'fixed'. To take an example from agriculture, we may consider either men being combined with a fixed acreage of land or more land being used in conjunction with a fixed number of men. The law of non-proportional returns then applies to whichever resource is considered variable. If we consider each to be scarce, then to avoid waste of any resource, they (men or land) must be combined so that there is a declining (though positive) marginal product accruing to each of them. This must also mean that each shows a declining average product.

Some practical considerations

So far, we have assumed that the only reason for increasing costs is the onset of diminishing returns. Table 7.1 indicates that it is possible to use increasing amounts of variable resource at a constant cost of £20 each. But, of course, this might not be so. Let us assume that there is more than one firm hiring these resources and increasing production. In such a case, the resources may become more and more scarce. The payment necessary to persuade them to work for any particular firm or organization would then have to be increased. Such a sum is called **transfer earnings,** and reflects the real cost, since more and more of the resource's alternative product is being sacrificed. In a period of full employment, for example, higher wages may have to be paid to attract a particular type of scarce manpower, especially of a skilled variety. Total costs then rise for quite a different reason.

We have also assumed that the units of variable resource are completely interchangeable, identical in all respects, and therefore **homogeneous.** Again, this may not be the case. It is likely that, as increasing amounts of this resource are used, the marginal quantities will be inferior and produce less than their more efficient counterparts already being used. Given an increased demand for foodstuffs in wartime, land which would otherwise not be used (i.e., marginal land), may be ploughed up. It is not likely to be so productive, however, as land under permanent peacetime cultivation. Because of the difficulty of increasing land supplies, earlier economists regarded agriculture as the classic case of diminishing returns, *land* being a *fixed resource.* As we have seen, this view has now been modified. However, it still remains true that the problems outlined in this Unit are at their most acute where agriculture and extractive industries, such as coal-mining, are concerned.

For most types of manufacturing industries, on the other hand, the fact of scarcity of resources, some of which are fixed, is much less troublesome. Resources used in these industries are much better substitutes for one another within the probable range of production. Consequently, over wide variations in output, marginal and average costs may remain constant. Finally, it is usually possible, *in the long run,* to increase the whole scale of production. In this case, the fixed factor itself may be increased. The response to a sudden increase in demand for a product may initially be that of using more men and materials on a shift system in a factory. If the demand continues, however, another factory may well be built. In this case, the problems become those of extensive as well as intensive production.

The time element

No firm can increase in size overnight. Indeed, in most cases growth is discontinuous or jerky. The decision to expand depends upon access to money capital, on the growth of sales, on the possibility of increasing the labour force, on the degree of uncertainty which management is willing to bear. There may well be two near-optimum sizes, one small or medium and one very large, with the near certainty of loss at any intermediate stage. Thus, we must now consider costs *in the long run,* after sufficient time has elapsed for changes to fixed resources as well as variable resources to be made.

Fixed and variable resources

In the long run, all resources (and all costs) are variable. Expansion of scale involves addition to factory floor space, installation of extra, and probably different, machinery, employment of more office staff and managers, and so on. Earlier in this Unit, that possibility was ruled out quite firmly. Production was assumed to be *intensive,* extra products being obtainable only by the use of more variable resources combined with fixed ones. On this assumption depended the law of non-proportional returns, with its effects on costs of production. Now we are considering the possibility of *extensive* production over time.

Let us return to the oversimplified assumptions of Table 7.1. We will now assume that it has been possible, given enough time, to double the amount of *both* the fixed and

81

variable factors of production. We will further assume that this has led to economies of large-scale production, so that doubling the scale leads to output being *trebled*. Line 1 of the table now reads as follows:

Variable resources	Total product	Marginal product	Average product	Total fixed cost	Total variable cost	Total cost	Average total cost
2	3	—	1½	£200	£40	£240	£80

A doubling of both fixed and variable resources has led to a trebling of total product. The average product arising from the use of each variable resource is now 1½. Total fixed cost and total variable cost are both twice what they were before, since the amount of all resources in use is doubled. (We are assuming that this has no effect on the price of the resources.) Total cost is therefore also doubled. The most interesting point, however, is that the average cost of producing any one of the three units of total product is now only £80, whereas, on the assumptions of Table 7.1, it was £120. To sum up, the effect of large-scale production has been *to produce more commodities at lower total cost per unit of commodity.* If the assumption of trebled output from doubled resources is carried on right through the figures of Table 7.1, a little arithmetic will show that both average total cost and marginal cost are consistently lower. We have a situation of *increasing returns to the scale of production.*

At first sight, this terminology may seem confusing. It is important to be quite clear on the difference between increasing returns and increasing returns *to scale.* The former situation arises when one or more resources are considered to be fixed in the short run and when, by the use of additional variable resources, extra products can be forthcoming at a lower average and marginal cost. In the latter case, all resources are considered variable in the long run. So it is the increase in the total scale of production (proportions between resources used remaining unchanged) which causes a fall in average and marginal costs.

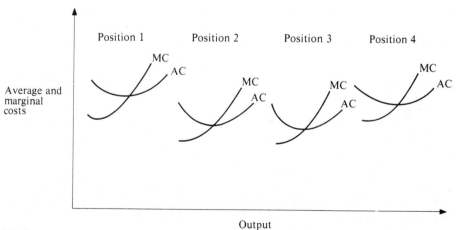

Fig. 7.3

Constant and decreasing returns to scale

As we have already seen, however (Unit 3), it is possible that there may be either no advantages in large-scale production or even that disadvantages may arise. An increase in all resources used may lead to either an increase in production in the same proportion or in a lower proportion. The situation then arises of either constant or decreasing returns to the scale of production; average and marginal costs either remain the same or increase—even though in each case output is greater.

The effects on costs of increasing, constant, and decreasing returns to scale may be illustrated by means of a graph. In Fig. 7.3, a firm moving from position 1 to position 2 over time achieves economies leading to lower costs. A further increase in size to position 3 would lead to greater output at the same average and marginal costs. A further increase in size to position 4 would lead to decreasing returns to scale. Output would again be greater, but at higher production costs.

Effects of changing technology on costs

A firm is seldom faced with production decisions as simple and clear-cut as those outlined in this Unit. In most cases the *laws of non-proportional returns* and *returns to scale* are operating simultaneously. Some years ago, for example, Pilkingtons, the glass manufacturers, wished to expand their production of plate glass. After much work on research and development, they discovered and patented a new process. By the nature of the technology involved, the new plate glass was called 'float' glass. The development costs have been immense, yet when the process was perfected, better glass could be produced at a lower cost per unit than before. Furthermore, somewhat fewer

New technology a threat to employment

A trade union study into the effect of technological advances upon jobs predicts five million unemployed by the mid 1990s. Even this figure is based on the assumption that every possible step is taken to expand the economy and thus create jobs.

Research for the report shows that the greatest impact will be from the use of micro-electronics and that jobs of all kinds and in all sectors of industry and commerce are at risk.

work people needed to be employed in the process. Thus, several things had happened at virtually the same time. The proportion of capital to labour had been changed; the scale of production had been increased, not merely by adding to existing equipment, but by a whole new technology. Initially, the glass was more expensive to produce because of the new massive element of fixed cost in its manufacture. However, because of the efficiency of the new process, as more and more glass was produced, its average cost fell both absolutely and in relation to its average cost when produced under the old conditions. In the short run the cost of glass rose, but in the long run it fell.

In this instance, improved technology paid off. However, it should not be assumed that this is always the case. Some inventions are never brought to a successful fruition. Others are technically sound, but languish because either there is insufficient capital to develop them or the market for their products is too small to warrant their use. The latter is one reason why British inventions sometimes have to wait for foreign innovators.

When we look at society at large, it is clear that *improved technology* has been an important factor in lowering costs and raising standards of living. This is because inventions have led to increased productivity, and as the labour force has had more power at its elbow, so its output has increased and wages have risen in consequence. It might be thought that the fruits of this improved productivity should go rather to the suppliers of the capital goods, but it must be remembered that the stock of capital goods has increased relatively to the labour force. Hence, there have been diminished returns to capital.

Summary

Resources are often specialized and immobile. Capital resources, in particular, often take a long time to produce. Thus, if production has to be increased, in the short run this is only possible by the more intensive use of fixed resources. This intensive use means that more variable resources are combined with fixed resources, leading eventually to diminishing output per variable resource employed. From the point of view of money costs of production, the last or marginal amounts of output begin to cost more. The law of non-proportional returns sums up the argument: *If more and more variable resources are combined with a fixed resource, then the marginal and average product first rise but later fall.* This may be illustrated, but not explained, by means of cost schedules and graphs. The important thing to know is the effect of increased production on costs in the short-run.

Given enough time, no resources are fixed, as it is possible to increase output by increasing the whole scale of the operation. Economies of scale (see Unit 3) lead to lower average costs of production. Diseconomies of scale lead to higher costs. Both short-run and long-run factors may influence costs simultaneously as an organization alters its production methods and size. Efficient production demands that an organization should be of such a structure and size that resources are used with the greatest economy.

Assignment

Your organization manufactures TV games, and your sales manager, reporting an increasing demand for the product, advocates greater production. He is confident that the increased production can be sold at the present price.

Write a report indicating, in general terms, the information required before a decision can be reached on whether or not to increase production.

Unit 8 Work and wages

The working population

In Unit 2, we discussed briefly the working population of the UK in the context of the total population and its geographical and occupational distribution. The time has now come to explore in greater depth the question of employment. We need to know why organizations employ people, why they pay different wages or salaries for different occupations, and why some people who are capable of work remain unemployed. The answers to these questions are highly complex. We can now make a beginning, leaving the complexities to Book 2.

The labour market

From the viewpoint of any organization, its workforce is a resource. It is insufficient for it to know that at any one time about 26 million people (16 million men; 10 million women) are available for work, or even that anything between 200 000 and 2 million of them are unemployed. It wants to know the state of the labour market in a much more detailed way. Are secretaries, plumbers, accountants, available, and what is the going rate of pay? At that rate of pay, can they afford to hire them? A good recent description of the labour market comes from a Manpower Services Commission document, 'Training for Skills' (Autumn 1977), from which the following quotation is taken (by permission of the MSC):

2.1 Industry needs skills if it is to be efficient and profitable or indeed if it is to operate at all. On the one hand, employers have needs, both in terms of numbers of workers and types of skill. These vary greatly between industries, firms and areas and over time, but the common thread is that it is in all employers' interests to have a management and a labour force with the right skills to do the work of the undertaking efficiently and well. On the other hand, it is in workers' interests to seek job opportunities which will enable them to find satisfaction in working life, to fit themselves through training and education for these job opportunities, and to earn appropriate monetary and non-monetary rewards for the training they have undertaken.

2.2 It is the labour market which brings together the diverse needs of enterprises in industry and commerce and employees' needs to have their skills used and rewarded. Good employment policies can help to reconcile these two sets of needs, but the question of what skills are needed or in demand at any time is decided by the interplay of many factors including, notably, technology and the supply of labour in areas where jobs are available.

2.3 The labour market (or, more accurately, the aggregation of many separate labour markets) is enormously diverse and dynamic. In addition to movement within companies there is a great deal of movement between employers—job changes are of the order of 10 million per year—reflecting both fluctuations in employers' demands and individual employees' decisions. Currently, over 650 000 school-leavers enter the labour market. People withdraw on retirement. People move into and out of employment. Women leave to have children and many return later.

2.4 At any point in time there are in the labour market imbalances of many kinds between the supply of and demand for labour. But the labour market is in a constant state of adjustment through the actions of both employers, in bringing their labour force size and structure in line with production requirements, and workers, who move around as their work needs change. As a result, most labour force imbalances are temporary and are easily accommodated, often with the assistance of manpower agencies such as Jobcentres. They do not have any substantial ill-effects on production or on the labour market.

This gives some idea of the complexity of the labour market facing organizations. In order to make a start on the analysis of that complexity, let us first concentrate on economic principles. Later in this Unit we see how these must be modified to take account of the operation of government organizations.

How wages are fixed: economic principles

Wages are the reward for work of all kinds, including running a business. Salaries, paid monthly rather than weekly, are included in this broad classification. Before going on to discuss the principles which govern the payment of wages, it is as well to know the possible methods which may be adopted.

Under a system of **time-wages** a number of hours' or days' work is given up in return for money. Time-wages thus include most salaries. They are paid whenever the work achieved cannot be measured. A teacher, for example, provides a service, the effect of which is not immediately apparent. Similarly, a manager cannot always be paid by results. Even where the product is measureable, weekly wages may be paid if the need for careful work is greater than that for speed in output. Nevertheless, the risk always remains that someone who is paid weekly or monthly may do the minimum amount necessary to save himself from dismissal.

The **piece-work** system relates payment to output and can thus only be used where such output is measureable. It can take many forms—like incentive bonuses, for example, which are paid when a man's output exceeds a given standard amount. Such a bonus leads to progressively increasing wages, giving an incentive to work harder (standards of workmanship may suffer as a result). Piece-rates in general, however, have the disadvantage that they are difficult to work out. Work study techniques are often necessary to establish what the standard output should be. These techniques are usually mistrusted by workers, who fear that the standard will be pitched too high, to prevent the earning of high piece-rates. Furthermore, not all workers are capable of producing the same output per hour: the slower ones (but perhaps the more careful) are penalized.

Although time work and piece-rates are the two main ways of paying wages and salaries, they do not necessarily constitute the whole of a man's earnings from work. Some firms have instituted *profit-sharing schemes* in an attempt to identify their workforce with the prosperity of the business. Such schemes may or may not go so far as to include *co-partnership,* whereby workers actually take a share in the running of the business. Although these schemes should improve relationships between management and the work people and may well lead to increased output, they often come to grief because workers are not necessarily skilled in taking management decisions and, in any case, are not willing to share losses as well as profits.

Wage payments may also be related to the general level of prices. The Index of Retail Prices, discussed in Unit 10 of Book 2, is used to regulate the wages of about one-twelfth of the total working force of the UK. Thus, **real wages,** expressed in terms of what money wages will buy, can be kept constant. The trouble is that the index is unreliable as a guide to changes in prices and is trusted by the workforce only as long as it is moving upwards.

Whatever the method by which wages are paid, there must be some principles determining the share of the *National Income* accruing to owners of work as opposed to owners of property. Supply and demand analysis must be brought into play.

In the last resort, the supply of work depends upon the size of the working population. In the short run, this must remain fixed and is, we will assume, fully employed. But the working population may be more or less able to work efficiently. In countries where living standards are low, *expectation of life* is short and the work people are often physically less able to carry out long and arduous tasks. Again, workers may be more or less willing to increase output by working either longer hours or more efficiently. As their *standards of living* rise they may wish to spend more of their time in leisure rather than in earning more money. Finally, they must be mobile.

The first thing to note about the demand for work is that it is *derived* from the ability of workers to contribute to production. Firms do not employ staff for themselves alone, but for what they will produce. Second, firms are more likely to be thinking of possible additions to their labour force than of their total employees. In other words, we are back to the concept of the **margin.** Given the scale of operations, successive additions to the labour force of a particular firm are likely eventually to lead to diminishing returns. When **marginal product** resulting from additions to the labour force falls, the firm has to establish whether or not it is worth while employing any extra hands. It can only know this if it has an idea of the **price** at which the marginal product is likely to sell. It is the **value** of the marginal product which is important. Suppose, for example, that one extra worker will result in 10 extra products, valued at £1 each, being produced each week. If the worker has to be paid £11, then it is not worth while employing him, since the value of his marginal product is less than the wage paid in producing it. If we assume that all workers are equal, then everyone will receive the same wage. Workers will be hired up to the point where the wage for each of them equals the value of the marginal product.

It is now possible to see how wages are determined, given certain assumptions. Let us suppose that the total working population is fixed, that each member of it is willing to work, and that everybody can do any job, being unspecialized. Then the wage payable will be that necessary to distribute the workforce between all firms in all industries. The more efficient firms have a marginal product higher in value than the others. So they are in a position to pay higher wages. Other firms are forced to pay the same wage, since the work force is unspecialized and presumably mobile. The wage paid determines how many workers each firm employs. It need not be exactly the same for all jobs, since some of these are more unpleasant than others. In the theoretical world which we are considering, it would be the *net advantages* of each job which would be equated. The teacher, with his short hours and long holidays, would be paid *less* than the dustman who, after all, could equally be a teacher and who would have to be compensated for the relative unpleasantness of his job. Again, changes in demand would be met quite simply by a switch in the working force from one product to another. When demand fell, the firms affected would find that the value of their marginal product was falling. They would release workers who would be absorbed into those firms the demand for whose product was increasing.

How wages are fixed: the real world

All the above analysis belongs, of course, to a theoretical world. In practice, *workers are specialized* and to some extent *immobile*. They cannot do whatever is to hand, but must find jobs for which they are suited. However, it is possible that we can make the theory of marginal productivity allow for this fact.

Instead of there being only one general market for workers, as we have hitherto assumed, let us now move closer to reality. There are many markets, often mutually exclusive. The chauffeur may be able to drive a lorry or pilot a plane, but is unlikely to be able to make a successful dentist. Chauffeurs and dentists are said to be *non-competing* groups. There is imperfect competition between such groups of workers for may reasons. Some people are born more 'brainy' than others or in more favourable circumstances. The influence of trade unions or professional bodies is directed towards restricting the number of workers in a particular field, by insistence on apprenticeship or other forms of training. Mobility is less than complete, as we noted in Unit 2, because of the difficulties of finding houses in certain parts of the country and because of natural reluctance to leave the part of the country considered as home.

The wage or salary paid to a worker must be high enough to cover the *transfer cost* of ensuring that the worker is attracted away from any alternative employment. Such a transfer cost (i.e. the worker's transfer earnings), is also a **real cost,** since the alternative employment is sacrificed. As a general statement, workers will have high earnings if the value of their marginal product is high, if they are relatively scarce, and if their transfer cost is high. They will earn relatively low wages if there are many of them, if their numbers can be increased quickly and easily, and if the community puts a low value on their marginal product.

The concept of **elasticity** plays an important part in this analysis. For a particular group of workers, the value of their marginal product is high if the demand for the goods or services which they produce is not only great but also relatively inelastic. This concept is discussed in detail on page 156. Meanwhile, an example will suffice. If, as a result of a rise in tobacco workers' wages, cigarettes double in price but sales only fall by a quarter, demand is said to be inelastic. Consumers would, in this case, be willing to finance the rise in wages. Equally, they are in a stronger bargaining position if their numbers can be restricted either naturally or artificially, i.e., if the supply of their work is inelastic and also if it is difficult or impossible for employers to substitute other resources, such as machinery, for them.

The doctor, for example, is usually paid more than the docker for two main reasons.

89

1. From the view point of demand, the community values the services of the doctor more highly and is prepared to pay for them. The value of the doctor's marginal product, though difficult to estimate, is higher than that of the docker.
2. The supply of doctors is restricted. By no means all people are qualified by ability to begin training. The training itself is long and arduous and there is always the possibility of failure. While learning his skill, the medical student is forfeiting earnings. Finally, the medical profession does not attract all those who might be able to follow it. For all these reasons, the doctor's eventual payment must be high enough to persuade him to undertake the training involved.

The theory of marginal productivity can help to explain why women often earn less than men. First, of course, we have to assume that the work done by men and by women is equal. In many cases, this is not so. Women, at least in the UK, are not expected to do heavy manual work and would not be employed on such tasks. This is merely a special case arising from the principle of non-competing groups of workers. Women are restricted to a smaller number of occupations than are men and, because their supply for these occupations is relatively great, their transfer cost is low. So their wages are correspondingly low.

Even where equal work is possible—as in nursing, teaching or the Civil Service—women have in the past been paid less than men. In part, this has been because employers have considered them less reliable than their male colleagues. In part, it was because they were less highly organized in trade unions and therefore more likely to be exploited. In recent years, however, the principle of *equal pay for equal work* has been largely conceded, although this may have led to men being preferred in open competition with women. Certainly it has given rise to a feeling of injustice in some quarters, the argument being that women are much less likely to have to support dependants than are men. Parliament has attempted to solve some of the problems of equal pay and opportunity by legislation. These matters are discussed later in this Unit.

When we come to consider how well the demand and supply analysis works out in practice, it becomes apparent that wage rates do not necessarily follow the pattern which might be expected. Even within the same market, for example, there may be wide variations in wages paid. To some extent, this is because the principle of net advantage is being preserved. A docker in Greenock may receive a lower wage than his colleague in the Port of London simply because it costs less to live in Scotland. Real wages are the same for both men. On the other hand, if workers are immobile, wide variations in wages become possible simply because the *market is imperfect*. Our theory also assumes that firms are able to calculate physical marginal products and their values. Where more than one commodity is being made by a firm, it may be that different interpretations by cost accountants may lead to widely varying answers. In many cases, the employer is not sure whether he will be able to sell extra output or not. Neither can he tell what price he will get. The idea of *marginal productivity* might work out neatly, given conditions of perfect competition. As we know, however, these conditions can never apply to their fullest extent. Given any degree of imperfect competition, the employer may be in a position to offer a wage lower than that which supply and demand determine. **Trade unions** exist to ensure that this does not happen. In many cases, therefore, wages are determined by the relative bargaining positions of organized workers and organized employers. In such cases, there is no one **equilibrium**

wage. The final outcome will be a wage somewhere between the lowest offer which would provoke a strike and the highest trade union demand which would precipitate a lock-out on the part of employers. Within this range, the most skilled team of negotiators will be the most successful.

Above all, the marginal productivity theory is a *micro-economic* concept. It deals with the determination of *particular* wages on the assumption that there will always be a tendency towards full employment. Under this assumption, unemployment can only arise in one of the following ways:

1. Through seasonal fluctuations—agricultural workers or builders may be unemployed in bad weather and football pools clerks during the cricket season;
2. Through immobility—this further subdivides into: (a) structural unemployment caused by basic shifts in the pattern of industry, e.g., a decline in the cotton industry, and (b) technological unemployment caused by the introduction of new labour-saving inventions and techniques.

In all these cases, it would be argued that, given enough time for things to sort themselves out, the labour force would overcome the 'frictions' of immobility and full employment would be re-established.

This argument may be criticized on two counts. In the first place, it ignores the fact that long-term and persistent unemployment can be caused by a lack of purchasing power. Economic fluctuations, investigated further in Book 2, may cause widespread distress through low wages *in general* rather than in any particular industry. Second, the argument overlooks the fact that if full employment is established there is a tendency for prices to rise and for levels of wages to follow them upward. The experience of the UK since 1945 has been that of a vicious spiral of prices chasing wages (and other incomes), wages chasing prices, and so on. Thus, no theory of wages can be complete unless it takes account of *macro-economic* analysis dealing with the determination of wages in general. Wage changes are part of the pattern of economic fluctuation; we have gone some way towards an analysis of the problems, and will leave a full discussion to Book 2.

Thus, the marginal productivity theory is merely the best one we have. Nobody would deny that it contains important truths. In particular, it is impossible to distribute in wages or other incomes what has not been produced. Pressures of demand and supply must have a large part to play in determining what shall be paid to a particular group of workers at any given time, but social customs, ignorance, monopoly pressures, and sheer inertia may be equally important. The spectacle of trade unions leapfrogging over one another in their quest for higher wages for members cannot inspire us with too much confidence that incomes from work are arrived at quite as neatly as the theory would have us believe. On the other hand, one may argue that the theory still holds good as long as we remember that many wage bargains are reached by negotiations between groups of monopolists or semi-monopolists. Organized labour confronts organized industry.

So far in this Unit we have examined the labour market in the UK and also some of the theories as to how wages are determined. This examination has resulted in broad conclusions which are of general application. At the other extreme, most workers are more concerned with their own job and its rate of pay, together with such matters as working conditions, holiday pay, safety, notice, and possibly redundancy. Some of these points are set out in the **contract of employment**. The parties to the contract—that is, the employer and employee—are invariably in what has been called an unequal bargaining position. For this reason, the State and the courts have intervened to protect the individual worker from this inequality. Thus, we now have to look beyond the immediate contract to several Acts of Parliament (particularly the **Employment Protection (Consolidation) Act 1978**) and to decisions of the courts, to fully establish the rights and duties of employer and employee.

The contract of employment

The employer–employee relationship is based on a contract. This is usually referred to as a **contract of service**. As such it must be distinguished from a *contract for services*. The reason for this is that the latter does not give rise to the rights and duties which are a feature of the contract of service. A contract with a heating engineer for the installation of central heating in a house would be for services; his workers would be employed by him under a contract of service.

In Unit 5 we examined the general law relating to contracts. The rules distinguished there apply to contracts of employment just as much as to any other form of contract. An offer of employment is made by a prospective employer, usually but not necessarily in writing. Acceptance of the offer, and all its terms, is made by the prospective employee. A contract is made and the parties are bound by it.

In the majority of contracts of employment, most of the important terms are set out in the letter offering employment. To do this gives certainty to the terms of the contract and, hopefully avoids some argument. However, not all offers are made in writing; even if they are, there are often matters of importance to the employee which are not included. As long ago as 1963, an attempt was made by Parliament, by means of the **Contracts of Employment Act**, to ensure that employees were given a written notice containing certain minimum information about their jobs. Although the 1963 Act has been replaced by a similar Act of 1972, which itself has since been twice amended, the basic requirement remains. The notice must be given to employees, 20 years of age and over, within 13 weeks of starting employment, thus excluding employees who only stay for a short while with an employer. Other major categories of employees excluded are civil servants, those in the National Health Service, and those working under sixteen hours a week.

The **written statement** must itself contain some of the details required. Other matters can merely be referred to, perhaps by directing the employee to a notice, or a rule book, or a collective agreement, details of which are accessible. The statement must record the *names* of the employer and employee, the *date* when employment began, and the *job title*. Sometimes, time spent in a previous job will count towards continuity of employment and this must then be shown. Another important area, details of which must be shown, is that concerning *grievances and disciplinary matters*.

The details mentioned so far are relatively simple and straightforward, and in general are personal to the employee. Other details, which need only be referred to in the statement, are of a more complex nature, and for this reason may well be in a lengthy separate document. Perhaps the most important of these other matters is *pay*; rates of pay, pay scales, bonus schemes, overtime pay, and special allowances are often enough to fill a booklet. So long as the information is accessible, that is enough. The same considerations apply to *hours of work* and *holiday entitlement* and pay. Rules regarding absence owing to *sickness*, and payment for such absences, must be detailed or a reference made to another source of information. Similarly, *pension* arrangements (if any) must generally be included by reference. The period of *notice* to be given by both employer and employee must also be mentioned.

Changes in the terms of employment are bound to occur. These must be notified to employees within *one month* of the change becoming effective. Depending on the form of the original term, the changes can be given either by a personal statement or by a general notice, referring to changes in another document—for example a new collective agreement.

The terms of the contract

We have dealt with those terms which, so far as most employments are concerned, must be included in a written statement given to an employee within thirteen weeks of starting employment. If the contract of employment is itself in writing, and contains all the statutory information, that is sufficient; otherwise there must be a special statement. The two should, however, be distinguished. The former is a contract which is binding on both sides; the latter is only evidence of some of the terms of a contract. As such, the statement can be added to, or contradicted, as not being a true record of the terms it purports to record. However, if the facts which it records have been accepted without argument for some time, any contradiction is not likely to be accepted by a court or an industrial tribunal.

In both cases, the terms are usually referred to as **express terms**. Any other terms of the contract which have been expressly agreed, either verbally, or in writing, can be similarly categorized. However, a little thought will show that no matter how long and how deeply the parties consider the contract, they are unlikely to foresee every problem which might arise. We have already seen that it is possible to refer to other documents and the detailed information which they contain. Such terms are said to be **incorporated by reference**; the document where they can be found is only referred to. Examples might include: nationally agreed salary scales, such as those included in the Burnham Report which applies to teachers; a collective agreement negotiated nationally by a trade union; locally negotiated productivity agreements such as those in the mining industry. There is also a third kind of term, that is, the **implied term**. Implied terms do not appear at all in the contract but the law will imply that they are there as necessary. So far as contracts of employment are concerned, these terms will arise mainly from those Acts of Parliament (Statutes), which relate to employment. In addition, many decisions of the courts have resulted in duties being laid at the door of both employers and employees. These duties are rarely expressed in contracts but are there, nevertheless. *Implied terms*, then, are the source of many of the *rights and duties* of employer and employee. We can now briefly examine some of the more important ones.

The major *common law duties* laid upon employees relate to competence, efficiency, and discipline. Employees must be able to perform the work for which they have been engaged and for which they are qualified. The work must be done carefully and competently, and with reasonable speed. It is accepted that orders are necessary and should be obeyed if within the terms of the contract. Employers, for their part, must ensure that fellow employees are competent and do their work in a safe manner. The system of working must be a safe one, and equipment provided must be of good quality and without obvious dangers and defects.

The above is just an outline of the common law duties imposed upon employers and employees. It holds good as a general statement of those duties. However, considerable additions and changes of emphasis have been made to them by Parliament in recent years. The Health and Safety at Work Act 1974 now incorporates most of the decisions of the courts on matters within its scope, thus giving them statutory force. It has also

Unsafe firms ~ call for tougher measures

THE HEALTH and Safety Commission has called for stiffer fines on firms who break the safety regulations. The Commission is also concerned that Crown bodies, including the civil service and area health authorities, are outside the sanctions of health and safety legislation.

The work of inspectors is reinforced by the fines which can be imposed.

placed a direct obligation on employers to concern themselves with safety, backing this up with enforcement procedures. The Act also tries to ensure that all employees will be more safety conscious. Some of the problems regarding defective equipment have been tackled by the Employers' Liability (Defective Equipment) Act 1969. This Act imposes what is termed a strict liability upon an employer, thus making him liable, whether or not he could know of the defect causing an injury to an employee. Finally, the more personal obligations of employer and employee to each other, which are outlined above, have become standards by which dismissals are judged to be fair or unfair.

There are two further major areas of legislation which partly relate to employment, and by which Parliament has broken new ground. The first of these, the **Sex Discrimination Act 1975**, is aimed at ensuring that the sexes are treated equally as regards employment, as well as in other areas. The Act applies, first of all, to advertisements for jobs; with a few exceptions, they must be aimed equally at persons of both sexes. Within employment, there will be an *implied term* that there are *no practices which discriminate* against either sex, for example in training and promotion. So far as pay is concerned, the **Equal Pay Act 1970** attempts to ensure that there is equality between men and women. This is done by *implying an equality term* in every contract of employment with a woman. This, broadly, gives a right to equal pay for 'like work' within the same organization. There is also an opportunity given to enforce this right, through an industrial tribunal, if necessary. The second major area is that of *racial discrimination*. Various **Race Relations Acts** attempt to ensure that discrimination, in the form of 'less favourable treatment' is not practised for racial or ethnic reasons. The Acts apply to employment as well many other possible areas of discrimination. Allegations of racial discrimination can be pursued by a complainant, helped, if necessary, by the Commission for Racial Equality.

No discrimination here!

Termination of the contract of employment

All contracts of employment must inevitably end at some time. Express terms will appear in most contracts regarding length of notice to be given by either side. Retirement arrangements are often spelt out in detail. The death of an employee, or the 'death' of a firm will end a contract. Some contracts will be for a fixed term anyway,

95

such as those of workers on a construction project. In addition, it is possible that a contract of employment may be ended in circumstances which amount to a breach of contract. Dismissal of an employee without notice may well be a breach and result in an award of damages for **wrongful dismissal**. An employee's conduct at work, or his walking out of a job, could both be breaches of contract. In addition, the test of 'fairness' must now be applied to all dismissals, whether or not they are otherwise within the rights of an employer. Finally, the termination of a contract by redundancy, and the rights and duties of employer and employee in such a situation must be considered. A significant feature of all these problems is the impact of legislation upon them. This has greatly increased the rights of employees in some of the above situations, and has added to the duties of employers. We can now deal briefly with each situation in turn.

Notice

Most employees must now be given a minimum amount of notice of termination of their contract of employment. This statutory period of notice ranges from one week (after four weeks' service), to twelve weeks (after twelve years' service). Of course, contracts may expressly provide for longer notice; even if they do not, the courts may judge that the statutory minimum is too short, for example in the case of a long-serving, senior employee. Notice from an employee need only be one week, but, again, this is subject to any express term in the contract specifying a longer period of notice. Payment of wages or salary in lieu of notice can, of course, be made to an employee. Notice once given by an employee cannot be withdrawn without the agreement of the employer.

Dismissal

As was mentioned earlier, all dismissals, whether in breach of contract or not, are now subject to the test: did the employer act fairly and reasonably in dismissing an employee, even though the dismissal was because of incapacity, misconduct, redundancy, or any other substantial reason? Failure to renew a fixed term contract may also constitute dismissal. So the employer is still able to dismiss an employee for good reasons. However, even then he must be able to show, to the satisfaction of an industrial tribunal, that the dismissal was fair and reasonable, to avoid having to pay compensation to the former employee.

Redundancy

One of the reasons for dismissal mentioned in the previous paragraph was redundancy, and it is worth discussing this further. This is because the problem generally affects larger groups of workers than questions of wrongful and unfair dismissal for the other reasons mentioned above. Even if the redundancy situation cannot be avoided, it is still necessary to protect the individual worker. This is done mainly be ensuring that he is compensated, at a minimum statutory rate, for the loss of employment. The **Redundancy Payments Act 1965** laid down a scale of compensation which relates weekly earnings, years of service, and age. This scale can be, and often is, improved upon by negotiation between trade unions and employers.

TAXMAN EASES GRIP ON GOLDEN HANDSHAKES

THE amount redundant employees will now be allowed to keep free of tax has been raised to £10 000. Above this limit redundancy payments are taxed as income.

The increase is intended to act as an inducement to employees to accept redundancy and to take another job, when available, in the same tax year. The concession will also help where employers and employees have agreed that obsolete plants should be closed and replaced by new technology, often with a smaller labour requirement.

Conclusion

The foregoing paragraphs, in the second half of this Unit, have given no more than an outline of the rights and duties of employers and employees. Although the basic principles which we have examined are relatively straightforward, they are just the tip of an extremely complex mass of legislation and case law. Almost every person at work is affected in some way or other. Because employment is so important, it has received a good deal of parliamentary time. As a result, the courts, and more particularly, the industrial tribunals, are hearing large numbers of cases. Each case is of extreme importance to a worker trying to establish a right and claiming compensation. These cases may include unfair dismissals, redundancy, equal pay claims, and hearings to establish contractual terms. Another aspect of each of these claims is that the employing organization could be seriously affected by the outcome. For example, an award in an equal pay dispute could result in the wages of a number of women workers having to be increased. Thus, we can see that legislation must be added to the economic factors which determine wages. However, this is only one aspect of the constraints which surround an organization in its activities. These and related matters will be examined in greater depth in Book 2.

Summary

The labour market is important to an organization in so far as the right workers are available at the right cost. A labour force must have the skills needed by an organization and individuals often seek training and education to meet this need. This is just one aspect of the constant adjustment in the labour market as the needs of employers and workers change. From the viewpoint of an organization, these imbalances may be temporary, and can be accommodated, often with help from government agencies.

Wages and salaries are the price of work and are largely determined by the forces of supply and demand. Some wages are relatively higher than others because of the existence of non-competing groups of workers, Demand for work depends on the value of its marginal product; supply depends not only on the available labour force, but also on its inclination to work and on the real costs of gaining skills. Wages for a particular job, in other words, must cover transfer costs.

These principles help to explain how some workers can gain an economic rent of ability, and why women may receive less pay than men. They are not wholly satisfactory, however, since they do not take economic frictions sufficiently into account and because they ignore the possibility of macro-economic changes in the economy. Also the existence of powerful trade unions and of legislation must be taken into account in any comprehensive theory of wages.

The rights and duties of employer and employee are regulated, partly by the contract of employment, and partly by legislation and case law. Most employees are legally entitled to a statement setting out the most important facts relating to their employment. Depending upon the circumstances, this statement may be held to contain express terms of the contract of employment. Other express terms are agreed between employer and employee. Terms are also incorporated by reference, and may be implied mainly by statute and common law. The most important implied terms are statutory and relate to safety, non-discrimination, and job security. In this way, some of the inequality between employers and employee is redressed.

Assignments

1. Using a local or national newspaper, look for and write a note on the following kinds of advertisement:
   (a) For a job which is normally carried out either by men or women.
   (b) For a job which, in the past, has usually been a man's job, but which is now stated in the advertisement to be open to applicants of either sex.
   (c) As in (b), but for a woman's job.
   (d) For a job which, in your opinion, could only be done by a woman, and where the advertisement does not specify that applications are acceptable from either sex.
   (e) For a job which has a masculine or feminine title, but which, it is stated, is open to applicants of either sex.

   In the case of advertisements which you find under categories (b) and (c), consider why applicants of the other sex have rarely taken up the occupation in the past. Consider also, the implications for an organization in now employing persons of the other sex.

2. Assume that you are a newsagent employing twenty persons. You have just engaged a manager for a small branch shop. Draw up the written statement required by the relevant Act of Parliament. Make up appropriate information which you consider necessary.

3. Mrs W. is a canteen assistant who has recently been ill and now seeks your advice. She has worked for her employer for five years. Apart from a brief maternity absence she has previously had only an occasional day off. However, her current illness has lasted for eight weeks, but she has regularly sent in medical certificates to her employer. The last certificate (at the end of the sixth week) stated that she would be fit to return to work in a week's time. She felt unable to return then and was absent for a further week. Her employer then asked her to say when she would be returning, which she was unable to do. She was then dismissed. With reference to the standards mentioned in this Unit, advise Mrs W. whether you consider she was dismissed fairly (in the legal sense of the word).

Unit 9 Property, interest and profit

In the previous Unit we examined some of the economic and legal implications for an organization in employing *labour*. The other resource in our classification —property—may, as we saw in Unit 6, include land, machinery, raw materials, and semi-finished and finished goods. The separate question of land use is dealt with in the next Unit. We turn now, first to the economic and then to the legal problems connected with the acquisition by an organization of other *capital goods* which are wanted not for their own sake but for their use in the production of consumer goods.

From the economic viewpoint, organizations require money capital in order to acquire capital goods. The means open to them depend on their nature. In Unit 3 we noted the difference between organizations in the private sector, including differences in the ways in which they are able to raise money capital from their own resources, by borrowing, or from shareholders. All this implies the existence of a market whereby lenders and borrowers are brought together. The structure of the money and capital market, including banks, the Stock Exchange, and many other institutions, is dealt with in detail in Book 2. So is the way in which public sector organizations acquire funds. Meanwhile there are broader matters to consider.

Property and saving

The provision of capital goods leads to more efficient production, but this can only be achieved by saving. From an organization's point of view, money must be forthcoming to finance investment because its receipts and payments are not evenly matched. A payment for new machinery may have to be made at once, even though that machinery will be useful only gradually over time. Furthermore, the income of trading organizations depends on sales, and since nothing can be sold before it is produced, the gap between production and income from sales has to be financed.

From the viewpoint of the economy in general, this saving to finance capital investment may or may not involve *sacrifice*. If, for the moment, we assume that all resources are fully employed, then sacrifice is inevitable. Men, raw materials, machinery, and land will have to be switched from the production of consumer goods to that of capital equipment. *Present consumption* must be sacrificed in order to provide a firm base for future expansion. Often, as in the case of the USSR, this can impose severe hardship on a whole generation. A similar problem faces most developing countries today. On the other hand, a situation may exist in which resources are under-employed. In this case, perhaps during the worst stages of a severe depression, there is no real sacrifice to the community in the provision of more capital. No saving has to be done collectively. Indeed, the making of new machinery may give incomes to the unemployed, thus enabling them to demand more consumer goods at a time when capital accumulation is also increasing.

From the standpoint of the individual, the financing of the waiting period between production and sales always involves sacrifice. A man who saves and lends his savings is said to be parting with liquidity. In other words, he is giving up command over his money and denying himself the ability to buy those goods and services which would give him immediate satisfaction. He is also giving up the ability to use his money in some future emergency. It is true, of course, that if his real income increases, he can both spend more and save more. Nevertheless, he will be prepared to use his savings to finance investment only if the total return to him over a period of years is likely to be greater than the amount originally lent. He must be offered a reward for the use of his property, a reward which can take the form of interest, profit or rent.

Interest

The above discussion has assumed that money is lent. In the case of profit or rent, the word 'lent' has been used rather loosely. As far as interest goes, on the other hand, it is a strictly accurate use.

Interest has been defined in many ways. From the viewpoint of the borrower, it is *the payment for the use of money* or a payment for the loan of capital funds. From the lender's angle, it is *the reward for parting with liquidity*. Who, then, are the borrowers and the lenders?

The lenders

1. Persons

Any income which individuals receive for the use of their work or their property may be either used to buy consumer goods or saved. The factors determining any single person's inclination to consume as opposed to save are extremely complex and must vary from person to person. Money 'burns a hole in the pocket' for some people. They naturally prefer consumables to money in nearly all circumstances. Others, more thrifty, 'save for a rainy day'. Having saved, and therefore put apart some of their current income to gain **liquidity**, even these take different views of the future. Some lend—i.e., part with their liquidity—only if they can be sure of recovering liquidity at short notice. Others, for a higher reward, may be content to lose control for a longer period over some or part of their savings. Commonly, when an individual first starts to save, he is very concerned to recover liquidity quickly. As his savings increase, he may be more inclined to 'tie up' his money for longer periods of time in order to secure a higher income. An individual saver, balancing his requirements, is able to recover some of his savings very quickly and some over a longer period of time.

The question of time is most important. The longer the period over which money is lent, the higher the risks involved. Quite apart from the possibility of a borrower defaulting on his obligations, there remains the question of what the money will be worth when it is repaid. During a time of rapidly rising prices, for example, the man who lends money in order to secure an endowment policy may find that at the end of twenty or twenty-five years, the capital sum which he receives has lost a great deal of its purchasing power.

Again, an individual's inclination to consume or to save depends very much upon his income. The very poor man typically consumes most of his income. His standard of living is so low that any extra income is almost certainly devoted to improving it in terms of current consumption. On the other hand, an extremely rich individual is likely to have a very high propensity to save. Having satisfied most of his current requirements, he is much more likely to devote any new income to saving. The supply of loanable funds from individuals, therefore, depends first on how much they are prepared to save, and second on how much they are prepared to lend.

2. Organizations

The second large group supplying loanable funds consists of organizations themselves. Quite commonly, part of the amount due to shareholders and arising from past trading is retained in the business rather than distributed in the form of dividends. Sometimes, indeed, government policy requires dividend restraint in the quest for an incomes policy, and this may lead organizations to retain loanable funds even in excess of their own requirements. Private sector joint stock companies building up excessive stocks of loanable funds which are not being put to effective use may find themselves the object of takeover bids by other companies. Alternatively, they may acquire capital assets which, to the country as a whole, may be less important than those which might have been secured had the loanable funds been freely available in other directions. However, in recent years, intercompany loans have become an important source of loanable funds. The growth of pension funds has meant that they have also become an important source of company finance.

3. Government

The central government and the local authorities taken together are large savers. In the case of central government, any supply of loanable funds comes from the difference between what it obtains by way of taxation and other income and what it disposes of currently to buy goods and services. If the government budgets for a surplus over current expenditure, it is in effect forcing the other two groups to save by withdrawing from them part of their disposable income.

The borrowers

The demand for loanable funds also comes from persons, firms, and the government.

1. Persons

Individuals borrow money for a variety of purposes, just as they save for many reasons. The very poor or the spendthrift may find it impossible to finance even their current consumption. As standards of living have increased, however, the most usual reason for borrowing is to finance the purchase of pieces of capital equipment which are too expensive to be bought in any other way. Among these, the most obvious example is a house, which, together with a car, is likely to be the most expensive item which any average individual will buy during his or her lifetime. Individuals also vary in their decisions about when and how much to borrow. Clearly, these decisions depend on their levels of current income. Building societies, for instance, rarely lend more than two-and-a-half to three times the borrower's annual income. Another important influence on borrowing is the estimated course of prices over the term of the loan. If house prices and incomes are expected to rise in future years, then, given the rate of interest, the would-be-borrower will calculate that he will be paying a smaller and smaller proportion of his income in real terms the further the loan stretches into the future.

2. Organizations

Organizations as a group, are the greatest borrowers. Plant and machinery wears out and must be replaced. Therefore, even to maintain capital intact and to provide for depreciation, funds are required. In addition, to ensure economic growth, fixed capital must be changed and added to; net new investment must take place. Yet again, some borrowing is, as with farmers, of the traditional 'seedtime to harvest' type, in order to provide working stocks of raw materials and semi-finished goods. Among the most massive users of loanable funds are the public corporations, where very heavy capital investment is needed to maintain and increase the provision of energy in the form of coal, gas, or electricity.

3. Government

Central government and local authorities borrow money to provide **social capital.** The provision of roads, hospitals, schools, municipal transport undertakings, and the like cannot be made entirely from current income from taxes and rates. Again, the government occupies a special position as borrower. It has a greater power to borrow overseas, for instance, thereby exerting an influence on the balance of payments. It also has a greater power to 'manage' its borrowing over time, and thereby, influence operations in the money and capital markets. (See Book 2.)

Interest rates

After much preamble, we are now able to turn to the question of what determines the *rate of interest* payable by an organization for the money capital which it borrows; in other words, the cost of acquiring capital goods. Lenders have to be persuaded to sacrifice immediate enjoyment of their property and also their inclination to hold money. Thus, the supply of what are called **loanable funds** depends on the rate of interest being attractive enough and that, in turn, depends on the strength of liquidity preference, the amount of money in the whole economy, the length of time of the loan, levels of income, the degree of inflation, and the risk of the organization defaulting. A well-known organization wishing to borrow for a year at a time when there is no inflation, full employment, and high general prosperity would no doubt pay less than another newly starting and requiring long-term finance during a period of depression and high unemployment. During the latter situation, however, neither organization might wish to borrow. Demand for loanable funds depends on those funds being put to profitable use, so that there is a return to the organization after interest has been paid. So a whole family of interest rates exists at any one time depending, as usual, upon supply and demand.

Profit

The first section of this Unit assumed, rather loosely, that liquid assets were always lent. In stricter terms, lending should only refer to those cases in which the terms of the loan and the time of repayment are clearly defined. In other words, loans, being *subject to contract,* attract interest. If a trading firm issues debentures, it has a legal liability to adhere to the terms of the issue. But, of course, it may decide to issue *shares* rather than debentures. In this case, shareholders become part-owners of the business, instead of creditors. They have again parted with liquidity, but their reward will take the form of profit rather than of interest. As another example, a man may decide to set up business on his own account, using accumulated funds in this way rather than putting them in a deposit account with a building society. If his business flourishes, his profit is an alternative reward to interest foregone. As in so many other cases, the question of real cost has arisen.

The peculiar nature of profit

Profit is best defined as *the reward for bearing uncertainty.* As we noted in Unit 6, payment for the organization and running of a business is best regarded as a salary—as a payment for a rather specialized form of work. We also made the point that risks, as such, are insurable, so that we are left with those business uncertainties which cannot be insured against.

These uncertainties must arise in the ordinary course of events. New inventions may render factory plant obsolete; new demands may enable it to run at full pressure. Competitors may arise or shut up shop. Wars and rumours of wars, more or fewer opportunities for trade abroad, government policies, all these must affect the trading position of a particular firm, and none can be forecast with any accuracy. People will, therefore, be prepared to hazard their money, supplying what is known (rather inaccurately) as **risk capital** only if they can see the chance of a reward greater than that forthcoming in the form of a relatively certain interest or rent.

Profits then are *uncertain* and *not subject to contract.* They remain after all contractual payments in the form of wages, interest, rent, raw material costs, and so on have been met. In the very nature of things, they must also fluctuate. In some years, a sole trader may find that his outgoings exceed his income; a public joint stock company may be unable to pay any **dividend** on its ordinary shares. Unlike other rewards, which are contractual in nature, the rewards for the use of economic resources which take the form of profit may be *negative.*

Profit: the accountant's view

An observant reader may have noted something of a paradox in the previous discussion. On the one hand, it has been said that profit, if any remains as a surplus after all costs have been met, is the difference between total revenue and total costs. On the other, we have argued that profit is a necessary payment to persuade people to part with risk capital. Yet any payment necessary to command the services of a factor of production is a cost. So it appears that, at one and the same time, profit is and is not a cost.

In an accounting sense, profit may be regarded as a surplus over costs of production. There may be some difficulty in computing costs, especially when problems of depreciation of plant and other assets are encountered, but this difficulty is one with which accountants are familiar. One may argue, as an economist, with any given interpretation of depreciation, but there is no theoretical problem involved. *Any surplus over costs, arising from whatever source, is profit in the accounting sense.*

Profit: the economist's view

The economist, more concerned with the nature of profit as a *reward,* looks at things from a different viewpoint. Not satisfied with the notion that the whole of the difference between revenue and costs is profit, he analyses this difference a little further, trying to isolate that part of total 'profit' which is the true reward for bearing business uncertainty.

Let us consider the case of a one-man business. Undoubtedly, a small shopkeeper, noting that his costs in the past year have been £1,000 and his income £3,000, will consider himself to have made £2,000 profit. His rival down the road may have produced only a £1,000 profit. Yet each may be equally efficient and have exactly the same result.

The first man may run his own shop, while the second employs a manager; the former may also own the freehold of his shop, as against his competitor's leasehold property. He may have put his own money into the business, while the second has borrowed, having to pay interest. If all this is true, then part of his so-called 'profit' is really wages, rent, and interest, *paid to himself.* Our example assumes that such payments amount to £1,000 a year. Thus, although his *paid-out* costs are less, total costs including *other costs* paid to himself are exactly the same as those of the other shopkeeper. *Gross profit* is higher, but net profit is not.

We argued above that profit can sometimes be negative. This is possible, even though there is an excess of revenue over costs. We may imagine that our shopkeeper, working as a manager, could earn £2,000 a year. If he works for himself and shows a 'profit' of £1,800, then he is bearing the uncertainty of his business for less than nothing. But the very large mortality rate among small shops and other businesses indicates that rather more people consider themselves to be good businessmen than is actually the case.

So called 'other costs' are likely to arise only in the case of one-man businesses or partnerships. However, in the case of all trading organizations, that payment necessary to attract risk-capital from shareholders is, to the economist, a normal profit. Finally, we should note that profit as a concept can only apply to trading organizations (as opposed to, for example, most local government departments).

Having dealt with economic considerations, we now need to examine some of the legal problems involved in the acquisition of property by organizations.

Contracts for goods and services

In Unit 5 we examined the basic rules of contract; we can now see how these rules are applied in commercial situations. In general, organizations are in fairly equal bargaining positions. Because of this, influence by the State on their freedom to contract has been limited. Where organizations are in an unequal bargaining position, and in consumer affairs, considerable protection is given by statute. Many of the rules which we shall examine are the result of decisions of the courts. They have stood for many years and will be followed as precedents unless overruled by a higher court or by Parliament. Names of cases are given for those wishing to read more deeply.

Invitations to treat

As we have already seen, an offer, once accepted, forms the basis of a contract. For this reason, it is often necessary to distinguish offers from what are termed **invitations to treat.** An organization, when purchasing goods and services, naturally seeks the lowest price if other things are equal. This is often done by means of an **enquiry** to a number of suppliers. Each one will then send a **quotation** for the goods, if they wish to supply them. They may also send a catalogue. The quotation and catalogue are merely an invitation to treat *(Partridge v. Crittenden).* If the quotation is acceptable to the enquirer, **an order** may well be placed. It is the order which constitutes an offer, and as such must be accepted by the supplier. He may not wish to accept it; by the time it is received the goods required may not be available, or prices may have gone up. But once the order is accepted, the supplier is contractually bound to supply the goods on the terms agreed, and the purchaser is bound to accept and pay for them if they are as ordered.

Forms of offer

When a direct order is placed, it is generally a simple matter to distinguish offer and acceptance. However, some further complications may arise. Instead of sending out letters of enquiry, an organization may invite **tenders** for the supply of certain goods or services. This method is frequently used for goods used in large quantities in local government. In this situation, the tender itself is an offer which will be submitted in the form required by the intending purchaser. A comparison of the tenders discloses the most suitable one, which is then accepted.

Even in this form of negotiation, two situations need to be distinguished. If a specific quantity of goods is required, the acceptance forms a contract for the whole quantity, to be delivered in accordance with the terms of the agreement. On the other hand, the requirement may only be for a maximum quantity, orders being placed for specific deliveries during the life of the agreement. In this case, the tender is merely a **standing offer,** each order being a partial acceptance of the offer. As we have seen, an offer can be withdrawn before acceptance, and a standing offer is no exception. The supplier in this instance is free to revoke the unaccepted part of the offer at any time before acceptance *(Great Northern Rail Co. v. Witham).*

Standard terms

Standard terms usually occur in commercial transactions when the seller imposes *fixed terms of contract* upon the buyer. They may also occur the other way round, particularly when the buyer is a large organization and the seller relatively small. The likelihood, in each of these circumstances, is that the standard terms will be largely favourable to the organization imposing them.

Standard terms of contract also frequently arise in everyday situations. These include making a bus or rail journey, parking a car, and taking clothes to be dry-cleaned. The contracts made for these transactions all have one thing in common; the terms are invariably standard ones, and the customer may well have to accept them or take his or her custom elsewhere. This, of course, might be difficult or impossible. No one would deny that standard terms are necessary in most of the situations envisaged. It would be impossible to agree special terms with each bus or rail passenger; queues at car park entrances would quickly grow as each driver negotiated a special contract. Needless to say, prices would fluctuate depending on the number of cars in the car park. So far as a dry-cleaner is concerned, special terms might be necessary for unusual articles or for delicate fabrics, and these are frequently arranged. In each of these cases, and others like them, it is essential that the standard terms are brought to the notice of the person entering into the contract *(Thornton v. Shoe Lane Parking* and *Thomson v. L.M.S. Rail Co.).* An examination of a bus or rail ticket, or a car parking receipt will show how this is done. Equally, this examination will show that it is relatively difficult to discover what the standard terms of such contracts really are, even when they are brought to our notice. Nevertheless, we are generally bound by them, whether or not we have read them.

It was suggested at the beginning of this section, that standard terms may well be favourable to the one who is able to impose them. The circumstances in which this is most likely are when the buyer is an individual, purchasing goods or services for private purposes, and thus, as we shall see later, 'deals as consumer'. Parliament has taken considerable steps to protect consumers on these occasions. How this is done is considered in Unit 15 (on consumer protection). Some protection is also given to business and other organizations when standard terms of business have to be accepted. This is considered later in this Unit when exclusion clauses are discussed.

Acceptance: some problems

We saw, when examining the basic rules of contract, that acceptance of an offer must generally be communicated to the offeror. If the negotiations are carried on face-to-face, there is usually no problem. However, the vast majority of business contracts are made, as a matter or routine, through the post or by telephone. Inevitably, problems have arisen, and the courts have offered solutions; in some instances such a solution has been merely a compromise.

Acceptance by post presents no difficulty if the letter of acceptance is received by the offeror, and it is in the same terms as the offer. A contract obviously exists. It is when the letter is posted but not received by the offeror that problems arise. It would be natural to conclude that no contract is formed in these circumstances. However, the general rule is that a contract comes into existence the moment the letter is posted. This of course assumes that it is correctly addressed. If this were not so, no business could assume that a contract existed until proof was obtained of the arrival of the letter at the offeror's place of business. This is essentially a rule of convenience, based on the assumption that most letters arrive safely at their destination, and that there is no control over a letter once posted. (*Adams v. Lindsell* and *Household etc. Insurance Co. v. Grant*). The same argument may be applied to the use of telegrams. Acceptance by telephone is considered as a face-to-face situation, as is the use of the Telex system (*Entores v. Miles Far East Corp.*).

The offer may sometimes specify the use of a certain method of acceptance. This   107 must be adhered to; for example, if a telephone call is requested, this must be made for the offer to be validly accepted. The use of the telephone, telegram, or Telex by the offeror would generally imply a sense of urgency. In these circumstances, in the absence of a more specific request, or any other regular method of dealing, an equally prompt acceptance should be made.

The rule relating to postal acceptance helps to solve another problem. If an offer is to be revoked, this must be done before acceptance. If the revocation of the offer is not received by the offeree before acceptance is made, a valid contract exists. Thus, where a letter of revocation was posted three days before acceptance by telegram, but received nine days after the telegram was sent, it could not operate to withdraw the offer (*Byrne v. van Tienhoven*).

Mistake which affects the validity of a contract

We saw in Unit 5 that some kinds of mistake do not affect the validity of a contract. In those cases the bargain stands although it may be that one or other of the parties loses by it. There are, however, some kinds of mistake which are so fundamental that the parties to a contract cannot be said to be in agreement. We can examine briefly, the most important of these with reference to business contracts.

If buyer and seller are both *mistaken* as to whether the *subject-matter of the contract exists,* there will be no contract. Thus, if part of a ship's cargo had been burnt and the remainder jettisoned, a contract for the sale of the cargo would be void if buyer and seller did not know of the loss (*Coutourier v. Hastie*).

A buyer and seller may each refer to what they understand to be the same subject-matter. If, in fact, they each mean something different, there will be no agreement and thus no contract. This may occur in negotiations over the telephone, and the parties are relieved of their obligations by this rule.

Finally we can examine the problem which arises when one party makes a mistake which is known to the other. If the mistake is over an important matter, for example price or identity, the contract will be void. If a retailer grants credit to **X**, who deceives him into thinking he is **Y**, the contract will be void if he would not have given credit to **X**. The effect of this is that the retailer can obtain restitution of any goods obtained by the deception. However, as was said in the discussion of the identity cases in Unit 5, the retailer must be able to prove that he intended only to contract with **Y** and with no-one else (*Cundy v. Lindsay*).

Consideration: discounts

Discounts are a feature of business life and may take one of several forms. *Special* discounts may be given to induce particular customers to place orders. *Trade* discounts are given to non-retail customers by wholesalers, merchants, and manufacturers. *Quantity* discounts are frequently offered to persuade customers to place larger orders; these may be cumulative and retrospective so that a discount is paid when total orders in a year reach a certain level. In this instance, consideration for the discount is the fact that the customer returns to the same supplier and continues to place orders. So far as the other discounts are concerned, they are merely part of a quoted price.

108   *Cash* discounts are often offered as an inducement to a customer to make an early

settlement of a debt. The terms of payment form part of the original contractual terms and therefore both sides are bound by them. Early payment is something the customer is not bound to do and is thus consideration for the cash discount. An attempt by a customer to deduct cash discount from a payment made after the due date is thus not supported by consideration, and for this reason has no legal basis.

Exclusion clauses

We have already noted, when considering standard terms, that these are likely to be more favourable to the organization which has drawn them up. If buyer and seller are in an *equal bargaining position,* and particularly if the buyer has alternative sources of supply, it cannot be said that one has imposed burdensome terms upon the other. Similarly, if the two organizations regularly deal with each other on the basis of the standard terms, it would be difficult for one of them to suddenly allege that the usual contract terms are unfair. The question of unfairness invariably relates to what the law calls *exclusion clauses.* By such clauses, an attempt is made to avoid liability for what would otherwise be a contractual obligation. So far as sales to a person who 'deals as consumer' are concerned, a great deal of protection is now given to individuals, largely by statute, and this is considered in Unit 15. Sales to persons who are *not dealing as consumers* are subject to rather less control, partly on the assumption that business and other organizations, when dealing with each other, can look after their own interests.

An exclusion clause in a contract for the sale of a second-hand bus might read 'no

Factory fire - security firm must pay

THE COURT of Appeal has ruled that a security firm could not rely on a clause excluding liability for damage when the damage was deliberately caused by its own patrolman. The firm was not doing what it contracted to do, said the Master of the Rolls; they were doing the complete opposite. The contract was to guard the premises and through a deliberate act of a security guard, the premises were burnt down.

condition or warranty, express or implied, is given as to the age or condition of the vehicle, or its fitness for any purpose'. The bus, when delivered, might be found to be a complete wreck, without engine, having been towed to the customer's premises. If this was what the customer had expected, there is no problem; if the bus was in better condition when inspected before purchase, it then becomes necessary to examine the effect of the exclusion clause. The courts, when considering a similar clause, in similar circumstances, concluded that there must be a performance of the contract on which to hang the exclusion clause. A bus was bought, but the vehicle as delivered could not by any stretch of imagination be called a bus. The seller had therefore not even begun to perform the contract, and for this reason could not rely on the exclusion clause. This is an extreme, although real, example, and although the exclusion clause as quoted is a very wide one, it might be perfectly acceptable in some circumstances. For example, if vehicles were being sold for scrap, such a clause might well be necessary. There are now statutory rules which apply a test of **'reasonableness'** to certain exclusion clauses in consumer transactions and when standard terms are used. (See page 12.)

Many exclusion clauses inserted into contracts for the sale of goods relate to some sections of the **Sale of Goods Act 1893.** The sections of this Act which we need to examine have been amended in recent years, mainly to incorporate some common law decisions. This was done by the **Supply of Goods (Implied Terms) Act 1973.** Each of the sections 12–15 introduces either an implied condition, or an implied warranty, or both, into most contracts for the sale of goods. It is possible for a seller to exclude some of these implied terms in certain circumstances. The extent to which this is now possible has been considerably restricted by the **Unfair Contract Terms Act 1977.** We can examine the effect of this Act on each section of the Sale of Goods Act (Sections 12-15), in turn.

Section 12. This section introduces an implied condition that the seller has the right to sell the goods; also an implied warranty that the goods are free from any charge not disclosed or known to the buyer. An example of such a charge would be the right of a warehouseman to sell goods if his storage charges remain unpaid.

This section cannot be excluded or restricted in any contract for the sale of goods.

Section 13. If goods are *sold by description*, they must *correspond with the description*; this is an implied condition. If the sale is by *sample and description*, then the goods must *correspond with both sample and description*.

A sale by description can take place even when goods are selected by the buyer and the section recognizes this. It may happen when packages are labelled as to contents—e.g., a central heating boiler in a carton. If the boiler was not as described on the carton, there would be a breach of the implied condition. Similar considerations apply when goods are sold on the basis of a description in a catalogue.

This section may be excluded in sales to a person *not* 'dealing as consumer'. That is to say, in normal business sales to other organizations. This rule, in the **Unfair Contract Terms Act 1977,** also applies to Sections 14 and 15, considered below. However, any exclusion is subject to a test of **'reasonableness',** and this term is discussed later in this Unit (page 112).

110   **Section 14.** This section introduces two further implied conditions. These are, that

goods are of *merchantable quality* and are *fit for the purpose* for which they are being bought. However, the general requirements are somewhat restricted by the same section. First, the sale must be in the *course of business,* thus excluding private sales between individuals. Second, *defects may be drawn to the buyer's attention;* in addition, or alternatively, the *buyer may perhaps examine the goods.* In these circumstances, defects pointed out, or which ought to have been seen, are not covered by the first condition. Merchantable quality means that the goods are fit for the purpose for which goods of that kind are commonly bought. Other factors to be considered, in deciding whether goods are of merchantable quality are: any description which is applied to the goods, and the price for which they are sold. Thus if goods are sold at a give-away price in a clearance sale, it is likely that the condition would not be implied, or at any rate would be interpreted loosely.

The second implied condition can now be seen to be similar to the first. However, its operation is limited by what is termed *reliance on the seller's skill or judgement.* This

CHAIN REACTION

An Essex cockle harvester was to blame for supplying seafood unfit to eat, the High Court decided yesterday. Over ninety guests of a Southampton firm of solicitors fell ill after eating a seafood cocktail at a hotel. This resulted in the hotel owners being sued by the solicitors, who were awarded over £15,000 in compensation, plus, costs. The hotel sued its suppliers who, in turn, sued their wholesalers. Last in the line was the harvester, who was sued by the wholesalers. This action resulted in an award being made against the man concerned, who was ordered to pay the agreed compensation figure together with the legal costs of all the organizations involved.

happens when, for example, a local authority consults a tyre manufacturer regarding the most suitable tyres for use on refuse collection vehicles. The reliance need not be so direct as this; buying from a reputable tyre manufacturer or wholesaler would be sufficient. Even though express reliance is not being placed upon the seller, it is nevertheless implied, since the tyres are being bought for use on a vehicle. Thus, he must sell tyres which are fit to be used in the usual ways that tyres of the kind bought are used.

Section 15. This section is concerned with sales, where there is either an express or implied term that the *sale is to be based on a sample.* Where a sample is used merely to illustrate the nature of the goods to be sold, this is insufficient to bring the section into operation. Conditions are implied that the bulk will correspond with the sample in quality, that the buyer will have a reasonable opportunity of comparing the bulk with the sample, and that the bulk will have no defects which would not be apparent from a reasonable examination of the sample. Thus, a traveller may obtain an order from a wholesaler on the basis of sample garments shown to the wholesaler. The wholesaler has the right to examine the consignment within a reasonable time of delivery; the garments delivered must be of the same quality as the sample; if they have any defects, the wholesaler can reject all the consignment if the defects are of such a kind as were not reasonably apparent in the sample. A sample should be carefully examined; however, a microscopic examination is not necessary, unless this is usual, or necessary in that trade.

It is worth repeating that the implied conditions and warranties of Sections 13, 14, and 15 can be excluded where the buyer is not dealing as consumer, and if it is reasonable that they should be excluded. We can now briefly examine some of the tests suggested by the **Unfair Contract Terms Act 1977,** to determine the question of reasonableness.

We have already seen that where a buyer has a wide choice of suppliers, or where buyer and seller regularly deal happily with each other, exclusion clauses in their contracts can be considered as quite fair and reasonable. These are now two of the tests set out by the 1977 Act. In addition, customs of the trade, the question of special orders, or the fact that buyer and seller are equal in bargaining power, are all other factors to be considered.

Finally, we can refer back to the very wide exclusion clauses discussed at the beginning of this section. These can go far beyond those excluding sections of the Sale of Goods Act. So far as exclusion clauses which avoid liability for breach of contract are concerned, *the reasonableness test is applied in two instances.* These are where the parties are *dealing on standard terms,* settled by one of them, or when one party is *'dealing as consumer'* (see page 167). In the case of business contracts, not on standard terms, the common law still applies. Where there is what amounts to non-performance of the contract, it is likely that an exclusion clause would not be upheld, (See press cutting on page 109).

Summary

Capital investment involves saving. This may or may not mean sacrifice for the whole community, but it certainly leads to the parting with liquidity as far as an individual is concerned. It is for this reason that rewards have to be given in order to gain command over property. This reward may take the form of cost—a profit, or rent—but it is in any case a cost payment necessary to persuade a resource to move from one use to another.

Interest, one form of payment for the use of money, varies according to the length of time of the loan and the creditworthiness of the borrower; if these factors are eliminated, then it is determined by the demand for and supply of loanable funds, as well as by government policy.

Profit differs from interest in that it is uncertain and non-contractual. It is the reward for bearing uncertainty. From the economist's viewpoint, normal profit is a cost of production, any greater profit being in the form of economic rent (see page 66).

Organizations, in their acquisition of goods and services, enter into contacts. The problems arising in these business transactions have resulted in intervention by Parliament, and also many decisions of the courts. The basic features of offer and acceptance, reviewed in Unit 5, in practice are more complex. Offers may be preceded by, and must be distinguished from invitations to treat. Tenders and standing offers are both special forms of offer. The offeree may be based on standard terms, and it is important that these are clearly brought to the attention of the offeree.

Acceptance by post is subject to special rules as a matter of business convenience. Mistake regarding the existence of the subject-matter, its identity, or the identity of the other contracting party when this is of importance, may render a contract void. Early payment, and the placing of a specified quantity of orders, are the consideration for cash and cumulative quantity discounts. The Sale of Goods Act 1893 implies several conditions and warranties in sales of goods. Section 12 (title) cannot be excluded. Sections 13–15 may be excluded in business contracts if it is reasonable to do this. Exclusion clauses, avoiding liability for breach of contract, are subject to the reasonableness test when standard terms are imposed by one party, or a person is dealing as consumer. Other exclusion clauses will probably not be upheld if they permit non-performance of a contract.

Assignment

Your aunt leaves you £1,000 in her will. What *could* you do with the money; what *would* you do, and why?

Suppose the amount had been £100,000. What would you now do, and why?

Unit 10   Property and rent

We can continue our examination of the resources used by an organization by looking at land. Land is a major part of the property used, and of course includes buildings on the land when it is acquired, or put up later. Other industrial structures, such as chemical plant, may be erected. Land may be derelict and acquired by a local authority for reclamation, later to be sold or let for industrial and commercial use. A change of use of land, or further development may be necessary for an organization to maintain or extend its activities. The new activities, or even the present ones, may be unaccept-able in the area for a variety of reasons. Finally, the cost of land, in the form of the purchase price or rent (refer back to Unit 6, page 64) is an important part of the costs of the organization and may therefore restrict its activities. We can begin by examining the ways in which land, or the use of land, can be acquired.

Acquisition of land: freehold and leasehold

When land is purchased, whether or not there are buildings on the site, the **freehold** is said to be acquired. The word freehold signifies that the land is held free of any superior interests, and is therefore the equivalent of ownership. The term freehold is still used, nevertheless, since all land is technically owned by the Crown; for this reason, land cannot be said to be owned in the usual sense of the word.

The second method by which organizations may acquire land, or at any rate, the use of land, is by means of a lease. **Leasehold** land is held under the terms of a lease. The lease must be for a fixed period of time or one that can be turned into a fixed period by giving notice. The effect of the lease is to give the lessee the *right to occupy the land for a period of time to the exclusion of all others,* including the lessor. Land in this case can include part of a building. At the end of a lease for a fixed term, or if the appropriate notice is given to the other by landlord or tenant, the landlord has the right to re-occupy the land. Because of the particular problems which this might give to a business, this right is subject to some statutory restrictions.

If the landlord can show that the tenancy has been an unsatisfactory one, he can oppose renewal of the lease. 'Unsatisfactory' might include *failure to maintain the buildings* in accordance with the terms of the lease, or persistently *late payment of rent*. If the landlord can offer suitable *alternative accommodation*, this would be another ground for opposition to renewal. If the court accepts the landlord's opposition, he can regain possession. Otherwise, the court is able to grant a new lease to the tenant on new terms, either agreed between the parties or fixed by the court. Alternatively, the tenant may propose a new lease, after giving notice in a special form. Even if the landlord is willing to grant a new lease, there may be disagreement over rent and other terms. In this event, the court can fix a rent, in accordance with what the premises would fetch on the open market. Any other terms not agreed are also decided by the court.

A lease always contains express terms imposing obligations on both landlord and tenant. If contained in a deed, these are termed **covenants**. The more usual ones concern rent, repairs, alterations, and a provision to allow the landlord reasonable access to carry out any repairs for which he may be responsible. There may also be terms regarding *sub-letting* and *assignment* of the lease to another person. There are, in addition, several conditions implied by common law. These impose obligations on the tenant not to damage or otherwise reduce the value of the property leased; the landlord, for his part, must allow the tenant to use the land, without hindrance, for the purposes agreed.

FREEHOLD NOW AVAILABLE

THE Community Land Act has now been amended to allow local authorities to sell small sites for industry on a freehold basis. Hitherto, only a lease could be granted and this has discouraged small industries who would prefer to own land and gain the advantage of development.

Sites disposed of in this way are limited in size to 0.5 hectares (about one-and-a-quarter acres) and having a value of not more than £25 000.

It is thought that the concession will encourage the development of rural industries thus providing badly needed employment opportunities.

A lease is normally granted by the owner of the **freehold**. However, if a lease does not stipulate against sub-letting, a sub-lease may be granted by a tenant. However, this does not relieve a tenant of his obligations under his lease, known in these circumstances as the head-lease.

Contracts for land: special features

It is necessary to distinguish two aspects of those contracts which are for the sale of an interest in land. The sale of a freehold or leasehold interest normally consists of two major steps. The first is the **contract of sale**; the second, **the delivery of the deed** forming the **conveyance** of the freehold interest, or the **assignment** of the leasehold interest.

The contract of sale, or for a lease, is normally in writing, and as such is enforceable by either party. Failing this, there may be additional *written evidence* of the contract

115

such as letters, cheques and other related documents. Other evidence may be provided by what is called a *sufficient act of part-performance* which relates to the contract. If any of these are present, an enforceable contract of sale will exist.

The deed of conveyance of a freehold interest is drawn up some while after the exchange of contracts by vendor and purchaser. Between exchange and completion the purchaser should satisfy himself, by questions and search, on many questions regarding the property.

A lease for more than three years, particularly for business lettings, is normally in the form of a deed, thus giving the creation of a long lease formality and certainty. Shorter leases often depend on other means of enforcement, such as we considered above. The fact of entering into possession, the payment of rent, and the record of those payments in a rent book, are sufficient acts of part performance. Thus, the contract is enforceable by landlord or tenant, without the formality of a deed.

Restrictive covenants

We have seen that a lease will contain several covenants agreed between landlord and tenant. Some of these may be what are termed *restrictive covenants*. In this case, the covenant will impose a restriction on the landlord, or more usually the tenant. One example would be a restriction on the kind of business allowed on the premises. So far as a lease is concerned, the parties to it naturally accept the terms which they have expressly agreed. With freehold land, different problems will arise in time.

Upon a sale of freehold land, the two parties to the contract may introduce any terms they wish, including restrictive covenants. As the land is sold and resold, perhaps being subdivided for building plots, new restrictive covenants may be agreed, between buyers and sellers. A feature of such covenants is that they must be for the *benefit of certain land*, and at the same time impose *restrictions on the use of related land*. Thus, an organization wishing to expand, may find that the land which it requires is subject to restrictive covenants limiting the use which may be made of the land. If the covenants are registered as a *land charge* at the Central Land Registry, a purchaser is bound by them; they are enforceable by the holder of the land which benefits from the covenant. However, it is possible for restrictive covenants to be removed, mainly by agreement, or by a tribunal if it is satisfied that the covenant no longer serves its purpose. This may happen when a neighbourhood largely changes character, for example as dwelling houses in a town centre are turned into business premises. Restrictive covenants in a long lease may also be discharged in a similar manner.

Easements

So far as business premises are concerned, easements frequently take the form of **rights of way**. These may be through parts of a building, or along private roads. Public rights of way exist because of long use, and of course must be considered by a purchaser of land. However, an easement, such as we are now considering, is created as part of a land transaction, or as a special agreement. For example, the vendor of land sold for building may reserve a right of way for access to his remaining land. In this way, a **dominant** and **servient tenement** come into existence. The vendor's remaining land is dominant, since he can enforce the right of way. Easements can be similarly created on a private industrial estate; access over private roads is granted to tenants of factories.

116

Planning restrictions

We saw in Unit 4 that it is the responsibility of the county to prepare a *structure plan* for the area. Districts are concerned with local planning and development within the overall county plan. In this way, the development of the area is considered as an integrated whole. The plans of any organization must therefore take the structure plan into account, together with the decisions of the district planning authority upon applications submitted. We shall see also, in Unit 11, that there is considerable government influence upon, and encouragement for, industrial and commercial development in certain areas of the country.

We can first look at the planning requirements for a new development needed by an organization. Firm decisions on the purchase of land are hard to make if planning consent has not already been given, or is not likely to be given, for the proposed development. To overcome this problem, it is possible for an application for *outline planning consent* to be made. This can be made by an owner of land, or by another person or organization, after giving notice to the owner. If outline consent is granted,

FREE PLANNING GUIDE

· THE Department of the Environment has recently published a new planning guide for businessmen. It gives advice on how to set about obtaining planning permission for industrial development in England and Wales. It is aimed at small and medium sized firms and copies are available free from local planning authorities. The department has issued the booklet as part of its industrial strategy to encourage firms to expand into new locations.

the purchase, together with detailed planning and development, can go ahead with some certainty. A *detailed planning application* must be submitted to, and be approved by, the planning authority before work actually starts on the site.

Alterations to existing buildings and other structures are permissible without planning permission, so long as the external appearance remains much as before. Internal alterations are allowed so long as they conform to the Building Regulations. Within industrial premises, structures other than buildings, may be erected as

117

replacement or new, provided they are *within certain height limits*. This would cover refinery or chemical plant developments, for example. *Small extensions* may be made to industrial buildings, without planning permission. In some instances, large industrial organizations have obtained *blanket planning consent* for any development within existing sites.

Overlying the physical aspect of planning is the question of *use*. A planning consent will be given on the basis of a particular use, called the *permitted use*. So long as that use continues there is no problem. However, even the smallest business does not stand still, and uses change. To avoid the necessity for repeated applications upon minor changes, uses are grouped within *classes*. So long as the change of use remains wholly within the class, it is permitted without planning consent. Thus, if a shop which sold shoes began also to repair shoes, this use would be within the same class. Similarly, the class covering offices is wide enough to allow an estate agency to act as building society agents.

From this brief review of the effect of planning legislation upon organizations, it will be appreciated that it is a major influence. We can now examine another—that is, the restriction placed on the day-to-day operations of an organization by the need to operate with a minimum of any form of pollution.

Operating restrictions

The restrictions imposed on the operations of all organizations have their roots in both common law and statute. Statutory controls, limiting the emission of noxious smoke, gases, and other substances from commercial and industrial premises have their origin in nineteenth-century legislation. In recent years, public opinion and the recognition of the importance of the quality of life, have led to a considerable increase in the control of pollution of all kinds. Running alongside statutory control has been the recognition of the rights of the individual where he suffers damage as a result of *nuisance* (in the legal sense of the word).

In considering planning applications, a local authority bears in mind the effect of the proposed activities upon the area. Even extensions to present activities may be detrimental because of increased noise, smell, and traffic to and from the site. New proposals may present even greater problems, particularly if they are alien to the general nature of the area. The problem of pollution by smoke is generally solved by the **Clean Air Acts** which control specific emissions of dark smoke from industrial and trade premises. In addition, local authorities have the power to create *smokeless zones*, and although heavy industrial sites are not likely to be included, light industrial and commercial premises may well be. Other controls cover industrial and commercial operations which pollute rivers and streams, the disposal of waste (particularly poisonous waste), and excessive noise and vibration.

The control of the forms of pollution which we have examined is largely the responsibility of local authorities. *Environmental Health Departments* have been given a wide range of powers through the various Acts, and by regulations made by Ministers under those Acts. Naturally, discussion and advice are used as a means of control wherever possible. Failing that, **abatement orders,** which may have the effect of closing down operations either temporarily or permanently, may be served on an offending organization. Fines may be imposed, following prosecution by a local authority. So far as the discharge of industrial effluent is concerned, this is subject to approval by a local authority. The treatment of the effluent and its method of disposal must be agreed with them. If no satisfactory method can be agreed, the authority deals with the waste, and the organization meets the cost.

The above methods of controlling pollution in all its forms are based on prevention and cure. Individuals, hopefully, will be protected in this way, and for most people it is the only way. Parliament has recognized this, and much of the legislation ensures that large numbers of people are not subject to nuisance for which, effectively they have no redress. Nevertheless, individuals and firms have the right to *sue for damages* and to seek an *injunction* to suppress a nuisance. The plaintiff in such an action must show that his *enjoyment of his land has been, or is being, interfered with*, and generally that damage has been suffered. An isolated act cannot constitute a nuisance, and the state of affairs must be unreasonable. Although nuisance is a **tort** (a civil wrong), it may also be a crime if the nuisance is of a particularly public nature such as unreasonable obstruction of a highway. One case involving a petroleum company illustrates the

Pollution experts under fire

FOLLOWING complaints to the county environmental health department, a resident on the south side of the town said he was not satisfied with their reply. Smokeless zones are being introduced, he said, but the council's own incinerator is belching thick black smoke.

A spokesman for the county engineer's department said that there was a fault in the smoke cleaner, but that this had now been put right. We are asking the manufacturers of the equipment to come and inspect it, he said.

problems which may be faced by an organization in carrying on its operations. The company had an oil distribution depot in an area designated for industrial use. The plaintiff occupied a house in an adjoining road which was in a residential area. Acid smuts from two chimneys in the depot damaged drying clothes and the paintwork of the plaintiff's car, which was kept on the road. A particularly nauseating smell came from the depot, which, although it did not affect the plaintiff's health, was more than a reasonable person could be expected to put up with. Noise from the boilers caused windows to vibrate; the plaintiff was prevented from sleeping. Also during the night, tankers arrived at and left the depot; the entrance and exit were near the plaintiff's house.

It was held by the High Court (Queen's Bench Division) that the smell, the noise made by the boilers, and the noise from the tankers while in the depot, all constituted a private nuisance for which the defendants were liable. The defendants were also liable for the damage caused by the escape of acid smuts, which are a harmful substance. This is known as the rule in *Rylands v. Fletcher*. The damage to the car and the noise of the tankers on a public highway constituted a public nuisance, and since the plaintiff had suffered more than other members of the public, he was entitled to damages on that score.

The account of this case has been given in some detail because it illustrates several aspects of the tort of nuisance. Since the case was heard, in 1961, many of the statutory controls reviewed in the early part of this Unit have been introduced. Nevertheless, the case serves as a reminder that, despite other controls, an individual may not receive any recompense for damage and discomfort caused by nuisance unless he brings a personal action.

Summary

Land may be acquired by an organization either by buying the freehold or by taking a lease. Both give exclusive right to land; in the case of leasehold land this is limited by the length of the lease. A lease contains many express terms agreed between the parties, together with several implied by common law. Contracts for land must generally be in writing, or at least evidenced by writing. There may be an act of part-performance accepted instead. Freehold land is conveyed by deed to a purchaser. Longer leases are usually in the form of a deed. A lease may contain restrictive covenants agreed between landlord and tenant. The purchaser of freehold land is also bound by restrictive covenants if they are registered. In some circumstances such covenants can be removed. Easements also bind a purchaser.

New developments, expansion, and major external alterations are all subject to planning consent. This also covers use. Changes of use which are outside the former class are also subject to local authority planning consent.

The operations of any organization are subject to considerable statutory control regarding many forms of pollution and the disposal of waste. Individuals and organizations are also restricted in their activities by the common law, and particularly by the tort of nuisance. Damages and an injunction can thus be obtained by individuals who have suffered unreasonably.

Assignment

A local authority has recently compulsorily acquired a block of houses in the central area of the town. The houses, which are substandard, will be demolished and the site redeveloped. A property company wishes to acquire the site, probably for light industry, and has approached the local authority. There are other firms also interested. The families from the area have been re-housed on an estate 2½ miles from the centre of the town.

Argue for/against the proposed development from the point of view of:

(a) a ratepayer
(b) the property company
(c) a local authority councillor
(d) a re-housed family
(e) an unemployed person.

All aspects of the problem—economic/legal/social/political—should be considered.

Unit 11   The location of industry

Where to produce is a question no less important than how or how much to produce. Production in the wrong place may lead to high costs. In this Unit we are concerned with the location of industry within the limits set by national frontiers, although the implications for international trade are of obvious importance and are the subject of discussion in Book 2.

Historic reasons for industrial localization

British industry in the nineteenth century was built up around the staples of textiles (predominantly cotton and woollen cloth), coal, iron and steel, engineering, and shipbuilding. For each of these industries, there was good reason for **localization**, the grouping together of firms making similar products.

The main forces making for initial localization were *natural resources, power*, and a local *labour force*. Coal, of course, had to be mined where it was found; shipbuilding had to be carried out on the coast; the location of the other industries depended also upon the availability of raw materials and of a skilled labour force. The main raw material of the metal and engineering industries was iron and, later, steel. This was produced from coked coal, iron ore, and limestone, and the relative transport costs of bringing these together determined the location of the industry. Textile production needed not only its raw materials, but also power produced initially from water and, some years later, from steam, the production of which depended on coal. Thus, there was an interdependence betwen these main industries. As a result, the basic industries situated themselves in south Wales, in the Midlands, in north-western and north-eastern England, and in the central lowlands of Scotland.

One further deciding factor was the nearness to important *markets*, so that transport costs could be kept low. A market, in this sense, is a centre of demand for a product. Where population is high, the market for consumer goods is likely to be expanding. Thus, as the nineteenth-century industries drew population towards them, they created their own markets.

Once established, secondary reasons for the location of industry appeared. These are the *external economies* noted in Unit 3. In Manchester, for example, the Cotton Exchange was established, thus centralizing the buying and selling of raw cotton imported from the US or from the Middle East. Communications became of great importance: it is no accident that both canals and railways first came into being in the industrial centres. In time, the labour force became even more specialized. Firms also started to specialize, each supplying the other. In some instances, the later causes of localization remained even after the earlier ones had disappeared. As the good clay around Stoke-on-Trent became worked out, that from Cornwall was imported for the pottery industry. It was easier to do this than to transport capital and skilled labour from the Midlands to south-western England. It is possible, eventually, for an industry to remain located in a particular area long after the original economic reasons for such location have disappeared. Were the cotton industry to be introduced into England today, it would not necessarily be located in Lancashire. Quite apart from any

122

remaining economic advantages, however, the cotton industry remains in Lancashire because of all the investment in factories and machinery which is already there and because that is its traditional home. This is an example of **industrial inertia**.

Even in the nineteenth century, however, there were many industries which remained scattered throughout the country. Retail shops, serving limited markets, existed wherever the population could support them. The provision of staple items of food, such as bread, made necessary countless local bakehouses. Tailors, lawyers, and medical men lived wherever there was a call for their services. Although the right location was important to the staple industries as one way of keeping down costs, it must not be overemphasized in terms of other industries.

Industrial localization today

The twentieth century has seen the decline of the old staple industries and the growth of many new ones, including electronics, oil refining, chemicals (including plastics and artificial fibres), car and aircraft construction, and new types of engineering. Furthermore, the growing use of electricity as a source of power has released industry from its traditional dependence on coal from direct energy. Whereas nineteenth-century industry might have felt the equal but opposite forces of markets, raw materials, and power pulling on it, today the predominant attraction is that of markets. Both population and manufacturing have tended to drift southwards and towards the other conglomerations of already high-density population. Although Northern Ireland, central Scotland and north-eastern England remain manufacturing centres, there is a striking concentration in the Midlands, Lancashire, and Yorkshire, while southern England and southern Wales are also clearly important.

This concentration does not account for the location of firms producing those items made for domestic use which have grown in importance as living standards have risen. A journey along any of the main arterial roads into London will reveal factories making cosmetics, packaged foods, domestic appliances, and all those other consumer goods on which we have come to rely. Within certain broad limits, it matters less today where firms are located. No businessman would willingly go to the sparsely populated and undercapitalized Scottish Highlands, except for a specialized purpose such as oil-rig building in deep-water lochs. On the other hand, there are not always the compelling reasons for 'togetherness' which existed hitherto. As in earlier times, service industries follow population patterns. So, to a large extent, the present industrial pattern is that of the old staples concentrated in their traditional areas with the newer industries much more widely dispersed.

Some examples

1. Oil-refining

The refining of imported crude oil results in its breakdown into scores of different products, each with its own market. The gradual replacement of imported oil by UK deposits will not affect materially the location of refineries, which are all on the coast. Such refining is less costly, since final products then have to be transported once only. Therefore refineries are found in the Thames estuary, in Southampton Water, on the Clyde, on the Tees, and in other estuaries near to markets. An interesting development

123

has been the establishment of refineries at Milford Haven, in the extreme west of Wales. Although this is relatively remote from distribution centres, it has very deep water so that tankers of more than 100000 tons deadweight may berth there. These tankers themselves transport each gallon of crude oil more cheaply than medium-sized ones. Thus, the economies of scale dictate location in this case, while pipeline development minimizes distribution costs.

2. Car manufacture

The main centres are at Dagenham on the outskirts of London, at Luton, in the west Midlands (Birmingham, Coventry, and Wolverhampton), at Halewood in Lancashire, at Linwood near Glasgow, and at Cowley near Oxford. Each of these sites is in or near a large centre of population. The West Midlands is traditionally connected with engineering and led the bicycle boom of the eighteen-eighties, while Halewood and Linwood owe much to government support for their existence. On the other hand, there is much in the argument that Lord Nuffield established Morris Motors in Cowley just because he happened to be in business there already, making bicycles.

3. Paper-making

The main centre is in the Thames estuary, although there are subsidiary centres in central Scotland and near Bristol. In this case, the main reason lies in the fact that wood, the raw material used, has to be imported (the main suppliers are the Scandinavian countries).

4. Distributive trades

There has been a marked movement towards the development of 'hyper-markets', on the edge rather than in the centre of conurbations. These stores cover large areas of selling space under one roof, often allow concessionaires in order to increase the variety of goods sold, and provide ample car-parking facilities. They allow shoppers to avoid mid-town congestion and often undercut other retail outlets, especially in the field of durable consumer goods. Economies of scale allow them to absorb the wholesaling function, although it may be that aftersales service is less good than that provided by more traditional retailers. They reflect the growth of car ownership and general affluence, but it is as yet too early to assess their permanent importance.

5. Government departments

The State has followed a policy of dispersal from London where possible. The Motor Vehicle Licensing Office at Swansea, and the Department of Health and Social Security in Newcastle-upon-Tyne are cases in point. The Location of Offices Bureau has had, until recently, the task of encouraging business out of London but now is encouraging the occupation of unused London office blocks. This graphically illustrates the dilemma which the government faces in deciding on a coherent policy in the face of determined opposition to re-location from trade unions in the public service area.

Problems of regional specialization in industry

Most of the economic and social problems of localization are connected with immobility of resources, particularly manpower, when staple industries decline. In the past, large centres of population have grown up around one or two main industries. Changes in demand and in the techniques of production have meant that the old skills are no longer required. Thus, in cotton production, in coalmining, in shipbuilding, **structural** and **technological unemployment** has developed. Structural unemployment arises when an industry declines and skilled men lose their jobs. The end of steel-making in Ebbw Vale is a case in point. Technological unemployment would have arisen if the same steel-making had continued with new methods. The regions most affected are those in which these industries once flourished. They include Cumberland (now West Cumbria), in the north-west, Northumberland and Durham in the north-east, the central lowlands of Scotland, south Wales, and Northern Ireland. We have already noted the differences in rates of unemployment in these regions compared with others such as the south-east of England. We have seen how population drift out of declining regions largely offsets any population increase from natural factors. Many workers, especially the older ones, are often reluctant to change jobs, particularly if this means leaving the area where they have always lived. Family responsibilities, age, or

SOUTH WALES – 800 NEW JOBS

A GOVERNMENT investment of £12 million on new sites and factories will bring around 800 new jobs to south Wales. The end of steel-making in some areas has brought particular problems. However, guarantees by the government and by the British Steel Corporation have resulted in a future for tin-plate making for the area.

World-wide, the steel industry has massive surplus capacity and the area cannot be shielded.

simply the feeling of belonging to an area can all play a part. But once a region has concentrated heavily on one or two industries, there is often little chance of alternative employment. The effect can be the emergence of what have been known variously as 'depressed', 'development', 'special development', and 'intermediate' areas, in which the level of unemployment is constantly above the national average, whatever the state of economic activity of the country as a whole.

Left to itself, the process of decline is likely to feed upon itself. One effect of unemployment and the relatively lower standard of living is that the social capital of the region falls into decay. Education, health, and transport facilities may become progressively worse as buildings, roads, and the like are inadequately maintained and replaced. Depressed areas are also likely to be scarred by the activities of earlier generations who were not so worried about the adverse effects of their activities on the environment. In 1971, for example, out of 97 000 acres of derelict land in England, 21 000 acres were in the north and only just over 5000 acres in the south-east.

Cost considerations apart, these areas of blight tend to discourage new industries for social reasons. There has been major resistance to the dispersal of central government departments and their attendant civil servants from the south-east to, for example, south Wales and Teesside. The problem, is, therefore, to improve the infrastructure, so that whatever the external diseconomies, at least a particular region is not socially run down.

It should not be thought that growth areas have all the social and economic advantages. A so-called declining region may have a readily available pool of skilled or trainable manpower, and there are unlikely to be the congestions associated with growth areas such as the south-east of England. In that area the external economies discussed earlier may well be partially balanced by the diseconomies of heavy transport costs, higher prices for building land, higher rents, and so on. Additionally, there are likely to be the social costs of commuting and crowds, which all dwellers in the growth areas must suffer. Anyone working in central London and living in dormitory suburbs during a rail strike will bear this out. 1975 population trends showed that just under 17 million people (out of the total population of England and Wales of about 49 million) lived in the south-east of England, a region which accounts for only little over 10 per cent of the land area.

State policy

Since investment initiative on the part of individuals may have its drawbacks, the State has thought it necessary to influence the decisions of organizations on where to locate or expand their production. Government action with regard to problems of localization has been a mixture of the stick and the carrot. On the one hand, there has been an attempt to prevent industry from settling in places which are already overcrowded and booming. On the other, an effort has been made to persuade organizations to go to those areas badly in need of diversification of industry.

Government concern first became acute during the great depression of the early 'thirties. Even though general unemployment was high, the decline of staple industries meant that south Wales, Northern Ireland, central Scotland and north-western and north-eastern England were particularly hard hit. **The Special Areas Act 1934** attempted, though with little success, to persuade new light industries to go to these regions. Since consumer demand was low, firms were reluctant to face the uncertainty involved. In any case, light industry often employs a higher percentage of women so that the hard core of male unemployment remained.

During the Second World War, the problem eased. Afterwards, however, it reappeared in a new form. General unemployment was low, but the development areas still had a persistently high average unemployment rate. This tended to be long term, in the sense that any one man might be unemployed for months or years at a time. The **Distribution of Industry Acts, of 1945, 1950,** and **1958,** gave the government power to buy land and to build factories in Development Areas, to improve their amenities (often first developed in the nineteenth century and subsequently run-down), to give financial assistance to firms moving in and to retrain workers. At the same time, firms were to be prevented from entering certain areas unless they could obtain an industrial development certificate from the Board of Trade.

The Town and Country Planning Act 1947 required local authorities to draw up *structure plans* for the development of their own areas based on a balance between open spaces, residential building, and industry. Such plans were, and are, reviewed by the appropriate Minister at regular intervals. Any development thus has to gain planning consent from either the local authority or, after appeal, the Minister. It must both fall within the plan for a local area and be consistent with overall development in respect of design and siting. In particular, a green belt must be preserved on the outskirts of large cities to prevent the indefinite sprawl of houses and factories.

New towns came into being as a result of the **New Towns Act 1946** and the **Town Development Act 1952.** Existing towns, lying outside green belts, were expanded into self-contained units, balanced between industry and social amenities. Some of the new towns were themselves subdivided into neighbourhoods, each with its own industrial site and residential area.

Unfortunately, these early post-war measures did not solve the problem. There was a continuing and unrelenting pressure on land within travelling distance of London, with the result that land prices and rents continued to rise (Unit 6, page 65). Higher than average unemployment continued in the development areas. In a temporary change of approach, the government repealed the Distribution of Industry Acts and replaced them by the **Local Employment Act of 1960.** This recognized Development Districts, smaller than Development Areas, and in need of special help on the basis of high unemployment. There was another Act in 1963, concentrating help where it was most needed, but by this time policy was undergoing a further shift.

In 1964, England was divided into eight **planning regions:** northern; north-west; Yorkshire and Humberside; east Midlands; west Midlands; East Anglia; south-east; south-west. Wales and Scotland become planning regions in their own right. Each region was provided with an advisory **Economic Planning Council** and a **Planning Board** to co-ordinate the work of government departments in formulating strategic regional plans. The tactics of attracting new industry are the responsibility of **Development Councils,** where constituent members are largely representatives of local authorities.

The 1966 Industrial Development Act superseded the Local Employment Act and returned to the concept of *Development Areas.* Within these, Special Development Areas, with particularly acute problems (e.g. parts of central Scotland, north-east and north-west England), were recognized, in 1967, while *Intermediate Areas* came into being with the **Local Employment Act 1970.** The present situation is roughly that the whole of England north of the Wash, plus Devon, Cornwall, Wales and Scotland, qualify as Intermediate, Development, or Special Development Areas.

Legal considerations

The working of the **Industry Act 1972** shows how the legal framework can encourage, rather than inhibit, the development of organizations. **Regional development grants** are available towards the cost of buildings over £1,000 in all three types of assisted areas at 20 per cent of cost in an Intermediate or Development Area and 22 per cent of cost in a Special Development Area. Grants are also available at the same rates for equipment and plant costing over £100, except in Intermediate Areas. Neither type of grant is restricted to projects creating new employment, but may be used to replace obsolete premises and capital goods. Selective assistance may also be given to organizations in assisted areas to create or safeguard employment. Low interest medium-term loans and interest free grants are available, together with payments of up to 80 per cent of removal costs of incoming firms. The **Industrial Estates Corporations** provide factories, either custom-built or 'advance' (of demand for them) rent-free for two years or on concessionary purchase terms. **Regional employment premiums** supplement wages and grants are paid in respect of employees moving in with the organization. Tax allowances of 100 per cent on the cost of replacement capital in the year of replacement are a further inducement. Finally, through the operation of the **Manpower Services Commission,** payments are made to firms who recruit unemployed school-leavers and, in the mid 'seventies, the rising rate of general unemployment brought forth a temporary employment subsidy in respect of every prospective redundant worker kept in employment.

The regions and the Common Market

The UK is not the only country in the European Economic Community which has regional problems. The starkest is probably in Italy where the *Mezzo giorno* in the south is a highly impoverished and run-down region compared with the heavily populated and developed north. France and Germany also have their difficulties— France with its inefficient agricultural areas, particularly in the west and south-west and in its congested Paris region, and Germany because of its artificial division and the isolation of its capital. The Community thus recognized the need for common action to prevent the possible economic advantages from particular location to individual firms being outweighed by the social costs to the community as a whole.

Up to 1974, the chief means by which the EEC provided regional assistance to member countries was through the European Investment Bank which, in that year lent nearly £300m for projects in economically deprived areas. In 1975, the regional development fund was established and is expected to make assistance worth £550m available in the period 1975–8. Of this, the UK share may be as much as £150m, the aid to be concentrated in Northern Ireland and the Development and Special Development Areas. Organizations cannot apply direct; they must make requests through the government, which will decide priorities. In any case, the aid, though substantial in money terms, is a small fraction of that spent annually by the State on the measures outlined above.

The effectiveness of State policy

Since the 'thirties, the government has adopted many different strategies in attempting to influence the location policies of organizations. It has itself been influenced by the evidence of differing rates of employment, economic activity, migration, and income and output per head between the regions. Yet evidence to date shows that it has been able to do little more than 'hold the line'. Regional differences in unemployment may have been some-what reduced, although the greater problems of structural, frictional, and cyclical unemployment experienced in the 'seventies have tended to obscure the underlying changes. Alterations in the regional migration patterns are also difficult to detect, because the whole country is tending to lose population rather than gain it, as in the past. Differences in average earnings have hardly been reduced; regional shares of production show little change. Perhaps the quality of life has improved in those Development Areas burdened by the legacy of the industrial revolution, but this cannot easily be measured. In any event, problems remain and the economic and political argument will continue about whether it is better to take work to workers or workers to work, and about whether the State, by its intervention, merely impedes the change brought about by natural economic forces. Does the subsidizing of 'lame ducks' prevent the move to industries of high technology, high potential, high capital usage, but employing fewer workers?

Summary

The localization of industry is another factor affecting costs of production. Historically, localization was determined by the forces of power, natural resources, labour, and the market for finished products. Supplementary forces, leading to external economies, were the existence of specialized facilities and the development of communications. Today, however, industry has been largely released from the necessity to locate itself on or near coalfields. While the nearness or otherwise of the market remains a force, there is no longer always the same compulsion for firms to settle in a particular area near their competitors.

Given changing economic conditions, heavy localization may lead to unemployment if the labour force is immobile. State policy has therefore been both to introduce new industries into the Development Areas (where the old staple industries have decayed) and to disperse industry from the large towns where congestion becomes yearly more apparent. This policy in its various forms has arrested, but not reversed the trends. It may, in future, be reinforced by joint action undertaken by EEC countries.

Assignment

A large food manufacturer is seeking a location for a distribution depot in your area.
Either:
As an employee in the industrial development department of your local authority, write a report to the manufacturer. This should contain sufficient information on which to base a decision to send a team to visit the location(s) reported upon by you.
Or:
As an employee of the manufacturer, sent to seek a location, write a report on your

129

recommendations. This should contain sufficient information on which to base a decision to send a team to visit the location(s) reported upon by you.

UNIT 12 The nature of supply

It is now time to bring together all the findings of Part 2 of this book. All the organizations with which we are concerned exist to supply either goods or services. This is true, whether they lie in the private or in the public sector, and whether what is supplied is wanted by individuals or by other organizations. They have to decide what, how, where, when, and for whom, to produce, and these decisions are influenced by economic, legal, social, and political considerations. In practice, the considerations are interrelated and cannot easily be disentangled. However, it is possible to view them in isolation by using the time-honoured phrase 'all other things being equal'.

Economic considerations

In purely economic terms, the amount of goods and services supplied depends solely on the cost of producing them relative to the price received for selling them. In earlier Units we explored the cost problems involved in the use of both human and non-human resources. Generally speaking, the more plentiful and versatile a resource is, the less will be its cost, both in real and in money terms. However, the cost of a product also depends on how many of it can be made from given resources—in other words, on how much output results from a given input. This in turn depends on the **proportions** of given resources used together in the productive process.

The short-run supply curve

Let us first return to the situation in which, following greater demand for a product, firms in an industry are unable to increase their scale of operations. Greater output may then only be obtained by more intensive use of existing capital. Eventually, through the operation of diminishing returns, marginal and average costs of production rise. Firms may, therefore, only be persuaded to produce more if their incomes rise in line with increased costs. In other words, more is usually produced at higher prices and less at lower prices. Under such circumstances, the supply curve for the whole industry is likely to resemble that of Fig. 12.1. This shows prices on the vertical axis and outputs on the horizontal one. Our conclusion is that such a curve will usually slope upwards. When the price rises, supply is said to *extend:* when it falls, supply *contracts.* The use of precise terminology is important, as we shall see in a moment.

Meanwhile, we must distinguish between a supply curve for a particular firm in an industry and for the industry as a whole. Any supply curve is based on a *supply schedule,* which indicates how much will be supplied at a given time at each of a series of prices. One firm producing a given commodity might have a supply schedule as follows:

Price (£)	Quantity of commodity supplied
5	250
4	200
3	150
2	100
1	50

Another firm, producing the same commodity under different cost conditions, might have a supply schedule as follows:

Price (£)	Quantity of commodity supplied
5	1000
4	900
3	800
2	700
1	600

Each of these schedules would produce a different supply curve. If they were added together, on the assumption that there were no other firms in the industry, then the industry's supply curve would result from the combined schedules.

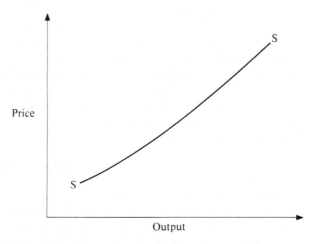

Fig. 12.1 The short-run supply curve

Elasticity of supply

In the short run, **conditions of supply** remain unchanged. There is no possibility of economies of scale, new inventions cannot be applied, and greater output can only come from more intensive use of existing fixed capital assets. Following an increased demand and a rise in price, the *amount* of extra output from the whole industry (including existing firms and any new ones which may start up), depends on the situation in which it finds itself. If fixed resources have been under-used in the past, then a situation of *increasing returns* exists. In this case, a small rise in price is likely to lead to a very great extension in supply. Similarly, if the proportion of variable resources to the fixed resource is very high, or if the resources are not specific, i.e, are reasonably good substitutes for one another, the same result is likely. In all these cases supply is elastic.

At one extreme, the price might not have to rise at all for more to be produced. Once a greater demand was forthcoming, it could be met, in such circumstances, without any rise in marginal costs. The supply curve would then appear as in Fig. 12.2. Supply is completely elastic.

132

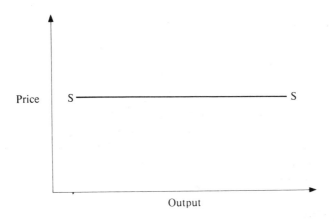

Fig. 12.2

At the other extreme, we may imagine a situation in which greater quantities cannot be produced, however high the price may rise. On any one day, for example, it might well be impossible to satisfy a greater demand for apples in a street market. The supply being wholly fixed, the supply curve would resemble that of Fig. 12.3 Supply is completely inelastic.

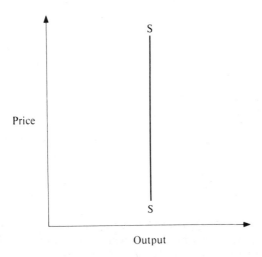

Fig. 12.3

Usually, short-term supply curves fall between these two extremes. The notion which we have been discussing, **elasticity of supply,** may be defined as the *responsiveness of supply to change in price*. A useful way of measuring such elasticity is as follows:

$$\frac{\text{Percentage change in supply following a change in price}}{\text{Percentage change in price}}$$

If, for example, a 5 per cent increase in price calls forth a 10 per cent extension in supply, then elasticity of supply is:

$$\frac{10}{5} \quad \text{equals 2}$$

In such circumstances, supply is said to be elastic, because a relatively small change in price has caused supply to 'stretch out' by a relatively large amount. On the other hand, if a 5 per cent rise in price engenders a 5 per cent extension in supply, elasticity of supply is one or unity. Finally, supply is inelastic if the percentage change in supply is less than the percentage change in price.

Supply in the long run

Given enough time, further developments in the supply position are possible, and these may have nothing to do with changes in price. At any time, inventions or innovations may be helping to lower costs in particular firms and industries. At the same time, firms can approach more nearly their optimum size, even if they can never attain it. Changes in costs of raw materials or in wages, changes in taxes, even changes in the weather may affect supply. In these circumstances, we say that the conditions of supply have changed. Firms, because of the changed nature of their costs, are willing to supply either more or less *at any one price*. If they will supply more, then supply has *increased:* if less, then it has *decreased*.

We must be very clear in our minds as to the distinctions between extensions, contractions, increases, and decreases in supply. If supply extends or contracts, then:

1. This is an *effect* of a change in price.
2. Conditions of supply have remained unchanged.

If supply increases or decreases, then:

1. This may *cause* prices to change.
2. Conditions of supply have altered.

Extensions or contractions of supply are shown by a movement *along* any given supply curve. If conditions of supply alter, however, and firms are willing to supply more or less at any given price, then a new supply curve is necessary. Figure 12.4, for example, indicates an increased supply. At each price within the range shown, firms are willing to supply more, O_1, as indicated by the curve S_1, than they were previously (curve S; output O). This supply curve has moved bodily to the right. Similarly, if long-term costs rise and supply decreases, the supply curve for the whole industry moves to the left.

The long-run supply curve

It has been commonly said that the long-run supply curve is more elastic than that relating to the short run. Given enough time, finer adjustments in supply may be

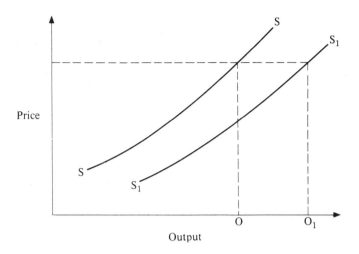

Fig. 12.4

possible. Economies of scale may come into play and outweigh the tendency towards diminishing returns and increased marginal costs.

Such a line of reasoning is based on a fallacy. While it is quite true that greater demand can lead to prices rising immediately only to fall back later, there can really be no such concept as that of a long-run supply curve. Any supply curve is an instantaneous photograph of supply in relation to prices *here* and *now,* before conditions of supply alter. Given enough time, supply which extended following a price rise may also increase, but a single curve cannot show the two effects simultaneously.

An example may serve to make this clearer. Let us suppose that, for some reason, more washing machines are demanded and that, following pressure on the resources of supplying firms, prices rise and output extends. If this state of affairs is expected to continue, the firms will enlarge their capacity to produce and may thus lower their costs. An *extension* of supply has been followed by an *increase* in supply.

Legal, social and political considerations

Economic influences, although important, are not the only ones which affect the supply decisions of organizations, as some examples will make clear. The British Steel Corporation, motivated solely by cost considerations, would no doubt have reduced its labour force by perhaps as much as 40 000 in 1977. It was restrained from doing so then by a mixture of government concern and trade union opposition. Steel-making is concentrated in areas, many of which have an unemployment rate higher than the national average. As we noted in Unit 11, the State's regional policy is aimed at reducing this disparity—hence the concern. Unit 8 considered some of the legal implications in dismissal on the grounds of redundancy. It is interesting to note that where unions and the British Steel Corporation have agreed on plant closure, redundancy payments, though amounting in some cases to £10,000 and over, have been a cheaper option than the losses incurred by keeping the plant operative. So legal, social, and economic interests have, to some extent, coincided.

In 1978 British Leyland, supported by the National Enterprise Board, was another

135

example of how purely economic supply considerations may be over-ridden. Left to itself, British Leyland might well have decided that in some of its divisions it was no longer covering the variable costs. The logic would have been to close these divisions in order to concentrate on the still viable lorry and specialist car production. Economists would have pointed to the diseconomies of large-scale production. However, the government was not prepared to see such a major employer and exporter go into drastic decline. Many hundred million pounds of public money were used in a rescue operation, the success of which is still in doubt.

Yet another case of public concern arose out of the proposition of the Atomic Energy Commission to extend its Cumbria plant at Windscale in order to reprocess nuclear waste. Cost considerations indicated that the supply of this facility would be profitable. Other countries would welcome it; foreign earnings would result. On the other hand, local residents, environmentalists, and people afraid of the spread of nuclear bomb know-how, objected vigorously. A government enquiry was needed to weigh the evidence; its decision in favour of the scheme received less than unanimous support.

Local and central authorities have their own problems of costs and supply. As we shall see in Part III, supply decisions are based, not only on economic, legal, social, and political considerations, but also on the likely demand by consumers for what is being supplied. This demand is expressed in terms of a willingness to pay. Such willingness is relatively easy to measure when single customers buy, or do not buy, coffee, or cars or candles. It is much more difficult to determine when the decisions are collective. What, for example, should be the criteria by which decisions are taken to supply defence, education, or welfare services? These questions are examined in detail in Book 2.

Summary

This Unit brings together all the conclusions of Part 2. These are, that both economic and non-economic forces influence the production decisions of organizations. Economic analysis alone indicates that there are both short-run and long-run factors affecting costs of production. The short-run situation is one where capital resources are likely to be fixed and where more intensive production is accompanied by diminishing returns and rising costs. The supply curve for a whole industry is, therefore, likely to slope upwards, showing that more will be produced only if prices rise. In the long run, however, economies of scale or a more effective location may lead to greater production accompanied by lower costs. These changing conditions of supply are represented diagrammatically by a new supply curve for the industry.

Higher prices usually mean that supply extends; lower prices cause it to contract. How great this movement is depends on elasticity of supply. Economies of scale, on the other hand, may allow supply to increase even without the stimulus of a price rise. Diseconomies of scale will usually mean higher average costs and a decreased supply. It is important to distinguish cause and effect. Thus, the *extension* or *contraction* of supply is the effect of a price change, while the *increase* or decrease of supply is the effect of changing supply conditions through economies or diseconomies of scale.

The above analysis, assumes that organizations operate in a society dominated solely by economic forces. In fact, other influences may be equally important in the determination of supply. The State—itself an organization—controls the policies of organizations in the public sector and, through the legal system, restricts the freedom of action of others in the interests of society in general. Trade unions influence the supply of workers; the monetary authorities influence the supply of capital. Foreign countries may influence, for political reasons, the supply of raw materials. In any case, supply decisions are not taken in a vacuum. Possible costs are balanced against possible revenue and so it is the question of markets and demand to which we now turn.

Assignment

Your sales manager has recently launched an advertising campaign for Product X which has been very successful. Stocks of the product had been increased to meet demand but they now prove to be too low. Orders have been flowing in, but the production manager is unable to promise much increase in volume of Product X without considerable disruption to normal production schedules.

Upon preliminary investigation you ascertain the following facts:

1. Excess orders received, over stock levels, amount to 10 000 units.
2. Production of Product X can be increased to 1000 units per week without seriously affecting other production lines, by some overtime working.
3. If some work on other products is displaced, 2500 units per week of Product X can be made.
4. Orders are in hand for all products.
5. An outside manufacturer is able to supply 500 units of Product X per week, at a price which will allow only half the normal profit margin.
6. The sales department reports that customers are making 'threatening noises' when informed that there may be 'several weeks' delay to their orders. Some orders have already been cancelled.

You have been asked to report to the general manager upon your investigation and to advise, with reasons, a course of action. Your report should also indicate why you advocate rejection of some plans. Also mention any lessons to be learned from the situation.

Part Three   The organization and its markets

A look backwards and forwards

People, we must now remind ourselves, are consumers as well as producers. Behind us lies a comprehensive discussion of resources, costs and production. Goods and services are only produced, however, if somebody wants them and can be brought into contact with the producer. In Part 3, we shall be looking at the ways in which consumers and producers are brought together, the responsibilities which each has towards the other, and the forces influencing people's buying habits. We shall also be looking at the special situations in which goods or, more often, services, are demanded collectively rather than by individuals.

UNIT 13　The nature of markets

Markets exist wherever something is exchanged. The 'something' may be a sack of potatoes, a washing machine, or a house. In all these cases there is a direct relationship between what is being bought and the payment for it. But the 'something' may be the collection of household rubbish, a new denture, state primary education, hospitalization, or an atomic bomb. All these items are collectively financed to a greater or lesser extent. A customer buying cheese becomes a client when in need of welfare services; commercial demand is not the same as social need. Since it is important to keep this distinction, we deal first with commercial markets, before turning our attention to collectively provided goods and services.

What is a commercial market?

To most people the word 'market' conjures up a picture of stalls grouped together, probably on one day each week, in a town or district. Indeed, in mediaeval times, the right to hold such a market was a town's prized possession. Into the market town came people from outlying districts, buying and selling their wares in some convenient spot. Fairs, much larger, attracted dealers from much farther afield and could usually be held only after the grant of a charter to the town. Market towns still exist, as do the historic markets in parts of London, such as Petticoat Lane, Leather Lane, and the Portobello market.

A little thought shows that the area served by a market depends upon the efficiency of communications. In this age of teleprinters, cables, and telephones it is possible to make contact with someone at the other side of the world swiftly and easily. Some markets may thus become worldwide. In the absence of artificial barriers, such as government restrictions, American shares could be bought and sold by an Englishman as easily and efficiently as by a citizen of the USA. Shares, of course, do not physically perish. It is much less likely that fresh vegetables could command more than a local market, although frozen fish may quite well be processed in Hammerfest, a Norwegian town well north of the Arctic Circle, and sold in your local shop. A market, then, in one sense, must be taken to mean *any mechanism by which buyers and sellers are brought together*. It is not necessarily a place.

In another sense, the market can be taken to mean **demand,** as in the expression 'the market for T.V. games'. In Unit 14 we explain this concept in detail. Meanwhile we can touch on the way prices are determined through the market mechanism.

Perfect and imperfect markets

A **perfect market** is one in which, at any one time, there can be only one price for identical goods. If we go back to our street market for a moment, it is possible to imagine many stallholders each selling apples of a given type and quality. Usually, each is selling apples at the same price. Any stallholder selling at less than the ruling price would be able to raise his price without necessarily losing custom. Anyone charging a higher price would have no sales. This analysis rests on the following assumptions:

1. There are many buyers and sellers, all with perfect knowledge of market conditions.
2. Both the buyers and the sellers compete among themselves.
3. There is free entry into the market of both buyers and sellers.
4. Goods are homogeneous (i.e., identical).
5. Buyers are willing to 'shop around', and sellers are willing to find out the ruling price and establish it themselves.

In practice, such a degree of perfection is rare. Sellers are not usually in such close proximity. Where they are separated geographically, they may be able to exercise some advantage—the housewife, for example, may be willing to pay a little more in the local shop rather than travel to the supermarket. Again, manufacturers are usually able to establish some goodwill for their product, which thus becomes differentiated from similar ones. On the other hand, where buyers and sellers are specialists, as on the Stock Exchange or in the foreign exchange market, there is a close approximation to market perfection.

On the whole, though, most markets are **imperfect.** One or more of the essential conditions being lacking, two prices are possible for a similar commodity. Anyone who has tried to sell a secondhand car by means of an advertisement in the local press knows that this is so.

Market functions and types of market

It is sometimes said that there is a 'chain of production'. Much of our discussion in Part 2 of this book centred around the problems of manufacturing organizations, the tacit assumption being that they sold their products direct to the consumer. This may sometimes be the case, but usually the product passes at least to a retailer, and possibly to a wholesaler first. Furthermore, the organization has to buy raw materials, machinery, and other capital goods, as well as hiring workers and managers. Thus, the marketing process is concerned with the bringing together of economic goods and services to a position where they may usefully be deployed and then distributing them or their derivatives until they reach the final consumer. During this process, those involved in marketing may perform some or all of the following functions:

1. *Financing*

The process of manufacture and/or distribution takes a greater or lesser time before the commodity or service reaches the final user. Before a jar of marmalade is bought in the shop, for example, costs have been incurred in the purchase of raw materials, in manufacture, handling, and distribution. It is thus necessary to have a market through which the producers can obtain credit ahead of sales. Institutions providing credit are said to be in the *money* and *capital* markets. These were outlined in Unit 9 and a full discussion of them must be postponed to Book 2. It is enough to repeat here that specialized institutions exist—including banks, issuing houses, and finance companies—whose function it is to bring together lenders and borrowers and thus provide credit.

2. *Concentration, the breaking of bulk, and storage*

These functions are typical of the **wholesale market.** It has often been asked whether a wholesaler performs any useful function at all. Is not the wholesale chemist, for example, buying from the manufacturer and passing on to the retail chemist, merely a parasite battening on both the producer and consumer? After all, he does not work for nothing. Are not final prices higher because of his activity? In some cases, there may be some truth in this accusation, but in the main the wholesaler's activities tend to be beneficial rather than harmful.

Production is the creation of form, time, or place utility. It is the task of the wholesaler to provide the last two services rather than the first. He becomes a specialist, knowing his market, buying in bulk, and distributing to retailers. In doing this, a wholesaler relieves the manufacturer of a detailed selling job, leaving him free to carry out his primary functions. By receiving large consignments, i.e., *concentrating them,* breaking them down ('breaking bulk') and reassembling other large, but mixed, packages, he saves transport costs. Often the wholesaler can provide specialist services: his sales staff, for example, often know what types of goods are in growing demand. Finally, he has the important function of *holding stocks* and making them available when and where they are required. While it is true that he is paid for his services, the net result may well be that goods are cheaper rather than dearer to the final consumer.

The amount which the wholesaler asks for his services depends to some extent upon the risks which he undertakes. Where demand is small or is likely to fluctuate wildly, there is a possibility that he will be left with unsaleable goods. In such cases, the difference between his buying and selling price is often higher than in trades where demand is constant and can be forecast fairly safely.

This defence of the wholesaler must not be carried too far. *Direct sales* of washing machines and refrigerators met with startling success in this country for a while. The manufacturer, by using much press advertisement and a large staff of salesmen, managed to cut out both wholesaler and retailer and, in so doing to reduce retail prices. There are, no doubt, other fields in which traditional methods need reassessment. Similarly, it is possible for wholesalers to work themselves into monopoly positions, extracting excessive amounts for their services. Nevertheless, if the wholesaler can be bypassed, manufacturing firms will usually do this in the end. Where wholesalers exist, it must normally be assumed that they perform productive functions.

3. *Advertisement and sales promotion*

We have just referred to advertisements and sales as marketing functions. Advertising may be undertaken on behalf of the whole industry, for example, 'Drinka pinta milk a day', in which case the aim is to increase the total sale of the product, or it may be undertaken on behalf of a particular firm which hopes to increase its share of the market at the expense of competitors. It may tell the public of a new product or merely publicize an existing one.

A distinction is often made between advertising which *informs* and advertising which *persuades.* Much controversy surrounds this distinction. It could be argued that, since the total market (i.e., demand) for Sunday newspapers is virtually fixed, competitive advertising by particular newspapers on television is merely wasteful.

141

Indeed, this is one of the 'wastes of competition' normally referred to in arguments about the benefits and disadvantages of nationalization—although it is instructive to note that nationalized gas, coal, and electricity also advertise competitively. Furthermore, it is not always easy to assess what is a new product and what is an existing one merely revamped. Others would argue that even the advertising of new products, particularly if they are durable consumer goods, merely raises consumers' expectations beyond the possibility of these being achieved. Nevertheless, goods such as man-made fibres would not have been in common use but for informative advertising concerning their properties. The difficulty is that much advertisement is a mixture of both the informative and the persuasive, and it is hard to disentangle one from the other.

Closely associated with advertisement is *salesmanship*. This, again, is both informative and persuasive, but is normally directed towards an individual rather than towards potential consumers at large. It may range all the way from the 'toe in the door' hard sell, through the distributive and informative activities of commercial travellers, to the soft sell of the pamphlet through the letter box. The salesman has a bad image. Often this is unjustified if he is legitimately promoting the product of his firm. However, aggressive selling, particularly when it is connected with the offer of credit, needs to be controlled, in the public interest. In Unit 15 we see how this is done.

Advertising and salesmanship are normally functions performed in the **retail market**—that is, the market for finished products. However, they may just as well be associated with the market for *capital goods*. By way of illustration, one need only be reminded of the hard bargaining which surrounded the sale of Concorde. One particular type of market connected both with capital goods and with costly durable consumer goods is the *trade fair*. This can range from the local agricultural show, through centralized exhibitions of, for example, catering equipment, to the Motor Show and Boat Show. External economies are achieved in these collective exhibitions of similar goods produced by a variety of manufacturers. Often they are international, thus having the additional advantage of promoting world information and world trade.

On the other hand these functions are not much in evidence in the *commodity markets*. These deal in raw materials and primary foodstuffs, and, far from differentiating between products by brand names, are much more concerned with sorting and grading into homogeneous lots. Among many examples to be found in London are the Wool Exchange, Corn Exchange, and the fish and meat markets at Billingsgate and Smithfield respectively. Another important market, the **Baltic Mercantile and Shipping Exchange,** deals with the buying and selling of shipping and air space, in addition to dealings in grain and other commodities.

4. *Transport*

Consideration of the Baltic Exchange leads us to yet another important market function, the provision of **transport facilities.** There is no point in producing goods unless they may be conveyed to buyers. Furthermore, since transport costs are an important element in a firm's total costs, relative cheapness as well as convenience enters into the calculation.

142   We do not need to be transport experts to know that the main forms of transport

available are *rail, roads, shipping, and air.* Canals and inland waterways, once so important, are now in sad decline. In 1971, they carried only 5 million tons of goods compared with the 1700 million tons carried by road, and 196 million tons carried by rail. However, it is not always recognized that *pipelines* are an important form of transport, and in 1971 these were responsible for the movement of 54 million tons of goods (mainly liquids and gases) compared with the 46 million tons moved by coasters. Aircraft on domestic routes are as yet even less important for the carriage of goods, and in 1971 accounted for less than 65 000 tons.

Clearly the main transport alternatives are road and rail. *Railways* are a form of public transport in the sense that they can be used by anyone and are also controlled by a public corporation, i.e., are nationalized. *The roads,* on the other hand, are publicly provided by a mixture of central and local government finance, but are used by both private transport (motor cars and other privately owned vehicles) as well as by public transport in the form of taxis and buses. Lorries may be either publicly owned public transport, through the National Freight Corporation, privately owned public transport or, simply, private transport. An organization wishing to transport its goods must, therefore, choose between the different physical forms of transport and between different providers of transport, including possibly itself.

To a large extent, such decisions are coloured by the nature of the goods to be transported. It is quite feasible for diamonds to be transported from Amsterdam to London by air because, although extremely valuable, they have relatively little weight or bulk. Tomatoes are flown from the Channel Islands for a different reason, that of speed in delivering a perishable commodity to the final consumer ahead of more local producers. More bulky, less valuable, or heavier European products, on the other hand, would almost certainly come by sea. If they were of a convenient shape, expensive to handle, and carried a high risk of damage, it is likely that they would be packed on to a large lorry which itself would then be transported by sea. Electrical and electronic goods manufactured in Eindhoven, Holland, could well come to Britain by this means. The increasing use of wooden pallets and of containers has reduced handling costs. These may be transported by rail, by road, and, increasingly, by air.

This increasing use of containers highlights the relative advantages and disadvantages of road and rail. The latter can carry large quantities of goods with *regularity* and *relative speed.* It is also an efficient means of transporting passengers. For bulky, weighty commodities, such as coal and coke, it remains unrivalled; for the speedy distribution of newspapers and mail it is essential. However, the rail system operates only between fixed points and must be supplemented by other forms of transport in the movement of goods to final consumers. Conversely, it is technically impracticable to transport loads weighing more than 30 tons by road, even by the use of so-called 'juggernauts'. On the other hand, roads offer a much more *flexible final delivery system.* If a firm decides to use rail transport, then it must deal with a single operator, the nationalized industry. Road transport requires a further set of decisions. It is possible to use the publicly owned National Freight Corporation, or a privately owned general haulage company, or to operate the firm's own transport fleet. The latter course is usually preferable when regular movements of large quantities of goods are involved. Oil companies usually run their own tankers and bakers their own delivery vans, although large general haulage companies can be specialized enough to undertake not only the distribution of oil, but also the carriage of long and difficult loads such as concrete beams, crane jibs, and structural steelwork. Less specialized general freight carriers become important where the main consideration is fairly rapid distribution between points not covered by the railway network and when it is uneconomic for an organization to maintain its own transport fleet.

Clearly, much competition exists between the publicly owned rail system and the largely privately owned road system. Recently, roads have been gaining traffic at the expense of the railways. In 1961, goods were carried to the extent of 63.9 thousand million ton miles (i.e., weight times distance carried). Using the same statistics, 32.3 went by road and 17.6 by rail, the remainder using other forms of transport. In 1971, the figures were as follows: total 82.1 — road 52.0, rail 14.9.

Government controls are necessary because of the importance of transport to the economy. In 1970, one-eighth of all capital investment was in the field of transport and communication. This was undertaken by the **Railways Board,** the **Department of the Environment** (which pays for the whole cost of motorways and trunk roads), *local authorities* (which together with *central government* pay for other roads), the **National Freight Corporation** and the **National Bus Company,** the **private road hauliers,** and **firms** operating their own fleets, the **port authorities,** and the **British Waterways Board.** Such investment decisions often lead to much public discussion. The recently completed London Underground Victoria line was known not to be economically viable before it was started. It was the subject of a cost-benefit analysis and was constructed on the basis that social benefits outweighed economic considerations. Similar discussions have surrounded the proposed and abandoned construction of the third London airport and the Channel Tunnel. It is partly because investment decisions are undertaken by so many bodies that conclusions are so difficult to reach. This is particularly so because we ourselves as private individuals are concerned in these decisions when we buy private cars. Our studies of transport must be concerned not only with the economic advantages to organizations, but also with the *social costs* in terms of congestion, pollution, and accidents. In 1951, there were roughly 4 million licensed motor vehicles, and in 1971, 15 million. In 1951, over 5000 people were killed on the roads, and in 1971, nearly 8000.

Channels of distribution

Producers market their goods in the way most advantageous to them. The simplest method of all is by making a sale **directly to the customer.** This method has clear benefits where capital goods are concerned. There are, for example, a relatively small number of both producers and buyers of large-scale generating equipment and thus little need for intermediaries. Similarly, expensive consumer durable goods can often be marketed by this method. The builder is often in direct contact with the prospective house buyer and the boatbuilder with the budding yachtsman, the latter often through specialized journals.

Direct selling is not limited to the field of capital or durable consumer goods. The **mail order** business is an extremely fast-growing sector of the retail trade. It may range in character from the small advertisement placed in a local or national newspaper to firms which specialize entirely in this form of retailing. Readers are directed to the advertisements appearing weekly in the colour supplements of Sunday news-papers.

The mail order business, however, does not necessarily imply direct selling from manufacturer to customer. The large mail order firms can as easily be the distributors of goods produced by others. In addition to national advertisements, they often produce large catalogues of their wares and employ local **commission agents** to help sell them. These agents are paid a proportion of the selling price or, in some cases, may obtain goods for themselves at favourable rates. Commission salesmen are also employed in other branches of distribution, notably the fruit and vegetable trade, and merge with the category of commercial traveller, who also earns commission but is usually an intermediary between either manufacturer or wholesaler and retailer.

Agencies also exist in other fields. The garage which is a main distributor for a car manufacturer is acting as an **exclusive agent.** As car dealers, garages are normally required to sell one manufacturer's cars only and to promote their brand image. In return they have exclusive territorial rights over a defined area and do not expect local competitors to be selling the same cars.

Another channel of distribution is directly from **manufacturer to retailer.** In such a

High Street move for Car Parts Giant

A MOVE into the High Streets is planned by a British engineering giant. The group is already a major supplier to the motor industry, with sales of nearly £750 million in addition to its vast interests in other fields.

The profitability of BL's own Unipart scheme has been a major factor in the decision, and the engineering group is now seeking ways into the retail market. The operation will require massive funding and although cash has been set aside, no firm decision has been made as to the precise way in which the operation will be carried out.

case, either one or the other or both shoulder the cost of distribution. It is quite common, for example, for the clothing industry to operate in this way. Large departmental or multiple stores employ buyers who can obtain whole ranges of dresses or shirts. This form of distribution is only possible if either the manufacturer or the retailer has sufficient storage space and sufficient capital. There must also be a steady and constant demand for the goods involved. There are sometimes disadvantages for the manufacturer, who may tie his production to the needs of a particular firm only to find later that his contract to supply is not renewed.

In spite of other channels of distribution, the one still most commonly employed is that of **manufacturer through wholesaler to retailer.** We have discussed earlier the advantages and disadvantages of the wholesaling system. It remains to analyse changing trends among retailers. In the 'seventies, *multiple stores, departmental stores* and *mail order businesses* have continued to gain ground as retail outlets at the expense of *independent retailers* and *Co-operative Societies.*

A *departmental store* is, of course, divided into areas dealing in specialist lines. Examples are to be found in Oxford Street, London, and in the main shopping areas of many other large towns and cities. *Multiples,* on the other hand, consist of retailers with many branches. There is nothing to prevent department stores also being multiples, so that there is no clear division between the two. Post-war developments among the multiples have included the increasing use of *self-service stores.* Although usually connected with the sale of provisions, a self-service store may sell a great variety of consumer goods. If it has a floor area of over 2000 square feet and at least four check-out points, a self-service store is usually defined as a *supermarket.* A *hypermarket* has even more check-out points and its floor area may be divided into miniature departments. The rapid growth of self-service arrangements is based on the saving of labour costs, but is also associated with the economies of large-scale marketing leading to possibly cheaper goods with the efficient use of space and with the offering of a more varied choice of goods to the consumer.

Two other conflicting trends are discernible in post-war retailing. One is the location of hypermarkets outside main shopping areas on the edge of large conurbations and with adequate car-parking space provided. It is hoped that purchasers, avoiding town congestion, will make regular journeys to buy all their needs in one place. The other trend is towards the provision of traffic-free *shopping precincts* in the centres of large towns. These were originally made possible by the need to rebuild after wartime bombing but have since become a feature in the redevelopment of the larger towns.

In many areas of retailing, it has become increasingly more difficult to establish and compare retail prices. Offers based on an undisclosed 'recommended price', the use of trading stamps, and the impossibility of comparing weights and qualities of competing goods, are all responsible for this state of affairs, to which we return in Unit 15.

Market orientation and market research

Successful selling demands that commercial firms must direct their attention very precisely to their probable markets. To produce hopefully, in the expectation of sales, is not enough. Even a good product does not necessarily sell itself. This is true of the **home market,** and even more so when we think of **international trade.** Brochures

146

produced in English, English-speaking salesmen, specifications in Imperial rather than metric measures do not impress the foreign buyer in Europe or elsewhere who is in a position to choose between English and non-English products. Tailoring the sales efforts to the potential market is essential and often so is market research.

One form of market research is passive and relies on the *projections of past trends* which are possible if statistics are available. Official statistics often indicate the growth or decline of overall demand for particular goups of products. However, these are of little help to the firm which wishes to protect or maintain its own market share, and which must therefore look to its own sales records. These sometimes give an indication of past demand. However, they are notoriously unreliable since the conditions of the past are rarely repeated. Trends in women's fashions, for example, are particularly unpredictable, even if one knows that heavier clothes are wanted in winter and lighter ones in summer. Again, even if a car manufacturer could be sure that the past growth of car sales based on rising incomes would continue, he would know nothing about the possible demand for his new model. History, therefore, is a rather poor tool for the researcher, who must also resort to more positive forecasting procedures.

Such a procedure is to carry out either a one-off or a continuing **opinion poll** similar to those used in the attempts to forecast voting patterns. A carefully selected group of consumers is asked prepared questions about their future buying intentions. On a continuing basis, this procedure may (but only may) indicate broad shifts in consumer spending, but is unlikely to be precise enough to indicate future demands for one particular competing product.

Particularly where the product is new, either in a real or in an artificial sense, it is sometimes useful to sell it in one selected **pilot area** before it goes on to the general market. This may give a better idea of the future popularity of, for example, a new brand of toothpaste, but problems still remain. It is almost impossible to select a 'typical' area of the country in which to conduct the experiment. What is popular in Yorkshire may be anathema to south London. In any case, by the time the product reaches the general market, selling conditions may have changed. The toothpaste containing fluoride may well have been popular in the test area. The decision to produce it in quantity would be disastrous if, meanwhile, anti-fluoride pressure groups succeeded in convincing the general population of possible dangers. We must conclude that whatever forecasting methods are used, the results, although better than nothing, can hardly be regarded as precise.

Customers and clients

Our previous discussion has been concerned with commercial markets. Now we turn to the markets for goods, or more likely, services, which are collectively financed. Most working adults pay taxes and many pay rates. The money so raised is used to fund expenditure by local and central government. In some cases, this expenditure is made through commercial markets. The Ministry of Defence buys armaments this way; so does a County Treasurer when purchasing a computer. On the other hand, Welfare State services are available to all of us, whether or not we finance them, on the basis of need rather than demand backed by the ability to pay. Prisons and the probation service cater for unwilling 'customers'; these are known as **clients.** So are those who are

147

helped by the facilities of the social services departments of local government. Teachers are also paid for their services by local government, aided by central government, and provide what is commonly thought of as a 'free' service. It is important to note that nothing provided is ever 'free' if the use of scarce resources is involved. Rather, it is a question of who pays. In the cases which we have been discussing, some people may pay more than they receive in benefits, and others less. In this way monies are redistributed, the mere payment of taxes entitling us to nothing at all.

The many sectors of local and central government providing collective services are not in a market situation because nobody is buying what they produce. Neither is there a yard-stick of price to regulate the exchange of goods and services. The use of resources must, therefore, be regulated in another way: by government decisions concerning levels of taxation and direction of expenditure. To these matters we return in Units 14 and 16.

Summary

Markets, concerned with exchange, are any mechanism by which buyers and sellers are brought together. In another sense, the market for a commodity is the demand for it. In commercial markets, the price of a commodity determines how much of it is exchanged. There can only be one price in a perfect market, but perfect markets are a comparative rarity.

Markets are of varying types and have different functions. Of these, among the most important is the transporting of goods, both for the organization and for the economy. Channels of distribution include direct contact between manufacturer and retailer, selling by the manufacturer, the use of wholesalers (who normally have a productive function), and of agents. Retail outlets are changing in relative importance.

Organizations producing goods and services for sale to other organizations or to individual consumers, must use market research to forecast future sales. However, other organizations, notably in central and local government, produce services for which there is a collective payment through rates and taxes and for which the market cannot be forecast by normal research methods.

Assignments

1. Your organization manufactures garden tools, and is approached by the inventor of a new type of spade which eliminates most of the effort involved in digging. The new spade will cost 25 per cent more per article to produce than the conventional tool.

   You are asked to make a recommendation about whether or not to adopt and manufacture the new spade. In the form of a report, indicate:

   (a) your market research methods
   (b) your conclusions, and on what you base them.

2. This assignment is based on the press cutting on page 145, which must be read

carefully. As a preliminary to the assignment a board of directors should be formed.
Members of the board might be:

> Chairman
> Managing director
> Sales director
> Marketing director
> Production director
> Finance director
> Company secretary
> Non-executive directors

(a) In discussion in a board meeting, consider the various ways in which the company might market car spares to retail customers. Existing methods of selling spare parts should be considered.

(b) Each member of the board should write a brief report recommending a method (or methods) of marketing.

(c) The next board meeting should consider the possible methods and choose one (by vote if necessary).

(d) Each member of the board should consider the chosen method from his specialist point of view, and briefly outline in writing any problems which the company might face in the short and long run.

(e) The final board meeting should consider the problems outlined by the individual directors and decide on a programme of action for the following year. This programme should be written up briefly by each board member.

Unit 14 Organizations, customers and demand

Introduction

In Unit 13 we discovered that markets bring together buyers and sellers. Part 2 of this book examined the problems faced by organizations in deciding what to supply. One of these problems is that of persuading their customers to buy. One meaning of the term 'a market' is demand by consumers of wealth. By consumption we mean the 'using up' of wealth. This may be a quick process, like eating an apple, or a longer one, like living in a house. In any case, the consumer has to possess the wealth before he can consume it. The process of coming into the possession of wealth is known as **demand**, for which a formal definition would be: *the amount of a commodity or service bought per unit of time at a given price.*

This may seem a long-winded way of putting things, but it has the merit of being precise. The definition covers demand for solicitors as well as that for sausages. It also covers the demand by organizations for resources; for steel and for steel-erectors. It ties down demand as being per day, week, month, or year. Most important of all, it relates it to **price**. *Demand*—effective demand—must be backed by the *ability to pay* and is by no means the same thing as need. Millions of people in the developing countries need food, but cannot buy it.

However, there are circumstances in which one group of people provides the finance to demand goods or services which are then consumed by others. State organizations, we noted earlier, can, through the taxation system, and by subsidies, redistribute wealth. The organizations which administer the Welfare State deal with clients rather than with customers, and clients are usually in need without being able to exercise demand. Since it is as well to separate the problems of organizations which operate in markets where there is a conventional demand from those organizations dealing with clients, we will first make the assumption that there is no State intervention leading to redistribution of wealth.

Given this assumption, demand is subject to many influences. People may, for example, buy more of a particular detergent because it has become cheaper, because they have more money to spend, because it has been widely advertised, or because they have become more convinced that cleanliness is next to godliness. British Leyland may buy less steel from the British Steel Corporation because fewer of their cars are being sold. The demand for steel is **derived** from the demand for cars; so, for that matter, is the demand for production workers in the car industry.

In spite of the many factors affecting demand it is possible, for the sake of simplicity, to take separately the influence on demand of changes in the price of the commodity or service in question. This we shall now do, assuming that all other things are equal—i.e., that nothing changes except prices. (The Latin expression for 'all other things being equal' is *ceteris paribus*.) Later, we shall consider the influence of other factors.

Price changes and demand

We all expect more of a particular commodity to be sold if its price falls and less to be sold at a higher price. But why should this be so? Consider the imaginary example given in Table 14.1. This records the possible reactions of five people to a change in the price of apples. The first thing to note is that not *everybody* buys more apples at lower prices. Man A will never buy apples in any circumstances, while E can only be persuaded to buy one more kilogram, however low the price falls. In total, however, more apples are bought at lower prices because existing buyers are encouraged to buy more and new buyers appear.

Table 14.1

| Price of apples per kg | Demand for apples per week (kg) | | | | | Total |
	A	B	C	D	E	
100p	—	—	—	—	4	4
50p	—	2	—	5	5	12
25p	—	6	5	8	5	24
10p	—	12	9	10	5	36

A dislikes apples. They are not on his *scale of preferences*.
E has bought almost as many apples as he can find use for at a price of 10p per kilogram.
B, C, and D find a price of 100p per kilogram too high but are prepared to buy apples at lower prices.
In total, more apples are demanded at lower prices and less at higher prices.

At a price of 100p per kg. only E buys any apples at all. But why 4 kg and not 3 or 5? The answer lies in the fact that he has a *limited income* to dispose of in the way which will give him the greatest amount of satisfaction. We must assume that all people distribute their income in this way, though usually without analysing what they are doing. E would rather have a fourth kilogram of apples than the 100p necessary to buy it. On the other hand, he is not prepared to spend a fifth 100p on more apples. Since he already possesses 4 kg of apples, an extra kilogram is less necessary. Furthermore, another 100p spent on apples means that 100p less is available for spending on other things.

When the price falls to 50p, E finds that he is better off. Four kilograms of apples now cost him only 200p instead of 400p. Although we have assumed that his money income remains unchanged, his *real income* (the amount of goods and services which his money income will buy) has become greater. At the same time, apples have become relatively more attractive than, say oranges, the price of which we assume is unchanged. For both these reasons, E buys another kilogram of apples, even though the extra usefulness of a fifth kilogram is probably less than that of the fourth.

At the new price of 50p, B and D start to buy apples. They also find that apples have become more attractive compared with some other substitute. At an even lower price, C makes his purchase; E, on the other hand, cannot find any use for more than 5 kg of apples, however far the price falls. He prefers to use his higher real income to buy other things.

Since all this seems a little involved when we meet it for the first time, let us go through it again, using rather more technical terms. We assume that all human beings

151

are rational and therefore know both what they want and the order in which they want things. Everyone has a *scale of preferences*. Although we usually put necessities at the head of the list, the actual amount bought of any particular thing depends on its price, all other influences remaining unchanged.

As we have more of a thing, the extra satisfaction we get from it, or the *marginal utility* of the additional amount, tends to become less. One loaf of bread has very high utility; a twentieth loaf at any one time would be a positive embarrassment. Thus, we continue to buy increasing amounts of any one commodity only as long as the marginal utility thus gained is at least as great as the usefulness of the money sacrificed which could have been used to buy other things. We come back to the idea first met in Unit 1 of *real cost* in terms of the sacrificed alternative. Furthermore, if we are to make our money go as far as possible, we have to ensure that it is not worth while switching spending from one commodity to another. Any penny must yield the same satisfaction whether it is spent on bread, beer, butter, ballbearings, or anything else. This is known as the principle of **equi-marginal satisfaction**.

If the price of any commodity falls, there is, first, an *income effect*. If we are already buying some of the commodity, our real income becomes greater. Second, a *substitution effect* makes itself felt. More can be bought of the commodity which has fallen in price relative to other things. The penny spent will thus give more satisfaction if spent on this commodity than if spent on any other. Part of total expenditure may thus be switched to buy more of this commodity and less of others. This, however, leads to *diminishing marginal utility* as we buy more of the commodity until we arrive back at a position of equi-marginal satisfaction.

Demand schedules and demand curves

Table 14.1 is an example of a demand schedule. From it we can construct a demand curve, showing exactly the same information in the form of a graph. Changes in price are plotted on the vertical axis, while changes in the total amount demanded appear on the horizontal axis. The result is shown in Fig. 14.1 on page 153.

The **demand curve** thus obtained slopes downwards and to the right, indicating that more is bought at lower prices and less at higher prices. The diagram does not show why this should be so, it merely records a fact. As the price falls, demand is said to *extend;* at higher prices demand *contracts*. Since it is important to distinguish the effect of price on demand from the effect of other influences, these terms should always be used.

Other influences on demand

There are many other things, quite apart from price changes, which can influence demand. Before analysing them in detail, we will examine their effect on a demand schedule and curve. The important point to note is that we are now assuming price to remain unchanged so that either more or less is being bought at each price. Assume, for example, that in Table 14.1, double the amount is demanded at each price. The effect on the demand curve is shown in Fig. 14.2 on page 154. Since the *conditions of demand* have changed, the demand curve has shifted, moving to the right. In this case, we say that demand has *increased*. Similarly, a *decrease* in demand would be

152

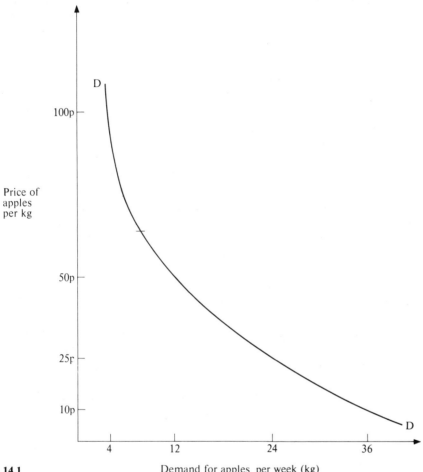

Fig. 14.1   Demand for apples per week (kg)

shown by a movement of the demand curve to the left. In summary, therefore, a demand curve is a sort of instantaneous photograph, showing what demand would be at each of a series of prices, conditions of demand remaining unchanged. The effect of a change in price is shown along the *slope* of a demand curve; the effect of a change in conditions of demand is shown by a change in the *position* of a demand curve.

Tastes and advertisements

It has been said that 'the consumer is king'. By voting with his spending power, he can encourage the production of one commodity and veto another. While this is true to a certain extent, we should also remember that the monarch is surrounded by many persuasive advisers. A change in tastes leads to an increase or decrease in demand; but such a change may be the result of an intensive advertising campaign. If enough people can be led to believe that 'an apple a day keeps the doctor away', then demand for apples will increase, quite irrespective of price. Through the media of hoardings, the

153

press, television, and the cinema, we are subjected to a daily bombardment of advertisements, some of them informing us of the qualities and relative merits of commodities, all of them persuading us to buy particular products. Serious doubts have been expressed as to the usefulness of much contemporary advertising, as we noticed in Unit 13. Its influence is, however, obvious to all of us.

Population changes and demand

We noted in Unit 2 that a population declining in numbers is likely also to be increasing in average age, while an increasing population is likely to contain a higher proportion of relatively young people. As people grow older, their tastes change, irrespective of any effect which advertising may have. A declining population is likely to be demanding fewer baby carriages and more bath chairs, fewer teething rings and more hair restoratives, fewer sweets and more indigestion tablets. Similarly, changes in the geographical distribution of population can affect demand. If, as some people fear, the UK is now in danger of becoming 'two nations', with greater prosperity in the south than in the north, there may develop a greater demand in the south for those commodities and services which appear necessary in order to keep up with the southern Joneses.

Changes in money income and demand

People sometimes complain that they feel very little better off even though their income has doubled over the past few years. It may be, of course, that prices have also risen, so that their real income has improved only slightly. It is as likely, however, that their standard of living has risen imperceptibly, and that they are now buying quite a different selection of goods and services. Margarine may be replaced by butter and

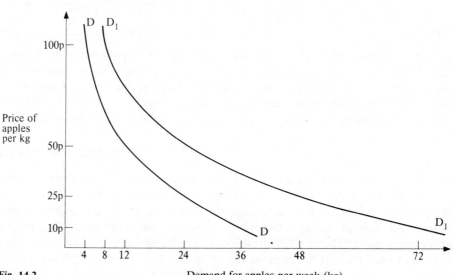

154   **Fig. 14.2**   Demand for apples per week (kg)

public transport by motor-cycle or car. Demand for pop records and coffee may increase as teenagers become more affluent; that for cheap cotton goods may decline in favour of man-made fabrics. Again, full employment and booming trade are likely to stimulate demand for a wide range of products, and, indeed, it is quite possible that more of these products will be sold under such conditions, even though prices are rising, simply because conditions of demand are changing so rapidly. On the other hand, when trade is depressed, demand may well decrease because people think it better to save for the impending rainy day.

Changes in the price of other goods

We shall meet, on many subsequent occasions, the notion that all prices are linked together into a **price system**. Changes in the price of one commodity can affect the demand for another, the price of which has not changed. Suppose that, because of more efficient production, the price of record players is drastically reduced. We have already seen good reasons why demand for them should *extend*. Demand for records is likely to *increase*, conditions of demand for them having changed.

The government and demand

Over 50 per cent of all production is in the **public** sector—i.e., it is controlled by central and local authorities, either by nationalization or in some other way. Furthermore, the government is the largest single consumer, making large demands even on the private sector of industry. Any change in government policy is thus likely to lead to large-scale changes in demand.

Price Commission lashed by Stores Chief

THE chairman of a large supermarket chain hit out recently at the activities of the Price Commission. He maintained that it should be disbanded as a benefit to the consumer. Competition among food traders is having more effect on reducing inflation, than any interference with the price mechanism. Fierce competition in the industry has resulted in the closure of 10 000 grocery shops in a three-year period, he said.

Price elasticity of demand

Price elasticity of demand may be defined as *the responsiveness of demand to changes in price*. It has previously been noted that demand is likely to extend as price falls and contract as price rises. We now go one stage further and ask *how much* it extends or contracts. If price falls only a little but demand extends a great deal, then, since it has 'stretched out' a lot, demand is said to be elastic. On the other hand, a great fall in price accompanied by a very small extension of demand occurs when demand is **inelastic**. This condition also holds good when price rises sharply but demand contracts very little; the notion of elasticity of demand can be applied, in other words, to the reaction of consumers following either a price rise or a price fall.

Measurement of elasticity

This general statement is hardly accurate enough. The precise degree of elasticity of demand can be determined only by reference to an actual demand schedule, such as that shown in Table 14.1. The same information appears in Table 14.2, with the

Table 14.2

Price of apples per kg		Demand for apples kg per week		Total consumer outlay
100p	x	4	=	400p
50p	x	12	=	600p
25p	x	24	=	600p
10p	x	36	=	360p

$$\text{Elasticity of demand} = \frac{\text{Percentage change in demand}}{\text{Percentage change in price}}$$

addition of another column showing total spending by all consumers at each price. When the price of apples falls from 100p to 50p, it can be seen that the consumers not only buy more apples, but also spend a greater total amount on apples. On the other hand, *total consumer outlay* remains unchanged when the price falls from 50p to 25p and actually falls when price drops to 10p. What we are examining is the *relationship* between changes in price and changes in demand. If the price falls, we would expect people to spend less in total on a commodity, and this will indeed happen unless the extension in demand is sufficient to outweigh the fall in price. If a 5 per cent fall in price is accompanied by a 10 per cent extension in demand, then total consumer outlay rises; demand is elastic. If a 10 per cent fall in price causes a 5 per cent extension in demand, then total consumer outlay falls; demand is inelastic. Finally, if a 10 per cent fall in price occasions a 10 per cent extension in demand elasticity is said to be **at unity**:

$$\frac{10\% \text{ change in demand}}{10\% \text{ change in price}} = 1$$

The measurement of price elasticity of demand can thus be expressed as *the percentage change (extension or contraction) in demand following a small change in*

156

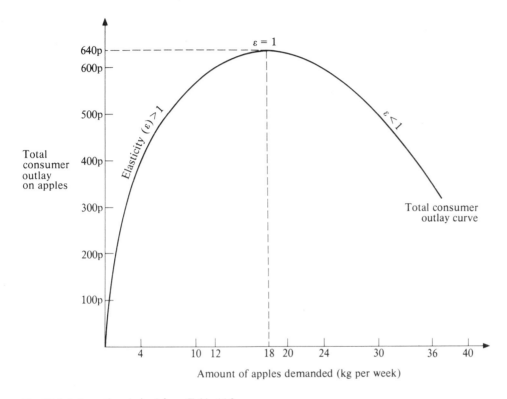

Fig. 14.3 Information derived from Table 14.2

price divided by the percentage change (fall or rise) in price. If demand is elastic, total consumer outlay increases with a fall in price and decreases with a rise in price. If demand is inelastic, the opposite happens. When elasticity of demand is at unity, changes in price leave total consumer outlay unaffected.

The best way to express this relationship in the form of a graph is by means of the **total outlay curve** (Fig. 14.3, above). When this curve is rising, demand is elastic; when it is falling, inelastic. When it is doing neither—i.e., at its peak—elasticity of demand is at unity. It is often dangerous to make any deductions about elasticity of demand from the slope of a particular demand curve, since this slope depends on the intervals selected on the vertical and horizontal axes. A glance back at Fig. 14.2 reveals that elasticity of demand is the same at any one price on each of the two demand curves, yet their slope varies considerably. Furthermore, since elasticity alters along the slope of a demand curve (i.e., between any two prices), it is best calculated as from one particular point. Figure 14.3 shows that price elasticity of demand is at unity when 18 kg of apples are bought and 640p spent.

Figures 14.4 and 14.5 show two exceptional demand curves. If people buy exactly the same amount, whatever the price, the percentage change in amount demanded following a change in price is nil. Elasticity of demand is also nil, the demand curve being a vertical straight line as shown in Fig. 14.4. If, on the other hand, there is an infinitely great change in demand, following a small change in price, the demand curve is the horizontal straight line shown in Fig. 14.5.

157

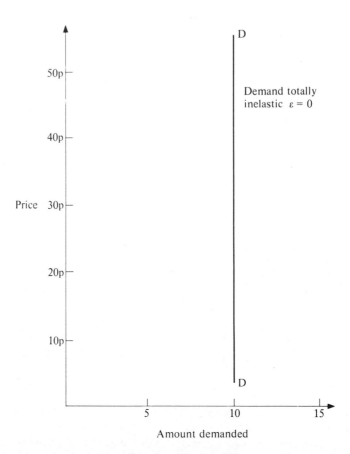

Fig. 14.4

Amount demanded

Reasons for different price elasticities of demand

Price elasticity of demand is likely to vary with any commodity or service according to its *price in relation to total expenditure*. If such a price is very high, then potential buyers are excluded and actual buyers can afford relatively little. Up to a point, as price falls, new buyers will enter the market and existing ones buy more. Eventually, if the price falls far enough, most buyers will possess at least some of the commodity, and extra amounts will give diminishing marginal utility. Demand can then only be encouraged to extend by relatively small amounts if there are relatively large price falls. As usual, of course, this argument holds good in reverse, demand often being more elastic at higher prices than at lower ones. Our imaginary example of demand for apples is a case in point.

It follows that demand for such items as matches or evening newspapers is relatively inelastic. Each forms a very small part of our *total expenditure*; each costs relatively little to start with, so that, for example, a $33\frac{1}{3}$ per cent increase in the price of matches, from $1\frac{1}{2}$p to 2p is likely to leave demand virtually unaffected.

Demand is also likely to be more elastic the greater the number of relatively close substitutes which exist. We may consider the problems which British Rail faces. If all

158

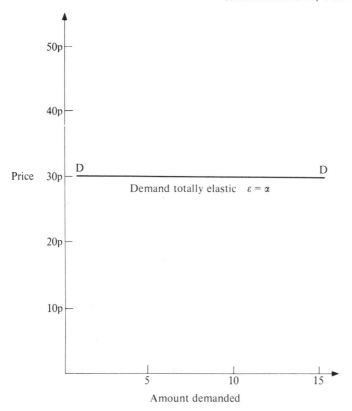

Fig. 14.5

Amount demanded

rail fares are increased, there will no doubt be mutterings from the hard core of commuters into London who, however, are likely to go on buying their season tickets because no practical alternative form of transport is open to them. Their demand is inelastic, as long as they travel into London to work. When it comes to holiday time, on the other hand, they are more likely to go by car or by coach, just as goods will go increasingly by road if rail freight charges are raised. The problem for British Rail is to know whether more is being lost on the swings than is gained on the roundabouts.

It is often said that demand is more inelastic for necessities than for luxuries. The extent to which this is so depends on the two factors already mentioned. Demand, even for bread, becomes elastic at high enough prices. On the other hand, it could hardly be argued that an evening newspaper is a necessity, even though demand for it is usually inelastic. These question-begging terms are thus best avoided. If demand for a good is inelastic within a given price range then, by definition, consumers consider the good to be a necessity.

Income elasticity of demand

The idea of elasticity can be applied to changes in demand caused by factors other than price. We have already noted that demand may increase or decrease because of changes in money income. Income elasticity of demand measures the *extent* to which demand alters as income alters. If, for example, a 10 per cent increase in money incomes leads to a 10 per cent increase in the demand for cars, other things remaining unchanged, then:

159

$$\frac{\text{Percentage change in demand}}{\text{Percentage change in money incomes}} = \frac{10\%}{10\%} = 1$$

Income elasticity of demand is unity.

In fact, all other things including price remaining unchanged, it is more likely that the income elasticity of demand for cars would be greater than unity in the UK. As we have become more wealthy, our demand for durable consumer goods and for services has been disproportionately high. On the other hand, our demand for some types of foodstuffs has actually fallen, producing a *negative* income elasticity of demand, while that for others, such as butter and margarine, has remained virtually unchanged. In the latter case, there has been a position of complete inelasticity, or zero elasticity.

Cross-elasticity of demand

This concept may be expressed as follows:

$$\frac{\text{Percentage change in demand for commodity X}}{\text{Percentage change in price of commodity Y}}$$

Suppose, for example, that the Post Office decided to increase telephone charges by 50 per cent, while leaving postal rates unchanged. Would it gain or lose from this move? It would depend upon the number of people who switched from communication by telephone to communication by post—i.e., upon the cross-elasticity of demand. Similarly, it would be possible to measure the cross-elasticity of demand for computer programmers following a substantial fall in price and extension in demand for computers. We return later to the idea of a price system wherein all prices are linked directly or indirectly. Meanwhile, the importance of cross-elasticity of demand should be noted.

Organizations and demand

Organizations are obviously interested in their customers' behaviour, since only by selling can they survive. The principles underlying this behaviour may be well understood, but, for an individual firm, very difficult to apply because of inadequate information. Business uncertainty is a fact of life.

What, for example, is the shape of the demand curve confronting an individual manufacturer of car tyres? What will be the effect of a 5 per cent reduction in his prices? Will the firm's *total revenue* increase or decrease? It is very difficult to answer these questions except on a basis of *market research*, referred to in Unit 13, and by trial and error. Some effort must be made to assess price, income, and cross-elasticities of demand for tyres. No doubt some more tyres will be sold, but how many more? Would the price cut be sufficient to win customers away from a competitive product in numbers more than sufficient to compensate for the loss of revenue arising from the cut in price? In other words, *is demand price-elastic*? Are consumers' incomes rising or falling in real terms? Are they likely to be buying more cars? Will an expensive advertising campaign increase sales sufficiently to more than meet its costs? Will such a campaign increase loyalty to the firm's brand of tyres and enhance its reputation and

160

the *goodwill* which attaches to its products? The questions are easy to pose; market research may or may not make them easier to answer. On successful answers depends the survival of the organization.

The same sort of questions face a supermarket. What will be the effect of 'special offers'? If the price of coffee is drastically cut, will this 'loss leader' entice customers in to spend on other goods as well? In Unit 15 we shall refer to fair trading and the special problem of price-cutting when the market price is not established and the 'recommended price' is not easily defined.

Organizations and need

Up to now, this Unit has been concerned with the problems of those organizations supplying products for which there is an effective demand. Now we turn to those which meet a **social need**. These include central government departments, such as the Department of Health and Social Security, local government organizations (including education and social services departments), and quangos (like the Manpower Services Commission). Important distinguishing features of all of them are that they cannot use price as an indicator of the demand for their services and that their resources are generated and supplied collectively. In other words, the normal market forces do not apply in their entirety.

How, then, is need assessed? The answer is, in the main, by law and by administrative rules. The provision of education is a case in point. Education, supplied by local authorities, is by law compulsory between the ages of five and sixteen. The 'demand' for it is thus dependent upon the number of children between these ages at any one time. This, in turn, depends upon the factors discussed in Unit 2. Above the age of sixteen, further and higher full-time education depends on the numbers of those both qualified for it and voluntarily seeking it. The uncertainties of demand are clearly even greater for organizations dealing with post-sixteen education than for those involved in the primary and secondary provision. Even in these areas, difficulty in calculating numbers has led to successive downward revisions of estimated numbers of teachers required. When we examine further education we find that demands fluctuate, not only in terms of total potential student numbers, but also in terms of the state of unemployment which influences numbers of those staying on in full-time or part-time education, of parental or employer desires, and of estimates of the future earning power of different occupations. On the other hand, the concept of price elasticity of demand has less part to play. Compulsory education is 'free'; further and higher education is subsidized.

Given the uncertain state of the education market, how are resources forthcoming? The answer is—mainly through the *allocation of taxes and rates*, which also go to finance the many other activities of the public sector. So the supply of education depends upon, first, that part of the *total national production* which the State takes for its own uses and, second, on the proportion of that part which is allocated to education as opposed to defence, health, roads, unemployment benefits or other uses.

The same considerations apply across the whole area of need. Organizations operating in this area are dependent for resources on centralized decisions. How much of total national production should be centrally controlled? What levels of need can reasonably be met and in which specific directions? Should all citizens be required to

161

provide for their own needs? If so, what happens to those who fall by the wayside? If not, do some aspects of the Welfare State allow people to opt out of being useful members of society? Are resources allocated inefficiently in the absence of market disciplines? Does that not apply with equal force to organizations in the private sector being helped out by the National Enterprise Board and to loss-making nationalized industries? These are complex questions, and they have no easy answers; we shall return to them in Book 2.

Summary

Demand is the amount of a commodity or service bought per unit of time at a given price. It is influenced both by prices and by other factors which cause *conditions of demand* to alter. People in general (the market) buy more at lower prices for two reasons. They can *afford* to buy more of *anything* if their real income rises, following a fall in price of any one item on their shopping list. Furthermore, they tend to *substitute* a cheaper commodity for a dearer one so far as this is possible. As in the case of supply analysis, demand schedules and curves illustrate rather than explain the theory.

Demand conditions may change, irrespective of any alteration in price because of changing tastes (influenced by advertisement), population movements, changing money income, changes in the price of other goods, government influence, and for a host of other reasons.

Price elasticity of demand is the term given to show the responsiveness of demand to changes in price. Such elasticity depends upon the price of a commodity, the proportion of this price to total spending, and the ease or difficulty of finding substitutes. Income elasticity of demand is the response of demand to changes in real incomes. Cross-elasticity of demand is the degree of change in demand for one commodity following a change in the price of another.

Changes in price cause the demand for a commodity to *extend* or *contract*. Changes in the conditions of demand lead to an *increase* or *decrease* in amounts bought.

Demand is not the same thing as need. Organizations in market situations have great difficulty in avoiding business uncertainty and in estimating future demand for their products; hence the need for market research. Organizations providing for needs are not in market situations in the sense that they can use prices as indicators; neither do they acquire resources in the same way but rely instead on funds from central and local government sources. The level of Welfare State provision depends on the collective decisions of the population as expressed through their elected representatives.

Assignments

1. You are a farmer. In 19X6, a given acreage of potatoes produced you a net income of £2,000. In 19X7, the same acreage produced an income of only £1,000. List all the reasons why this may have happened. What would you need to forecast before deciding whether or not to grow potatoes in 19X8?
2. You are employed as a clerk in a local office of the Department of Health and Social Security. Your friend, a clerk in a shipping firm, makes the criticism that you are one of an army of unproductive civil servants. How would you answer?

Unit 15   Consumer protection

State influence in consumer affairs

We have looked already at some of the sections of the **Sale of Goods Act 1893,** which give protection to buyers of goods. Although the Act is dated 1893, it was in fact an Act which codified, or collected together, many of the past decisions of the courts on problems relating to the sale of goods. The decisions themselves would often be the result of applying customary law; that is, commercial customs of merchants such as would be accepted by them in fairs and markets. In this way, the Sale of Goods Act ensured that the best mercantile rules were applied throughout the country. So far as sales to individuals, or consumers, were concerned, its major drawback was that those sections which apparently gave protection could be excluded.

While it was hardly practicable to exclude the implied terms of Sections 12 to 15 (see Unit 9) in sales of small everyday items, larger purchases were a different matter. The growth of the department and multiple stores organizations led to a wider ownership of consumer durable goods. Mainly by the use of guarantees, which were generally anything but, a customer's rights under the Act were often taken away. This was done by asking a customer to sign an order form, which, while apparently offering considerable advantages, in fact removed a customer's basic rights under the Act, and also under **common law.** We saw in Unit 9 that the courts attempted to preserve some rights when *exclusion clauses* were used. In practice, very few disputes reached the courts, and many consumers were deprived of those rights which the 1893 Act purported to give to them.

Of course, cash and credit sales were not the only ways of selling goods. The *hire-purchase system* was firmly established by the 'thirties. This coincided with the economic depression of those years. This coincidence exposed some of the evils and perils of an unregulated hire-purchase system. One serious problem was the right of repossession, often with a right of entry to premises, which customers unwittingly gave when signing agreements. The right of repossession was sometimes exercised even if only the last payment was outstanding. Hirers might suffer penalties if they ended an agreement because of payment difficulties. Another problem which arose was that of the so-called 'end-on' agreement. In this instance, further goods were added to an existing agreement; failure to pay instalments would result in all the goods being repossessed.

It was only in 1938 that, largely due to the single-handed effort of a woman MP, the Hire Purchase Act of that year was passed, eliminating at least some of the worst abuses of the system. However, one major drawback remained—the transaction was not a sale, and therefore, the Sale of Goods Act did not apply to the hire aspect of it. So far as the *option to purchase,* to be exercised at the end of the agreement, was concerned, it was not an agreement to buy, but merely an option to be exercised or not as the hirer wished. In practice, of course, unless the agreement was terminated, the hirer invariably exercised the option to purchase, but without any real protection regarding the quality of the goods. The Hire Purchase Acts of 1964/5 were a further step forward, giving further protection to hirers as hire-purchase and other forms of credit

163

transaction multiplied. Although the Acts have been largely repealed, most of the provisions have proved eminently satisfactory and now appear in the **Consumer Credit Act 1974.** This Act also extends the protection to all forms of consumer credit agreement, and is considered later.

Parliament has also intervened to solve problems regarding descriptions which, when applied to goods and services, are false or misleading. This was done by the **Trade Descriptions Acts of 1968 and 1972.** Another problem which often causes distress, that of receiving goods which have not been ordered, followed by pressure for payment, was met by the **Unsolicited Goods and Services Act 1971.** A major step forward, and a positive attempt to co-ordinate consumer protection was taken by the **Fair Trading Act 1973.** This Act, among other things, created the office of the **Director General of Fair Trading.** We also need to examine further the **Unfair Contract Terms Act 1977,** which also strengthens consumer protection.

Our starting point was a situation in which the State left consumer affairs largely to the parties involved. We are now at a point where not only is there considerable consumer protection, but consumer affairs are kept under constant review. It is now possible to look more closely at these important matters.

Trade descriptions

The 1968 Act was a major attempt to give a broad protection to consumers in three areas. These are: false trade descriptions applied to goods, false or misleading pricing of goods, and false statements applied to many kinds of services. Although the Act was mainly intended to protect retail customers, it applies equally to sales by one business to another. However, it does not apply to private sales. The 1972 Act adds a provision to the 1968 Act regarding the marking of imported goods. They must not have a name or mark likely to be taken as a UK mark.

The 1968 Act lists several characteristics of goods; if a description relates to one or more of these characteristics, and is false, the Act applies. The major items in the list relate to quantity or size, the composition of the goods, fitness for purpose, and related matters, and method of manufacture. The description, to be 'false', must be false to a material degree—minor differences in quantity, for example, are not false. If goods are

MILEAGE FRAUD

Two car dealers today pleaded not guilty to charges relating to false trade descriptions. The men were alleged to have cut a total of 450 000 miles from the mileage recorders of 19 cars before entering them in north country auctions.

described in such a way as to be misleading, rather than false, this is also covered by the Act. A 'Jumbo' sized packet must be considerably larger than others in the range, otherwise the description is misleading. Descriptions such as 'waterproof', 'hand-made', 'woollen' and 'cream', must now mean exactly what they say. Similarly, goods such as glues, oils, paints, and cleaners must now be fit for the purpose as described on packages, or in notices and advertisements. Some of the provisions relating to descriptions and marks had been in existence for a long number of years in other Acts; the 1968 Act consolidated and clarified them, and made them more easily enforceable. It also added important provisions regarding pricing of goods and we can now examine these.

It is natural for a seller of goods to indicate that they are being sold at a fair or even a bargain price. So long as this is done without false comparisons, it is perfectly acceptable. However, the Act specifies three ways in which a price indication may be considered to be false. The first of these is concerned with situations where a price is indicated to be equal to, or less than, *a recommended price*. So long as the price is one generally recommended by a manufacturer for goods sold in that area, the comparison is considered to be a fair one.

The second restriction concerns *indicated prices* which are, in fact less than the price at which a supplier is willing to sell. This provision covers situations where a low price is charged so long as a large quantity is bought, but this is not made clear. The third restriction concerns itself with apparent *pricing bargains*. Indications that prices have been reduced must be genuine and generally based on the fact that higher prices have been charged previously for the goods. The Act provides a measure for this—any higher price which is indicated must have been charged continuously for twenty-eight days in the preceding six months, unless a statement to the contrary is expressly made. If this is done, it is usually by notice, and customers are thus able to draw their own conclusions about such bargains.

The third major area of the Act relates broadly to false statements made in relation to the provision of services. If a statement is made which is known to be false, an offence is committed. Equally, if a statement is made 'recklessly', and it is false, an offence is still committed. Thus statements regarding '2 hour cleaning' or 'shoe repairs while you wait', must be backed up by such services.

It will be appreciated from the foregoing paragraphs that the Trade Descriptions Acts give considerable protection to consumers and others. The Acts serve as a deterrent and their provisions are enforced by the **consumer protection departments** of local authorities. Even though no additional contractual rights are given, there are provisions for compensation in the Acts. Following conviction of an offender under the Act, a compensation order may be made by the court. Thus, a person whose holiday has been spoiled because it did not meet the description in a brochure may receive some financial recompense.

Unsolicited goods and services

The need for further consumer protection in this area was disclosed by a growing business practice of sending out to customers goods which in fact had not been ordered. In the same way, a service might be provided unasked for, such as an entry in a trade directory. This practice had several consequences. Despite the absence of an order, some firms would pay, perhaps thinking that a verbal order had been placed by someone. In the same way, once the goods had arrived, it was sometimes easier just to pay up; indeed the goods might even turn out to be useful. So far as private customers were concerned, the consequences were sometimes more serious. A failure to pay for unwanted goods was invariably met by demands for payment couched in rather threatening legal terms, and this frequently frightened a customer into paying. Legally, the goods belonged to the sender, and even if unwanted, had to be kept reasonably safely or sent back. The distress caused, often to elderly and poor people, led to the abuse being stopped by Parliament. This was done by the **Unsolicited Goods and Services Act 1971.**

Now goods received unordered may be kept, without payment, after six months. At any time within this period the recipient can notify the sender that the goods are not wanted and should be collected. If not collected within one month, the goods may be kept without payment. Further provisions deal with the demands for payment which were a feature of this practice. It is now a criminal offence to demand payment of a debt unless the person making the demand has reasonable cause to believe there is a right to payment. The presence of an order form or letter would, of course, give reasonable cause, but the absence of any form of order would be fatal.

Implied terms in consumer transactions

In Unit 9 we examined some of the terms which are implied in contracts for the sale of goods. These relate to title, description, merchantable quality, fitness for purpose, and correspondence with sample. We noted that, apart from the implied condition as to title, the terms may be excluded in business contracts for the sale of goods, and also that this right is subject to the test of *'reasonablesness'*. One of the tests suggested by the **Unfair Contract Terms Act 1977** is that exclusion of the terms is reasonable when buyer and seller have equal bargaining power. By implication, when buyer and seller, even in business, are not in an equal bargaining position, the exclusion of the implied terms may not be reasonable. This protection of inequality is taken a stage further by the 1977 Act, when the buyer is *'dealing as consumer'*. In this event, *the terms implied by Sections 12–15 of the Sale of Goods Act cannot be excluded*. Similar protection is given to persons acquiring goods under consumer credit agreements. In this way, Parliament has given considerable protection to individuals as consumers. At the same time, it has imposed statutory restrictions upon organizations selling goods to consumers either for cash, or by means of consumer credit agreements. We can now identify 'consumers' in this context.

The Unfair Contract Terms Act stipulates a three-part test to determine whether a party to a contract 'deals as consumer'. He or she must not be making the contract in the course of a business; the other party must be making the contract in the course of a business; the goods must be of a type ordinarily supplied for private use or consumption. If this test can be met, any clause excluding the implied terms of Sections 12–15 is void. Equally important is that provision which states that if a business (which includes local and central government departments and others) claims that the buyer is not dealing as consumer, the business must prove this. If it cannot, any exemption clause of the type under discussion will not be enforced.

In Unit 9 we also looked at the problem of exclusion clauses. We saw that, in the case of *'standard term'* and *'consumer'* contracts, a test of reasonableness is applied to *clauses avoiding liability in contract.* The 1977 Act sets out three categories of such clauses. These are:

1. *Exclusion or restriction of liability for breach of contract,* e.g., 'The Company shall not be liable for loss, damage, or delay to, or misdelivery, of property however caused.'
2. *A claim to be entitled to perform the contract by doing something different from what could be reasonably expected,* e.g., 'The Company reserves the right to provide accommodation in any other hotel in the resort.'
3. *A claim to be entitled not to carry out the contractual obligations, or part of them,* e.g., 'The Company shall not be liable for any loss, damage, inconvenience, or injury arising from the failure of the vehicle to start, or arrive at the times specified in the Time Tables, or at all.'

It is important to note that the restriction applies to any type of contract and not just those for the sale of goods. Thus, it takes in a very important area of consumer activity, that relating to services.

Consumer credit

We saw in the first section of this Unit that the former law relating to hire-purchase and credit and conditional sale transactions has now been incorporated into the **Consumer Credit Act 1974.** This includes the rules relating to the form of agreements, cooling-off periods, rights of cancellation, and return of goods. However, the previous Acts were restricted in their operation to certain kinds of transactions, as noted above. The rapid growth of all forms of credit during the 'sixties led to a general review of this form of trading by a government appointed committee. The report of the committee concluded that there were many features common to all kinds of credit transactions. From this conclusion it then recommended that further protection was required for consumers in credit transactions, in addition to that already given. The government accepted most of the committee's recommendations, which it implemented by the Consumer Credit Act 1974. At the time of writing (1978), not all the provisions of the Act have been brought into force.

Briefly, the 1974 Act brings under the umbrella of protection such methods of granting credit as bankers' and other *credit cards, bank loans* and *overdrafts, credit arrangements with shops, check trading,* and *second mortgage business.* In addition, *hire agreements* are brought under statutory control by the Act. A restriction is placed upon individuals and organizations wishing to carry on consumer credit, or consumer hire, business. A *licensing system* for such businesses has been introduced by the Act. Advertising and canvassing for business is strictly controlled, as are the activities of what are termed ancillary credit businesses, including debt collectors and credit reference agencies, which must be licensed. The definition is wide enough to include shops which sell goods by means of consumer credit agreements. If the shop, or any similar business, introduces customers to a finance company, it is acting as a credit-broker (i.e., arranging credit), and needs to be licensed for this.

Licences are of course, required for any consumer credit or hire business, even

£45 credit licences a must for many firms

THE THIRD and final stage of licensing under the Consumer Credit Act 1974 is now in operation. The first two stages were concerned with the licensing of credit reference agencies and debt counsellors and collectors, and also of businesses providing consumer credit up to £5,000 on sale or hire agreements. The present stage is concerned with firms and individuals acting as brokers by arranging credit facilities.

The word 'broker' is wide enough to include, for example, garages arranging credit with finance companies for their customers. In the same way, stores selling higher value consumer goods by means of consumer credit agreements with a finance company, must be licensed. There are many more examples of firms who will be 'netted' by the system, and already finance houses are reminding those who place business with them of the need to be licensed. This is particularly important for them, as their agreements will generally be unenforceable if arranged through unlicensed brokers.

though the credit is financed by the shop or other retail establishment. The licensing system is operated by the Director General of Fair Trading (see below), who is also given additional powers under the Act. These relate to the form of documents and their contents, and also to the enforcement of the Act. This in practice is done by local authority consumer protection offices. The penalties for an offence under the Act include fines and imprisonment.

Any organization operating consumer credit business without a licence finds itself handicapped. Any agreement which it makes with a customer (debtor) is unenforce-able without the agreement of the Director.

Office of Fair Trading

We have just seen that the Director General of Fair Trading plays an important role in the operation of the Consumer Credit Act 1974. This is just one aspect of the functions of the Director and of the **Office of Fair Trading,** but this function is so important that one division of the Office is devoted to it. Another one, the **Consumer Affairs Division,** is, as its name suggests, concerned with those matters which directly affect consumers. These include the enforcement of the Director's powers to obtain assurances from traders that they will cease to operate in such a way as to persistently break the criminal law, or who have disregarded their obligations to consumers under the civil law. Failure to give such an assurance may result in prosecution. In any event, the assurances, with names, are widely publicized, and this in itself is a considerable deterrent to traders. The division also keeps under review, and makes special investigations into, particular trading activities affecting consumers. These have included methods of selling, advertising, methods of pricing, and guarantees. *Codes of practice* are negotiated with trade associations to ensure clarity of rights and obliga-tions for consumers. The **Competition Policy Division** is concerned generally with monopolies, mergers, and restrictive trade practices, particularly in so far as they restrict competition. This is examined in Book 2.

As may be seen from this brief review of the work of the Office of Fair Trading, it is of particular value in consumer protection. It is able to bring pressure to bear upon

Package deal for shoppers

THE Parliamentary Under-Secretary for Prices and Con-sumer Protection announced the formation of a government sponsored body, the Packaging Council. The council will fol-low the well-proven method of laying down a code of conduct for packaging companies and this will be voluntary. The council's chairman considered that the power to issue reports should operate as a sanction against organizations failing to follow the spirit and terms of the code.

Many consumer groups have expressed concern about pack-aging standards and methods. Most complaints concerned packages which give a mislead-ing impression of the quantity or size of the contents, and of wasteful decorative packaging which appeared only to in-crease prices.

organizations to fulfil their contractual obligations, thus ensuring that individual consumers get a fair deal, although it does not deal with individual complaints. Its monitoring and investigation of particular consumer affairs often ensures that practices against the general interests of consumers are eradicated. The codes of practice negotiated—for example, regarding dry-cleaning and laundry services—help to avoid misunderstandings between organizations and customers. There is a side-effect also, which is that the standards of all engaged in a trade are brought up to those of the best. The Office has also published a large number of leaflets giving information concerning many aspects of consumer affairs. These are aimed not only at the general public but at shopkeepers and others, so that both sides may be better informed.

Conclusion

The rapid extension of ownership of consumer durable goods has led to growing demands for more certain consumer protection. The growth of 'consumerism', through local and national consumer groups and associations exposed many deficiencies in consumer legislation. Also exposed was the widespread use of exclusion clauses which we have already examined. In addition to the exclusion of implied terms, such exclusion clauses would often limit or remove contractual liability from the seller. Added to this was the David and Goliath situation of the individual against the organization. The press was quick to take up the consumer cause by turning a spotlight on particularly bad cases. The result of this mounting campaign was a recognition by government that consumer affairs were of growing importance. We have charted the development, by legislation and other means, of considerable protection for consumers of both goods and services. In this way, some of the inequality between individuals and organizations has been redressed. In Book 2 we shall examine this whole question further, with particular reference to the constraints which are placed upon organizations by legislation, local and central government departments, and by public opinion and pressure groups.

Summary

Historically, the State has played little part in consumer affairs, leaving the parties broadly to make their own bargain, on negotiated terms. New selling methods, and particularly hire-purchase, led to some protection being given to individuals. The growth of the economy and rising personal affluence caused consumer sales to rise dramatically. Protective legislation began, post-war, with the Hire Purchase Acts in 1964/5 and the Trade Descriptions Act of 1968/72. The latter creates criminal offences regarding false description and pricing of goods and services. The Act also provides for compensation to be paid to a person misled.

The problem of unsolicited goods and services, coupled with pressure for payment, was solved in 1971 by the Unsolicited Goods and Services Act, which gave the right to keep unordered goods, and made demands for payment for these and unwanted services a criminal offence. The exclusion of Sections 12—15 (Sale of Goods Act) implied terms was stopped in 1973, so far as consumer sales of goods were concerned. Their exclusion in business sales was subject to a reasonableness test. The Act also applied to hire-purchase transactions. These provisions are now in the Unfair Contract Terms Act 1977. This Act also contains provisions limiting the use of exclusion clauses which seriously restrict liability under a contract; this applies to all contracts, thus giving protection under contracts for services.

The growth of credit trading and the need for control has led to the Consumer Credit Act 1974. This Act, which has incorporated former hire-purchase legislation, extends consumer protection to all forms of credit trading. A licensing system has been established which applies to all organizations carrying out credit transactions with consumers, or offering ancillary credit services. The licensing system is operated by the Office of Fair Trading, whose work also includes consumer protection in many other areas. The Office reviews and investigates consumer matters and is able to anticipate problems by consultation, agreement, and information.

Legislation, the activities of local and central government departments, and public opinion and pressure groups place some constraints upon organizations, and these are considered in Book 2.

Assignment

'Regulations for the carriage of passengers and goods' issued by many bus companies, and often included in their timetables, contain a regulation similar to the following:

No right of action shall be maintained against the company by a ticket holder or any other person in respect of (i) death or bodily injury to any person unless sustained while the passenger is being carried in, or is entering, or is alighting from, a stationary public service vehicle, or (ii) any other loss, damage or delay to any person however caused, or (iii) any loss, damage or delay to, or misdelivery of property however caused or (iv) death or bodily injury or loss sustained while entering or leaving a public service vehicle while in motion.

(a) Do you consider that the above regulation covers all circumstances in which passengers might board or alight from buses?
(b) The Unfair Contract Terms Act 1977 forbids the exclusion, by a contract term, of liability for death or personal injury resulting from negligence. How far do you consider that the terms of the extract meet this requirement?
(c) Mrs T., a typist and regular bus traveller, boarded a bus operated by a driver–conductor. She was last in a small queue; a few moments after she had paid her fare and received her ticket, the bus moved quickly away from the stop. The sudden jerk caused Mrs T. to fall to the floor. She broke her wrist, her coat was torn, and in the confusion her purse was stolen. She missed a dental appointment, but had to pay for the appointment nevertheless. She was away from work for two weeks, but was paid during her absence. The bus company's regulations included the extract shown above. Advise Mrs T. regarding any possible claim which she might wish to bring against the bus company.

Unit 16   A summing-up and a look ahead

We have now arrived at both an end and a beginning. This book has been concerned with a somewhat simplified account of organizations and the environment in which they operate. It may perhaps be summarized by a discussion of the various propositions within it.

The laws of demand and supply

1. Markets bring sellers and buyers together

Unit 13 described the nature of markets. Many—probably most—organizations concerned with the production of wealth are sellers; all individuals and organizations are also buyers—of raw materials, capital goods, and consumer goods. However, it is important to remember the assumptions implied. The first of these is that organizations sell their products at a **price** and that buyers pay that price, thus exercising effective demand. The assumption is that of a freely operating and unrestricted **price system,** through which consumers 'vote' for what they want and organizations produce because they find it most profitable. Given this assumption, the consumer is king and what cannot be paid for is not produced.

Our society is not like that. Some organizations deal with clients instead of customers and satisfy needs instead of demand. The services which they provide are financed collectively and do not carry a market price. Nevertheless, they are wealth producers and resource users; there are methods other than commercial markets by which decisions are made on what, how, when, where, and for whom, to produce.

2. More of a commodity is demanded at lower prices and less at higher prices

Unit 14 explained the reasons behind this statement. Again, we are dealing with demand rather than need and, even given that assumption, we discovered that it is very difficult for organizations to determine just what their customers' reactions will be to a price change. And prices can tell us very little about people's behaviour in situations where individuals do not themselves pay for what is supplied. Perhaps individual attitudes are bound up with views about property. If I buy a car it is 'mine', and I look after it; if I sit in a bus-shelter it is communal and I may pay it scant respect.

3. More of a commodity is usually supplied at higher prices and less at lower prices

Part 2 of this book was concerned with organizations, resources, and costs. Most resources are scarce; their use in one form of production means that alternative uses are sacrificed. This sacrifice is called **real cost.** Unit 7 indicated how real cost can be translated into money terms and Units 8 and 9 discussed the particular cost problems associated with human and non-human resources respectively. It is important to note that any barriers to the free movement of resources from one use to another have cost implications. To that extent, trade unions and legal or contractual rules affect costs by creating artificial scarcities or surpluses of particular kinds of workers. It may be socially or politically necessary for State organizations to intervene in the labour market, for instance, to prevent unemployment; as far as organizations are concerned, such intervention may lead to higher production costs. Higher prices may then have to be paid if production is to take place.

Again, the statement applies only to commercial markets. More State education, health facilities, local government services or job centres may be forthcoming because of a collective political will; prices do not directly determine their supply, although, in the final analysis, more of them may mean more taxes, less money for consumers to dispose of themselves, and thus a reallocation of resources and of wealth.

4. *If demand increases (because of a change in conditions of demand), the price of a commodity usually rises and its supply extends. If demand decreases, the price usually falls and supply contracts*

This proposition, applicable to commercial markets for resources and consumer goods and services, combines the findings of Units 7, 13, and 14. We have learnt to distinguish between changes in demand caused by price changes and those caused by anything else, such as advertisement, changing tastes, or increased money incomes. It should be noted that changing conditions of demand *cause* the change in price and, hence, supply. Organizations faced with an increasing demand for their product usually try to meet that demand. In doing so, their average costs of production possibly rise, at least in the short run, because of diminishing returns. Figure 16.1 illustrates the position in respect of the total market (total supply from all organizations and total demand from all consumers) before and after an increase in demand. Conditions of demand having altered, a new demand curve is necessary (see Unit 14). D is the old demand curve and D_1 the new one. P is the old price and P_1 the new one.

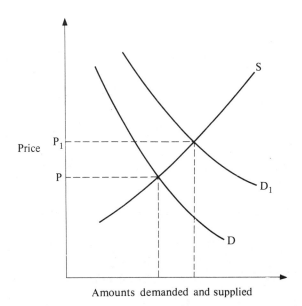

Fig. 16.1   Amounts demanded and supplied

In real life, matters are not so simple. As usual, the analysis does not apply except in commercial markets, which Fig. 16.1 illustrates. Even here, it is difficult for organizations to estimate the extent to which demand is changing permanently, as opposed to merely fluctuating; their response, in terms of changed production, must take account of this business uncertainty. Those that guess best profit most if profit maximization is indeed their objective.

5. *If supply increases (because of a change in conditions of supply) the price of a commodity usually falls as demand for it extends. If supply decreases, the price usually rises and demand contracts*

In this case, the *cause* of the change in price and demand is an alteration in conditions of supply. Such an alteration may come about because resource costs have themselves changed. Workers may be hired for more or less wages; imported raw materials may have become scarcer or more plentiful; a new industrial location may have yielded external economies; new production methods or increased scale of production may have had beneficial or adverse effects; new laws may have imposed extra costs either directly or indirectly, for example by more stringent control of the health and safety of workers; all these factors, and many more besides, can alter supply conditions.

Figure 16.2 shows what may happen when costs rise and total supply of a commodity decreases. S is the old supply curve and S_1 the new one. P and P_1 are the old and new prices respectively, demand having contracted. Again, this is a simplification. Organizations, it is repeated, cannot know the total market conditions, including the degree of price elasticity of demand for their products. And when the cost of centrally-provided services rises, it is not price but committee decision which usually regulates the amount of that provision.

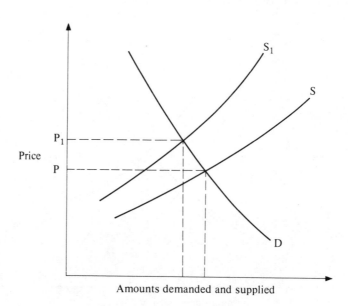

174   **Fig. 16.2**

Amounts demanded and supplied

6. An equilibrium price is one at which organizations are just willing to offer for sale the quantity of a commodity which buyers are just willing to purchase

This situation is illustrated in Fig. 16.3. Customers of the supplying organizations are unwilling to buy more at the ruling market price; at the margin they would rather keep their money or spend it on something else. Suppliers are unwilling to produce more since, if they did so, their marginal costs would be greater than the selling price. The community as a whole is measuring the extra real costs involved in devoting more scarce resources to a particular product against the extra utility to be gained from larger quantities of that product.

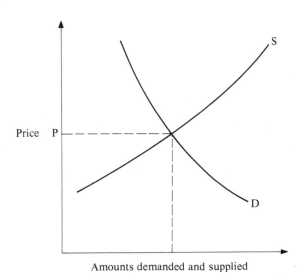

Fig. 16.3   Amounts demanded and supplied

Price and value

The six propositions above are sometimes known as the laws of demand and supply. Prices, it appears, perform several functions. From the viewpoint of the consumer they allow him to measure *utility,* personal to him, against the *value* which the market puts on a commodity. Utility and value should never be confused. The former is the power to give satisfaction. For a particular commodity or service, this power varies from person to person. The latter, on the other hand, should really be called value *in exchange.* It measures the real cost of resources used in terms of money. For example, if a completed Concorde is valued at £30 million and this same amount could provide thirty schools, then the value of Concorde is thirty schools—or anything else costing the same amount. Put another way, utility is **subjective** to the consumer, 'inside him', while value is **objective** or 'outside' him and determined by the interaction of total demand and total supply. In trying to obtain the greatest satisfaction from limited means, he measures utility against value in money terms. It follows, therefore, that in a market economy, prices act as a rationing mechanism, goods and services going to

175

those consumers who, having purchasing power, find that the commodities have the greatest utility at the margin.

All this is of great significance to the organizations supplying the goods and services, and it might be thought that 'the consumer is king'. Prices, however, act equally as a guide to producers. Measured against costs, they indicate the directions in which resources should be allocated, the size and scale of production required (and hence the size of organizations). In a market economy, the questions of what, how, when, where, and for whom to produce are answered, at least partly, by prices, which to the producing organization represent revenue.

Thus value in exchange, measured by prices, is determined by demand and supply acting in opposition to each other. A famous economist, Alfred Marshall, once likened the determination of value to the operation of a pair of scissors. Each blade does part of the work; costs of production and utility each play their part in fixing price and value.

The complex society

The market economy, in its extreme form, presupposes *'laissez-faire'*. In such a system the State would stand aside, providing for basic defence and little else, while individuals and organizations pursued their own enlightened self-interest through the operation of prices. Consumers, it would be assumed, *care* about obtaining maximum satisfaction; organizations *care* about obtaining maximum profit—and the devil take the hindmost. Prices alone, interlocking and affecting one another (that is, forming a *price system),* would be instruments of resource allocation.

This system, in such an extreme form, does not exist in the UK. The first half of the nineteenth century was the time when it was most nearly in operation. However, it became apparent that along with the economic advantages of laissez-faire came social evils. Wealth became very unevenly distributed, leading to extremes of poverty for many and of wealth for few. People, having unequal bargaining positions in the market economy, became exploited and exploiters. The market economy presupposes competition among supplying organizations, but monopoly and imperfectly competitive situations became common. Perfect markets presume perfect knowledge; without this consumers may not achieve maximum satisfaction. Worst of all, trade cycles developed, leading to successive and regular waves of boom and slump, to inefficient resource allocation, and to large-scale unemployment.

It was possible to argue, with Karl Marx, that the market economy, which he called the **capitalist system,** was productive of social division. **Communism,** in its pure form, would argue for the proposition, 'from each according to his ability; to each according to his needs'. Under such a system, prices would have little or no part to play. **Resource allocation** would be decided by committee to achieve socially desirable ends. Of course, this in itself begs many questions. Who would decide what was or was not socially desirable? What yardsticks would be used if the price system were to be abandoned? Would society work if self-interest were totally ignored?

In the UK, society has steered a middle course. The market economy, and the society implied by it, has been controlled but not abandoned. State intervention has taken two main forms. Working through the price system, the State has sought itself, through its organizations, to become a producer. Reference has been made earlier to nationalized industries and to quangos. The state has also sought, through the legal system and other controls, to restrain the activities of the private sector. We have seen how laws regulating employment, the use of land, the retail trade and other contractual situations, have sought to limit the freedom of action of organizations in the interests of one group of citizens or another.

Outside the market situation, the State has also recognized needs which unrestricted laissez-faire would not meet. Through its *welfare provision 'from the cradle to the grave',* it has sought to remove many of the uncertainties of life. This collective provision is not regulated by prices entirely, as we have noted on many earlier occasions. The organizations which administer it are centrally funded; their activities lead to a redistribution of wealth.

Some would argue that State control has not gone far enough and would centralize all 'means of production and wealth'. Others would say that, by sapping 'initiative', the State has already gone too far in creating an inefficient bureaucratic and dictatorial society. This is one of the fundamental differences of opinion between political parties of the left and the right.

Objectives; policies; accountability; constraints.

Whatever view individuals may take, it is clear that economics, politics, (and therefore degrees of State control), and sociological trends are inextricably linked. Society is dynamic, is constantly changing. Within it exist organizations, large and small, publicly and privately owned, operating inside and outside market forces. Each of these organizations has one or more objectives and pursues policies to meet these objectives. Each of them is accountable to one or more 'masters'. Each of them is subject to economic, political, and legal constraints. The actions of each of them interact with those of the others. This is indeed a complex society. Having laid the groundwork in this Book, we go on to explore these complexities in Book 2, thus setting organizations in their environment.

Summary

This book has been an account of organizations and their environment. Organizations sell to each other and to individuals, and we have examined the theory of the market, and the price system operating in a market. Organizations operating outside the price system deal with clients, and satisfy their needs through decisions made other than in commercial markets. Within a market, more of a commodity is demanded at lower prices, and less at higher prices. Equally, more of a commodity is usually supplied at higher prices and less at lower prices. However, the reaction of organizations to changes in demand is affected by many restrictions not of their own making. Outside the commercial markets, changes in supply depend largely on political decisions. Changes in demand in the markets are usually accompanied by prices changes and supply extends or contracts as prices rise or fall. Changes in supply are usually accompanied by price changes and demand extends or contracts as prices fall or rise. Theoretically, an equilibrium price eventually establishes itself, when demand and supply are exactly equal—in equilibrium. The laws of supply and demand thus outlined help us to understand the functions of prices. Utility, measured subjectively, can, through prices, be compared with value in the market, and the consumer can thus obtain the greatest satisfaction from limited means. To the producer, prices measured against costs, assist decisions on the allocation of scarce resources, the scale of production, and hence the size of organizations.

The market economy, with no State intervention, does not exist in the UK. The lessons of history show that the first half of the nineteenth century, a time of laissez-faire, produced extremes of wealth and poverty, with successive waves of boom and slump and large-scale unemployment. The other extreme, pure communism, would allow prices to play little or no part in resource allocation, which would be decided by committee. The UK, at present steers a middle course; State intervention comes through production in the nationalized industries and quangos, and by statutory and other controls on the private sector. In addition, the Welfare State has resulted in needs being met by resource allocation by the State, which would not otherwise be met.

Organizations today exist within a dynamic and constantly changing society. Whatever their objectives, organizations must inevitably take into account economic, political, and legal constraints. So far we have laid the groundwork and in Book 2 we can examine the complex society, thus setting organizations in their environment.

Unit 17   Cross-modular assignments

1

A. Ford is the owner of a shop with three departments. He provides the following information for the year ended 31 December.

Cost of goods sold	£
Department X	45,000
Department Y	165,000
Department Z	290,000

Sales	
Department X	90,000
Department Y	180,000
Department Z	360,000
Wages	40,152
Rates	20,000
Administration	29,995

Wages and administration expenses are to be apportioned in proportion to sales.

Rates are to be apportioned in accordance with floor space, which is Department X 450 square feet, Department Y 1800 square feet, Department Z 2250 square feet.

A. Ford is considering closing down Department Y and leasing the vacated space. Half the staff employed in Department Y could be absorbed into the other two departments; the remainder would no longer be required, which would reduce wages by £5600. The administration expenses would be reduced by 20 per cent, but the rates for the whole shop would still be paid by A. Ford.

(a) Prepare a statement showing the net profit or loss for each department.
(b) Calculate, on the basis of your statement and the additional information given, the minimum charge per square foot at which Department Y floor space must be leased to compensate the business for the closure of Department Y.
(c) Prepare a report for A. Ford outlining the legal implications of
   (i)   the change of use of part of the premises
   (ii) the terms which might be included in the lease
   (iii) the reduction in numbers of staff and the redeployment of some staff.

2

TO THE ORDINARY SHAREHOLDERS:

Following the passage at the Extraordinary General
Meeting held on .... of the resolution for
the capitalization of part of the amount standing to
the credit of the Share Premium Account, the Directors
have allotted you one new Ordinary Share of 10p credited
as fully paid for every 4 Ordinary Shares of 10p held
at the close of business on .... Attached is
a renounceable certificate for the new Ordinary Shares.'

The above extract from a Company Secretary's letter concerns a capitalization issue of shares. This is sometimes known as a scrip issue.

(a) Is the public joint stock company giving shares away for nothing? If not, why not?
(b) Why are debenture holders not participating?
(c) Does the stated price of 10p mean that shares are necessarily bought and sold on the stock exchange for 10p? If not, why not?
(d) What may be the effect of this issue on the price of the shares?
(e) Why should a public joint stock company take this action?
(f) Why was a general meeting necessary before the directors could act?
(g) What does 'renounceable' mean?

Prior to the proposed scrip issue the summarized Balance Sheet of the company was as follows:

Authorized capital	£		£
2000,000 ordinary shares at 10p each	200,000	Fixed assets	205,000
Issued capital			
1400 000 ordinary shares at 10p each	140,000		45,000
Share premium account	50,000		
Profit and loss account balance	10,000		
Debentures	30,000	Current assets	
Creditors	20,000		
	£250,000		£250,000

(i) Rewrite the Balance Sheet showing the effect of the scrip issue.
(ii) What would be the effect of the scrip issue on the shareholders net worth and why?
(iii) What profit will the company need to earn in the next financial year to maintain its rate of dividend at the present rate of 12½ per cent?

3

Your advice has been sought by a successful shopkeeper, John Beckman, who now wishes to expand his business. He envisages opening a second shop in another area of town where property values are similar to his present shop.

In his shop he sells do-it-yourself materials, mainly for wood-working, including tools. He has one full-time assistant who has worked with him for four years. He himself works almost the whole week at the shop. There is also a part-time assistant who works on Fridays and Saturdays.

Mr Beckman has given you the following information about his business, relating to his previous financial year:

	£
Sales	50,000
Gross profit (av.)	25%
Stock (average)	8,000
Wages	3,750
Business expenses	3,250
Drawings	3,500

His assets and liabilities in his business are:

	£
Premises (at cost)	3,000
Fixtures and fittings	1,250
(J.B.'s valuation)	
Van (trade-in value)	750
Bank and cash	2,000
Creditors (average)	1,500

You ascertain that property values have risen four-fold since he bought the shop. The fixtures and fittings are in very good condition. The van is five years old. Mr Beckman has a house worth £20,000 on which he has an outstanding mortgage of £5,000. He also has investments worth £2,500.

(a) Write a financial report to a bank, setting out the basis for a request for finance to open the new shop.
(b) Mr Beckman has also considered seeking a partner. Set out the main points which you consider should be included in a partnership agreement for him.
(c) Consider the problems which Mr Beckman might encounter in his first year of trading in an enlarged business.

4

Situation You are the Assistant Manager of a large carpet department of a Supermarket. You have been asked by a customer to supply a carpet, 4 metres × 3½ metres, in a green and brown pattern shown in Murchison & Co.'s catalogue as design no. 32/Y/4. Your firm has not dealt with this manufacturer before. The manufacturer is the sole producer of this pattern and deals directly with retailers.

Task 1 To write the appropriate letter of enquiry on behalf of the customer. You will also wish to know trade discounts, manufacturer's recommended price, date of delivery, and if any cash discounts are offered.

Task 2 Write the manufacturer's reply.

Task 3 Prepare an invoice to the customer. (Assume £6.50 a sq m). (You charge £10.00 for fitting and there is 8% VAT).

Task 4 After three weeks the customer returns to complain that the carpet is of inferior quality and showing signs of wear and fading. The General Manager deals with

181

complaints, but needs a memo giving details of the situation and information regarding the customer's emotional state.

Task 5 Write to the customer as from the General Manager dealing with the complaint.

Task 6 The customer has failed to pay the account after several weeks. Write the appropriate letter dealing with this situation.

Task 7 The customer telephones you. Advise the General Manager by memo what the nature of this conversation was.

Task 8 Assuming that the firm of manufacturers will not replace the carpet, advise the customer what his legal rights are (if any), and what action he should take.

Task 9 Advise the General Manager of the problems arising from dealing directly with a sole supplier and make recommendations.

Add What copies of what information should go to whom, for filing.

5

Your company is reviewing its purchasing policy regarding raw materials which it uses in large quantities. At present, purchases are made shortly before they are required. Prices are those ruling at date of despatch, and tend to fluctuate. It is therefore difficult to budget costs and fix selling prices with certainty.

You have been asked to investigate the possibility of placing long-term contracts at a fixed price. Delivery quantities under such contracts will be much larger; it is hoped that prices will be fixed.

You are asked to:

(a) Using appropriate source material ascertain the movements in a commodity price, plot the values in the form of a graph and assess the probable trend.
(b) Briefly report on other factors your company will need to take into account before entering into a long-term contract.
(c) Draw up a brief contract for the purchase of a material. Show clearly the points which you consider are important in such a long-term contract. Make up any figures which you think should be shown.

Index

INDEX